CGO . . . . CONGO
CHA. . . . . CHAD
CIV. . . . . IVORY COAST
CMR . . . . CAMEROON
ETH. . . . . ETHIOPIA
GHA . . . . GHANA
GUI . . . . GUINEA
KEN . . . . KENYA
LBR . . . . LIBERIA
LBY. . . . . LIBYA
MAD . . . . MADAGASCAR
MAR. . . . . MOROCCO
MLI . . . . MALI
NGR . . . . NIGERIA
NIG . . . . NIGER
NRH. . . . . NORTH RHODESIA
RAU. . . . . UNITED ARAB REPUBLIC
SEN . . . . SENEGAL

TAN . . . . TANGANYIKA
TUN . . . . TUNISIA
UGA. . . . . UGANDA

Asia

AFG . . . . AFGHANISTAN
BUR . . . . BURMA
CAM . . . . CAMBODIA
CEY . . . . CEYLON
HKG . . . . HONG KONG
IND . . . . INDIA
IRN . . . . IRAN
IRQ . . . . IRAQ
ISR . . . . ISRAEL
JPN . . . . JAPAN
KOR . . . . KOREA (SOUTH)
LIB. . . . . LEBANON
MAS . . . . MALAYSIA
MGL . . . . MONGOLIA

NEP . . . . NEPAL
PAK . . . . PAKISTAN
PHI. . . . . PHILIPPINES
THA. . . . . THAILAND
TUR . . . . TURKEY
TWN . . . . TAIWAN
VET . . . . VIETNAM

Oceania

AUS. . . . . AUSTRALIA
NZL . . . . NEW ZEALAND

THE OLYMPIC CENTURY
THE OFFICIAL 1ST CENTURY HISTORY OF THE MODERN OLYMPIC MOVEMENT
VOLUME 16

THE
XVIII OLYMPIAD

TOKYO 1964
GRENOBLE 1968

BY

CARL A. POSEY

WORLD SPORT RESEARCH & PUBLICATIONS INC.
LOS ANGELES

1996 © United States Olympic Committee

Published by:
World Sport Research & Publications Inc.
1424 North Highland Avenue
Los Angeles, California 90028
(213) 461-2900

1st Century Project
The 1st Century Project is an undertaking by World
Sport Research & Publications Inc. to commemorate the
100-year history of the Modern Olympic Movement.
Charles Gary Allison, Chairman

Publishers: C. Jay Halzle, Robert G. Rossi,
James A. Williamson

Senior Consultant: Dr. Dietrich Quanz (Germany)
Special Consultants: Walter Borgers (Germany), Ian
Buchanan (United Kingdom), Dr. Karl Lennartz
(Germany), Wolf Lyberg (Sweden), Dr. Norbert Müller
(Germany), Dr. Nicholas Yalouris (Greece)

Editor: Laura Foreman
Executive Editor: Christian Kinney
Editorial Board: George Constable, George G. Daniels,
Ellen Galford, Ellen Phillips, Carl A. Posey

Art Director: Christopher M. Register
Production Manager: Nicholas Pitt
Picture Editor: Debra Lemonds Hannah
Designers: Kimberley Davison, Diane Farenick
Staff Researchers: Mark Brewin (Canada), Diana
Fakiola (Greece), Brad Haynes (Australia), Alexandra
Hesse (Germany), Pauline Ploquin (France)
Copy Editor: Elizabeth C. Graham
Proofing Editor: Harry Endrulat
Indexer and Stat Database Manager: Melinda Tate
Fact Verification: Carl and Liselott Diem Archives of the
German Sport University at Cologne, Germany
Statisticians: Bill Mallon, Walter Teutenberg
Memorabilia Consultants: Manfred Bergman, James D.
Greensfelder, John P. Kelly, Ingrid O'Neil
Staff Photographer: Theresa Halzle
Office Manager: Christopher Jason Waters
Office Staff: Chris C. Conlee, Brian M. Heath,
Edward J. Messler, Elsa Ramirez, Brian Rand

International Contributors: Jean Durry (France),
Dr. Antonio Lombardo (Italy), Dr. John A. MacAloon
(U.S.A.), Dr. Jujiro Narita (Japan), Dr. Roland Renson
(Belgium), Dr. James Walston (Ombudsman)

International Research and Assistance: John S. Baick
(New York), Matthieu Brocart (Paris), Alexander
Fakiolas (Athens), Bob Miyakawa (Tokyo), Rona Lester
(London), Dominic LoTempio (Columbia), George
Kostas Mazareas (Boston), Georgia McDonald
(Colorado Springs), Wendy Nolan (Princeton), Alexander
Ratner (Moscow), Jon Simon (Washington D.C.), Frank
Strasser (Cologne), Valéry Turco (Lausanne), Laura
Walden (Rome), Jorge Zocchi (Mexico City)

Map Compilation: Mapping Specialists Inc., Madison,
Wisconsin
Map Artwork: Dave Hader, Studio Conceptions,
Toronto
Film Production: Global Film Services, Toronto

Customer Service: 1-800-451-8030

Bookstore and Library Distribution:
Firefly Books Ltd.
3680 Victoria Park Avenue
Willowdale, ON M2H 3K1
(416) 499-8412

U.S. Offices
230 Fifth Avenue, #1607
New York, NY 10001

Printed and bound in the United States by R. R.
Donnelly Co.

ISBN 1-888383-00-3 (25-volume series)
ISBN 1-888383-16-X (Volume 16)

Library of Congress Cataloging-in-Publication Data

Posey, Carl A., 1933-
    The XVIII Olympiad : Tokyo 1964, Grenoble 1968 / by Carl Posey.
        p.   cm. -- (The Olympic century ; v. 16)
    Includes bibliographical references (p. 172 - 173) and index.
    ISBN 1-888383-16-X (alk. paper)
    1. Olympic Games (18th : 1964 : Tokyo, Japan) 2. Winter Olympic
Games (10th : 1968 : Grenoble, France)   I. Title. II. Series.
GV722 1964P67   1996
796.48--dc20   96-33366
                                                                        CIP

CONTENTS

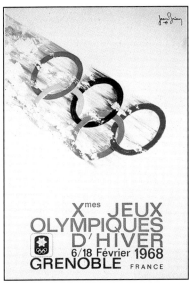

I

UNDERDOGS

᾿7᾿

II

UNDER THE VOLCANO

᾿51᾿

III

A SHADE OF DIFFERENCE

᾿93᾿

IV

UTMOST GRAVITY

᾿113᾿

APPENDIX 150

ACKNOWLEDGMENTS 172

BIBLIOGRAPHY/PHOTO CREDITS 172

INDEX 174

NEW LIGHT IN THE EAST

Orimpikku metsu—Olympic fever—had a grip on Japan, and by noon of October 10, 1964, Tokyo's 75,000-seat National Stadium was filled beyond capacity. At the stroke of 1 p.m., bands rolled onto the stadium infield from the north and south gates. Guns boomed, the "Olympic Overture" played in the background, and national flags rose on poles around the stadium. Then the crowd grew quiet, almost reverential. The gentle peal of bells and the throb of gongs broke the silence—a sign that Emperor Hirohito had arrived. With a lineage purported to date back 2,624 years, the diminutive monarch was a symbol of old Japan. He walked to the imperial box and stood, bowing politely as 5,700 athletes and officials from 94 delegations marched past him in the Parade of Nations.

But these Olympic Games were not about the old; they stood for the new—the first Games in Asia, the first to welcome athletes from the newly independent nations of Africa. There was no greater symbol of renewal than the presence of Yoshinori Sakai, a 400-meter runner and university student who trotted onto the stadium track, torch in hand. The 19-year-old Sakai was born 42 miles from Hiroshima on the day the atomic bomb fell there. The crowd cheered feverishly as he ran around the track and up a flight of stairs. For a brief moment he triumphantly held the torch aloft, then plunged it into the cauldron. Pigeons were released from baskets around the stadium. A squadron of jets lazily traced five interlocked rings in the perfect blue sky. It was a momentous beginning for the Games, an impressive symbol of the new Japan.

UNDERDOGS

Toying with an opponent had never been Joe Frazier's style. A thick, heavily muscled 195-pounder not quite 6 feet tall, Frazier had neither the legs nor the reach for much choreography in the ring; his style, like his life, could afford no such frills. A young man with a wife and three kids and few marketable skills had to fight the way he had to work, and he worked in the Cross Brothers slaughterhouse in Philadelphia, doing the hard, hand-wrecking labor of carving the carcasses of recently slain beef. "Don't worry about the guys over here," he had written Florence, his wife. "They fight like girls."

"Over here" meant Tokyo, and on this night in October 1964, under the conical glare illuminating the ring in the Korakuen Ice Palace, the 20-year-old from Philadelphia seemed to be toying with a 30-year-old German giant named Hans Huber, a powerful boxer a head taller than the American, blessed with the long frame and limbs of the true heavyweight. The three 3-minute rounds would be the most important

nine minutes in either man's short life. But, trapped in the cosmic irony that seemed always to dog him, Joe Frazier wasn't able to wade in like a compact armored machine, as had been his custom. Circumstances beyond his control were making him fight the way Huber did—like a girl, as Frazier had put it.

Only two years earlier, Frazier had walked into Philadelphia's 23rd Police Athletic League Gym at 22nd Street and Columbia, a shortish, fat black kid with no experience. He had come up from Beaufort, South Carolina, a couple of years before, first to join an older brother in New York, and then to Philadelphia, where he found work and summoned his little family north. He was tough—indeed, his slaughterhouse work would have exhausted most men—with a left arm as powerful as a very strong leg. His sharecropper father had lost his own left arm in a shotgun accident, and Joe had taken up the left-side slack around the farm—"my left-hand man," Rubin

Joe Frazier, U.S.A., and Hans Huber, Germany, boxing heavyweight gold-medal bout, Tokyo 1964

THE GAMES AT A GLANCE

	Oct 10	Oct 11	Oct 12	Oct 13	Oct 14	Oct 15	Oct 16	Oct 17	Oct 18	Oct 19	Oct 20	Oct 21	Oct 22	Oct 23	Oct 24
OPENING CEREMONY	■														
ATHLETICS (TRACK & FIELD)				■	■	■	■	■	■	■	■				
BASKETBALL		■	■	■		■	■	■		■	■	■	■		
BOXING		■	■	■	■	■	■	■	■	■			■		
CANOEING											■	■	■		
CYCLING						■		■	■	■	■	■		■	
DIVING		■	■	■	■		■	■							
EQUESTRIAN							■	■	■	■			■	■	■
FENCING				■	■	■	■	■	■		■	■	■	■	
FOOTBALL (SOCCER)		■	■	■	■		■		■			■			
GYMNASTICS										■	■	■	■	■	
HOCKEY		■	■	■	■	■	■	■	■		■	■	■		
JUDO											■	■	■	■	
MODERN PENTATHLON		■	■	■	■										
ROWING		■	■	■	■	■									
SHOOTING							■	■	■	■	■	■			
SWIMMING		■	■	■	■	■	■	■	■						
VOLLEYBALL		■	■	■	■	■		■	■	■		■	■	■	
WATER POLO		■	■	■	■	■		■	■						
WEIGHT LIFTING		■	■	■	■		■	■	■						
WRESTLING		■	■	■	■		■	■	■	■					
YACHTING			■	■	■	■				■	■	■			
CLOSING CEREMONY															■

Frazier had liked to say. The muscle behind one of history's famous left hooks, Joe used to tell people, "That's all from my dad, not from lifting weights or hitting a bag or anything like that."

Later, Joe would explain that he had gone to the gym to lose weight—a matter of economics, not vanity: He couldn't squeeze his fat thighs into regular-size trousers, and he couldn't afford tailor-mades. But police sergeant Duke Dugent, the boxing instructor at the gym, knew it was more than big legs that had brought Joe to him. "He said," Dugent would recall, "he wanted to learn boxing to see if he could make a living at it."

Dugent had signed him up, put him on a diet, and started kneading 240 pounds of soft clay into 190 pounds of hard muscle. Gradually, the young man who had walked into the gym too fat, too short, and too slow to be a boxer—the clumsy kid who couldn't throw a punch without losing his balance—metamorphosed into a fighter.

Dugent taught Frazier to discard the long comic-strip left, telegraphed from a mile away, and to concentrate on short jabs and hooks, on combinations, on throwing volleys of quick, hard punches instead of the single haymaker. A barrage of hooks would open a man's defenses, along with the skin around the eyes, the mouth, the nose. Frazier was a quick study. "At first he was bad," said Dugent, "the next day he was good." Nothing got in his way. Up at 4:30 a.m. to run, Frazier did his wearying shift at Cross Brothers, then went to the gym until 8 at night, when he dragged himself home to his little house on Somerset Street near 12th. Sometimes, inside the gloves, his hands were laced with cuts from the slaughterhouse. He didn't seem to care. Joe Frazier had become a new man, powerful and graceful and deadly in the ring, with less and less time to think about minor discomforts.

For a while, he had looked unstoppable. Frazier won 35 of 37 amateur bouts, losing decisions twice to Buster Mathis, a 6-foot-9, 295-pound Grand Rapids housepainter turned boxer—a man of unexpected agility and speed. Still, Frazier won the Middle Atlantic Golden Gloves heavyweight championship in 1963 and 1964, and many in the game thought him the best contender around. These bouts were not the 15-round endurance contests of the professional ring, but comparatively tame matches of only three 3-minute rounds. You had to win quickly, and there was little time to show such added value as stamina, determination, and the imponderable quality known as heart. The bouts paid nothing, but for Joe Frazier, as for every other strong young man trying to fight his way into the light, these were the first rungs of the climb to another, better stratum of life.

Early in 1964, Frazier entered the trials for the Olympic Games to be held in Tokyo that October.

In New York he fought six fights and tallied six knockouts. He wanted to win a gold medal for his country in Tokyo, but he also could see where the Olympic trail might lead. Floyd Patterson had leapt from a middleweight gold medal at Helsinki 1952 to the world heavyweight championship four years later. And Patterson's successor—lumbering, indestructible Sonny Liston—had just lost the crown to another Olympian, Cassius Clay (soon to be known as Muhammad Ali), who had won the Rome 1960 light heavyweight gold. Manifestly, gold in Tokyo could mean gold at home. Frazier badly wanted to be part of that equation.

On May 20, with his six KOs tidily in hand, Frazier stepped into the ring with his huge nemesis, Buster Mathis, and lost 2-1 in a narrow decision. "It's back to the abattoir in Philadelphia, instead of on to Tokyo, for heavyweight Joe Frazier," reported a Philly sportswriter, and indeed, the loss to Mathis seemed to warrant the

The Korakuen Ice Palace boxing ring is empty except for Choh Dong-kih, who protests his disqualification. The South Korean flyweight made his point about what he deemed unfair judging by sitting in the ring for 51 minutes. Choh was ousted from his quarterfinal match against the Soviet Union's Stanislav Sorokin for holding.

Hungarian referee György Sermer takes a left to the chin from Spain's Valentín Loren. Sermer had disqualified Loren for repeated holding. The Spaniard's outburst prompted the international boxing federation to ban him from amateur boxing for life.

epitaph. With his hand just grasping a crucial rung of the ladder out of the slaughterhouse, Frazier had slipped and fallen. He had become once more the young father of three, drawing a hard-earned $100 a week, a once-promising amateur boxer who had failed to make the Olympic team. For the first time in his life—maybe the only time—Joe Frazier despaired. "I don't want to ever fight again," he said. "This is it."

But it wasn't. Pat Duffy, boxing chairman of the Middle Atlantic AAU, asked Frazier to come to Tokyo anyway, as a sparring partner. Maybe something would happen to Mathis. Maybe Frazier could compete as a middleweight. So Frazier went to Tokyo, paying for his own passport and inoculations, carrying so little cash that he couldn't afford to buy his own soap. He left his family a small cache of savings to see them through what he had once thought would be the most important October in his life. But the Fates didn't seem to be smiling. Before the trip, Frazier had gashed a hand with a meat cleaver at work, threatening the Tokyo pilgrimage. The wound had healed on time, though, and—perhaps

deciding this tenacious boxer was overdue for a break—destiny began to relent.

In San Francisco en route to Japan, Mathis and Frazier squared off in an exhibition bout for the troops at nearby Hamilton Air Force Base. One of Mathis' surprisingly soft, slapping rights clipped Frazier on the head—and jammed a knuckle on the big man's fist. For Mathis, it meant a cast until October 10—the day before the Games opened in Tokyo. For Frazier, it meant his hands were back on that rung, on that ladder to the gold. The stand-in would step into the lead role under the hard lights of the Ice Palace.

His first trial came on October 15 against George Oywello of Uganda; Frazier knocked the African out midway through the first round. On October 19 the American stand-in went against Australia's Athol McQueen, who dropped him to one knee early in the fight. But 40 seconds into the third and final round, Frazier was so clearly beating the Aussie that the bout was stopped. Joe's third encounter—the last match of the semifinals—buzzed with political as well as pugilistic excitement. In the Cold War frost, Frazier was fighting hulking Soviet boxer Vadim Yemelyanov, who looked ready to join seven other Russian fighters marching toward the finals, three of them over the defeated forms of American semifinalists. Never in Olympic history had the United States been shut out in the ring; now it was clear that if any boxing medal was going home to America from Tokyo, Joe Frazier would have to win it.

Frazier charged Yemelyanov, pummeling him in the fearless style that had won all those other amateur matches. In turn, Frazier absorbed some staggering blows from the Russian. But Frazier really opened up in the second round, smashing the larger man to the canvas twice. After Frazier landed a particularly devastating left hook, just one second short of the two-minute mark, the battered Russian's handlers threw in

the towel—literally. The white flag of surrender fluttered out of the Soviet corner like a dove of peace.

But Joe Frazier hardly noticed. He focused entirely on the brightening flare of pain in his left hand, where, even as he had felt the punch connect, the thumb had broken.

Frazier let the broken thumb remain his little secret. He mentioned some pain in his left hand but refused to let medics take X rays; he had seen what a broken knuckle had done to Buster Mathis. Frazier had advanced to the finals, and now, on the last night of the Games, he shuffled across the ring at Korakuen Ice Palace, dancing around the big German he hoped to destroy with one hand. There was no escaping the slaughterhouse without pain. Joe Frazier had always known that.

Frazier's imperative to break out of the abattoir was something his Japanese hosts would have understood perfectly. Japan was now not quite two decades from the vaster killing field of a devastating world war fought across the Pacific half of the planet—and the spiritual slaughterhouse of unconditional defeat in August 1945. The island nation had emerged into the postwar era as an occupied colony, governed through the military apparatus of the Supreme Commander, Allied Powers. The peace treaty of April 1952 had been duly ratified; indeed, during the Korean conflict of the early 1950s, Japan had become a crucial base of United Nations military operations and home to thousands of Allied troops, especially Americans.

Back from the ashes of World War II, the Japanese economy had revived during the Korean War and flourished since. Japan in the 1960s was an economic power to be reckoned with, a hotbed of technological innovation. And yet the aura of the aggressor nation, crushingly defeated,

Frantic spectators stampede for the exits at Peru's national stadium in Lima during a riot at the Peru-Argentina Olympic qualifying soccer match. Spreading into the streets, the rioting caused the deaths of 328 people.

MAD FOR SOCCER

Soccer is so passionately popular worldwide that, traditionally, more national teams have applied for Olympic berths than the Games can accommodate. Beginning in 1952, therefore, international soccer federation officials instituted qualifying matches to whittle down the field. For the Tokyo tournament, no fewer than 48 countries applied for the 16 slots, and in South America seven nations took part in a round-robin tournament to pick the two teams that would fill the continent's two allotted berths. Predictably, perhaps, in a sport that inspires fanaticism like no other, things eventually turned ugly.

As the tournament progressed, Argentina, Brazil, and Peru appeared to be the likely Olympic candidates, making the May 24, 1964, match pitting Peru against Argentina pivotal. With two minutes left, Peru scored to tie the game at 1-1. The referee, however, had called a penalty against Peru, and the goal was nullified. Fans were outraged. Two attacked the referee and were arrested, whereupon the crowd stormed the field. The game was called, igniting a riot that spilled into the streets and all the way to the Peruvian presidential mansion. The South American tournament had to be abandoned. Argentina, leading on points, was awarded one berth; Brazil defeated Peru in a one-game play off a month later for the second spot.

The Olympic tournament itself was far calmer. The field was reduced to 14 teams: Italy had to drop out when several players on its squad were revealed to be professionals, and North Korea left the Games completely in a dispute with the International Olympic Committee over the eligibility of some of the North Korean athletes. The tournament lasted 32 games without incident. Hungary defeated Czechoslovakia 2-1 for the championship.

A twig broom and a zebra-striped outfit denote a member of Tokyo's Olympic cleaning crew. The Japanese were so conscientious about sanitation during the Games that when one worker at the Olympic Village complained of being bitten by a poisonous moth, the sanitation department launched a wholesale moth-extermination effort.

had clung to the country, to the Japanese spirit, persistent as a poison vapor.

Some powerful agent was needed to disperse that malaise of the national spirit. To many, it seemed that playing host to the Olympic Games—the first to be staged in Asia—would provide the cleansing agent. *Orimpikku made ni*—by the time of the Olympics—became a kind of watchphrase of Japanese society. That time was itself a matter of considerable debate. Staging the Games in late May or early June would have provided perfect weather but would have limited opportunities for student athletes to train between school and competition. Midsummer was too hot and humid for athletic competition. Early autumn brought the annual season of typhoons. In the end, typhoons seemed the least problematic, and October was chosen.

By October 1964—Orimpikku made ni—social problems would be resolved, traffic snarls eased, Tokyo reborn as a clean, uncluttered city. "With all its flowering streets, Tokyo makes a fresh start as a new Tokyo this year," sang the popular lyricist Sayuri Yoshinaga. At the end of the fortnight between October 10 and 24, 1964, Japan would shake off the mantle of defeat and take its rightful place among the great nations of the world. Tokyo 1964 was, as one observer put it, "the end of the postsurrender era," the "opportunity to mingle in the society of nations with new clothing."

This new clothing had to be cut to heroic proportions, for the problems of hosting the Games well would have daunted the Immortals. Tokyo was not just a big city with bad traffic. To the Western visitor especially, it had too few roads, rooms, subways, sports venues, and even public toilets. And it was ugly, unsanitary, and, some believed, vulgar besides. It was a vast urban smear; one reporter said that from the air in daylight it looked like "an enormous coffee stain" shrouded in a woolly smog against the green undulations of the Kanto Plain.

The city had begun in 1437 as a feudal fortress and was known until the mid-19th century as Edo. It had taken something over five centuries for its urban tissues to spread between villages and towns, forming the modern chaos of tangled neighborhoods, open drains, and glutted roads; by the 1960s a metropolis of 10.5 million people stretched over some 800 square miles. Those who loved Tokyo thought it one of the planet's great original cities, a place of elegantly executed parks and urban forests and temple grounds, its nights a galaxy of animated neon. To others, it was a sea where islands of affluence floated in archipelagoes of ragpickers' villages, a place without street lamps, adequate water, or even sidewalks, its conglomeration of 24 towns, 15 villages, and 23 wards huge, chaotic, and incurably dysfunctional.

Curiously, Tokyo had been offered an uncommon number of opportunities to start over. The city was nearly destroyed by fires in 1657 and 1772. The great earthquake of September 1923 had shaken Tokyo to a flammable rubble that quickly ignited; the temblor killed some 2,000 people, the ensuing fires 57,000 more. During World War II, Allied bombs destroyed perhaps two-thirds of the city, much of it with incendiary raids that left the metropolis flickering like a great bed of coals. While the scars of such disasters were swiftly erased, the city never took the chance to plan its rebirth. It kept re-forming like healing tissue, following its nature toward unfathomable complexity.

However beautiful the result, a face-lift is a painful business, and Tokyo's was wrenching. By 1961 the diggers had begun ripping open major traffic arteries to extend the subways. Bulldozers flattened homes, stores, and temples to create

Gaudy neon signs illuminate Tokyo's Ginza district. Once considered the most expensive real estate in the world, the Ginza features upscale shops and restaurants. It was much patronized by Olympians and visitors to the Games.

the city's first elevated expressway, and the bay-side area between Tokyo and Yokohama was tortured into a monorail route. The great metropolis reverberated with jackhammers and rivet guns—a 24-hour-a-day ruckus that proved unbearable for some. One university student committed suicide by pushing his head under the hammer of a pile driver. More than a hundred workers would die readying Tokyo for the Olympics, and 2,000 people would be injured in related accidents.

Despite the rigors of reconstruction, new temples of sport began to rise across this mainly horizontal city. Near the central area of the Ginza, on the quilt of cedars and pines of Meiji Park, a national stadium had been built to accommodate the Third Asian Games, played in Tokyo in 1958—a kind of regional rehearsal for the Olympics. For the 1964 Games, the stadium was refurbished with a soaring, winglike superstructure that raised its capacity to 75,000.

A few blocks to the southeast, the Yoyogi Sports Center acquired a stunning centerpiece: the large, graceful, suspension-roofed structure of the new National Gymnasium. The larger part of this intriguing complex housed the swimming lanes and diving pools. "It was," observed one swimmer, "the kind of space you would expect after you died and went to heaven." Connected to the natatorium was a smaller annex, a stadium for Olympic basketball, enclosed in an otherworldly whorled structure resembling a conical seashell. The National Gymnasium was a unique contribution to architecture, one of the great buildings of the modern world.

Komakawa Olympic Park appeared some five miles to the south, a complex of stadiums and gymnasiums dominated by a 250-foot "control tower." Although built of concrete beams, the tall, vertical oblong evoked the traditional timber construction of Japan. By night, sheathed in blue and white lights, the tower became a skyscraping torch for the Games of the XVIII Olympiad.

On a bluff overlooking a river in Kito-no-maru Park in northeastern Tokyo, the Olympic debut of judo was celebrated with Nippon Budokan Hall, an eight-sided Buddhist hall built to modern fire- and earthquake-proofing standards.

The 600-odd low-rise structures of Washington Heights—a cluster of family dwellings built after the war for American servicemen and their dependents—became an Olympic Village. In all, a score of venues were either created or refurbished for Tokyo 1964, some as far away as the Karuizawa Equestrian Track, four hours by train to the south; the Omiya soccer field some 40 miles northwest of Tokyo; and the Enoshima yachting center on Sagami Bay, to the southwest on the Pacific coast. But most of the competition sites were sprinkled around the metropolitan sprawl of Tokyo itself.

It was not enough to alter the venerable city's landscape: Certain social dimensions also required change. As much of the reconstruction followed the Japanese estimate of Western expectations, so did the tinkering with attitudes and behavior. The government and the press went to work urging the people of Tokyo—a population as attentive to such stuff as that of New York or Paris—to behave properly toward the 60,000 foreign visitors drawn by the Games. "Will our people bump into foreigners," asked the *Yomiuri Shimbun* rhetorically, "step on their toes, and otherwise give them unpleasant moments?" Would merchants pressure visitors to buy goods they didn't want at inflated prices? Pamphlets were published with such titles as *What Foreigners Are Like*. Americans, for example, were "usually honest and friendly and like jokes. But some Americans are very demanding." Etiquette had to be reconstituted along Western lines: ladies first in restaurants; ask if they want sugar and cream before adding it. Signs urged Tokyoites to be polite in other ways as well. "Let's stop urinating in public," one suggested. "The Olympics are nigh."

WHERE THE GAMES WERE PLAYED

National Stadium

Komazawa Gymnasium

National Gymnasium

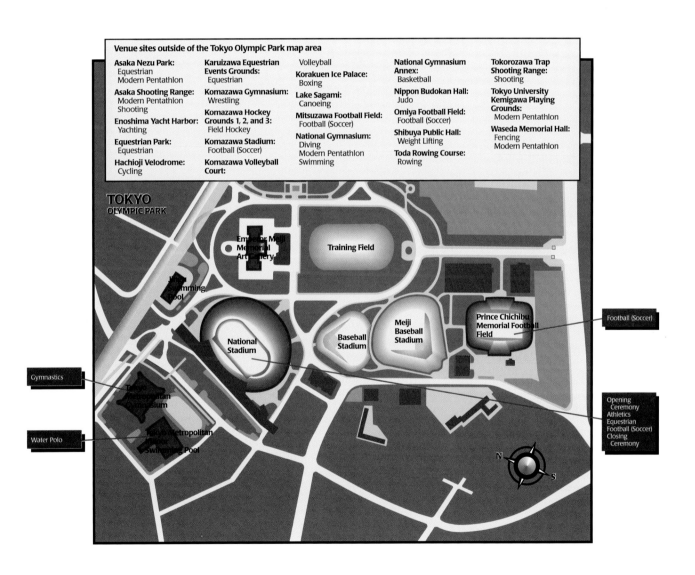

Venue sites outside of the Tokyo Olympic Park map area

Asaka Nezu Park:
Equestrian
Modern Pentathlon

Asaka Shooting Range:
Modern Pentathlon
Shooting

Enoshima Yacht Harbor:
Yachting

Equestrian Park:
Equestrian

Hachioji Velodrome:
Cycling

Karuizawa Equestrian Events Grounds:
Equestrian

Komazawa Gymnasium:
Wrestling

Komazawa Hockey Grounds 1, 2, and 3:
Field Hockey

Komazawa Stadium:
Football (Soccer)

Komazawa Volleyball Court:
Volleyball

Korakuen Ice Palace:
Boxing

Lake Sagami:
Canoeing

Mitsuzawa Football Field:
Football (Soccer)

National Gymnasium:
Diving
Modern Pentathlon
Swimming

National Gymnasium Annex:
Basketball

Nippon Budokan Hall:
Judo

Omiya Football Field:
Football (Soccer)

Shibuya Public Hall:
Weight Lifting

Toda Rowing Course:
Rowing

Tokorozawa Trap Shooting Range:
Shooting

Tokyo University Kemigawa Playing Grounds:
Modern Pentathlon

Waseda Memorial Hall:
Fencing
Modern Pentathlon

TOKYO OLYMPIC PARK

Emperor Meiji Memorial Art Gallery

Training Field

Indoor Swimming Pool

National Stadium

Baseball Stadium

Meiji Baseball Stadium

Prince Chichibu Memorial Football Field

Football (Soccer)

Gymnastics

Tokyo Metropolitan Gymnasium

Water Polo

Tokyo Metropolitan Swimming Pool

Opening Ceremony
Athletics
Equestrian
Football (Soccer)
Closing Ceremony

N S

A market in Hachioji, a suburb of Tokyo, hawks films, books, and memorabilia. The Hachioji area was host to the Olympic cycling events.

Japanese by the hundreds of thousands turned to English-language records and radio broadcasts, struggling to learn such things as "May I help you?"—and, for the inevitable crunch, "What's the matter? We offer at reasonable fixed price so we cannot offer any discount." Tokyo cabbies, noted for their furious disregard of traffic safety, put up signs: I Am Not a Kamikaze Driver.

Although not known for its restraint, Tokyo, through a greatly reinforced police force, went about suppressing some of the other elements of urban society—the pimps, prostitutes, exotic dancers, and purveyors of pornography, erotic baths, and erotic movies. To old Tokyo hands, it meant downgrading the world's raciest city into

its dreariest. Of course, as always, Tokyo remained immutably itself.

For a time, the rash of construction, physical and social, seemed more like a pox, however, and the optimism one had heard in Orimpikku made ni gave way to a fatigued derision; "by the time of the Olympics" was a time few believed could come. Yet, by the time of the Olympics, the giant apparatus and its accompanying infrastructure were in place, and the tired sneer had become once again an expression of pride. Beneath this beautiful new face, Tokyo no doubt continued irredeemably to be Tokyo, but—Orimpikku made ni—the city was ready. At 2 p.m. on October 10 some 5,700 participants from 94 countries followed their flags into the National Stadium at

The Tokyo torch relay, which began on August 21, 1964, with the traditional lighting ceremony at Olympia, Greece, made stops at 12 Asian cities before arriving in Japan on September 7. Once in Japan, the Olympic flame was divided among four torches, such as the one shown here, and relayed along four separate routes toward Tokyo. The fires were reunified in a rite at the Imperial Palace Plaza on October 9, 1964.

Meiji Park. The emperor of Japan declared open the Games of the XVIII Olympiad, cannons fired, and 12,000 colored balloons climbed cheerfully into the cloudless autumn sky.

Then, from the stadium's northern entrance, the final runner of the Olympic torch relay entered the field, bearing flame from the ruins of ancient Olympia in Greece, a torch carried across half the world in a 12,000-mile journey. After trotting half a lap of the 400-meter track, the runner bounded up the steps of the backstand to plunge the torch into a cauldron of oil and ignite the Olympic fire.

The torchbearer was 19-year-old Yoshinori Sakai, a 400-meter runner of some repute. But it had been his value as a symbol, more than his running ability, that had made him the final bearer of the Olympic flame. His life had begun with another kind of fire. Yoshinori Sakai had been born on August 6, 1945, near Hiroshima,

just two hours after the sky above that city had flared with the first atomic explosion to be used in war. Inscrutable to some observers, his selection was evidently intended to demonstrate Japan's survival and renewal, its national will toward peace in a world polarized by ideology.

As deftly as they had rebuilt their capital, the Japanese had shown their hearts to a world they now rejoined. Orimpikku made ni, Japan had accomplished the impossible, and done it with such good humor that journalists dubbed Tokyo 1964 the Happy Games.

This achievement of impossibilities would become the theme of these Games for many athletes as well. From across the world, determined young men and women had followed their national flags—and their stars—to Tokyo, expecting

The undulant rooftop of Komazawa Stadium, a building by architect Eika Takayama, is a signature component of Komazawa Olympic Park. The stadium, a stage for soccer during the Tokyo Games, is part of the 101-acre Komazawa complex that contains swimming pools, three field hockey arenas, an archery range, and a multipurpose gymnasium.

17

An athlete's badge at Tokyo 1964

to compete against the best, but with little hope of being best themselves. A gold medal for them was not in the cards; it was impossible—like Tokyo's face-lift, like Joe Frazier's being there at all.

In the Korakuen Ice Palace ring with Hans Huber, Frazier took what the German threw at him—and he was throwing plenty. Clearly, Frazier wasn't going to beat Huber one-handed, or without firing the most potent weapon in his arsenal, that explosive left hook. So Frazier began using his left, the hand that could have lit a dark room with its pain, and connecting, then letting the agony wash through him; when the hot coal throbbing in the glove cooled off, he would launch the left again. But the hook knew about the pain and often went wide of the mark or became a pawing jab: In 20 tries during the second round, the left connected only three times. During the third and final round, Frazier waded in. "I'd gone all that way," he would tell people later, "I couldn't let one hand pull me back."

Huber stayed with the American, not in the least ready to forfeit his own shot at the gold. As Frazier moved in on him, Huber fired a stunning left into the vacuum behind one of those wide left hooks, then hammered a strong right into Frazier's face. But the round turned toward Frazier, who put a punishing right to Huber's body, then connected with two perfect lefts—lefts that hurt both men—to the face. In the end, the willingness to endure the globe of pain filling his left glove gave Frazier the narrowest of victories. Of the five judges, three gave the fight to the American.

Frazier won the only American gold medal in boxing that year. He would remember the moment as a high point in his life, higher, he would say years later, than taking the heavyweight title from Jimmy Ellis in 1970, and confirming it with that decision over a derisive Muhammad Ali in 1971. From the sometime ice palace in northeastern Tokyo, Frazier may have discerned the faces that waited in his professional future: Oscar Bonavena, the Argentine giant; veteran Eddie Machen, knocked out just once in 61 professional bouts; his old nemesis, Buster Mathis; Jerry Quarry, the California contender; Mexican champ Manuel Ramos; George Chuvalo, Canada's man of steel. They hovered like pugilistic spirits, and perhaps Frazier felt their dangerously exciting gravitation.

He was, however, ill prepared to follow his destiny on that October night in 1964. He was an amateur champ with a busted hand. The job Cross Brothers was holding for him back home was a job you couldn't do with a broken thumb, so he was an unemployed 20-year-old without the price of Christmas presents for his wife and three kids. Perhaps he also knew in his heart that he was a good boxer who needed considerable finishing to compete in the professional ring: Arithmetic notwithstanding, 15 rounds are infinitely more than five times as tough as three.

Things would work out for Joe Frazier. A Philadelphia sportswriter would organize a drive to bring in Christmas money for the family, and the Reverend William Gray over at Bright Hope Baptist had a janitor's job to tide him over. In a year, the broken thumb would come out of the cast and Frazier could begin climbing the professional ladder. A few Philadelphia businessmen would create a corporation called Cloverlay—clover for luck plus overlay, which in gambling parlance means a perfectly hedged bet—and sell 14 shares of Joe Frazier for $250 each. In a year, Frazier would be what they called cocktail stock, the property people talked about at cocktail parties: a piece of a racehorse, or a piece of a fighter. There would be the fame and fortune that had drawn him to the Police Athletic League Gym on 22nd.

But at the moment of victory in the Korakuen

Playing records helped speed Joe Frazier's recovery after surgery on his thumb. But the cast and a gold medal won Frazier no sympathy from his bosses at the Cross Brothers slaughterhouse in Philadelphia when he returned from Tokyo. Because he couldn't use his hand, he was laid off from work.

Haskell Indian Institute track star Billy Mills tightens his shoelaces before a 1958 track meet in Lawrence, Kansas. Mills' alma mater was founded in 1884 as a boarding school for Native American elementary-school students. It continues its educational mandate today as the Haskell Indian Nations University.

Ice Palace, one can imagine Joe Frazier, the young unemployed father of three, the boxer with a broken thumb, shaking his head in bitter wonder. So this was the top of the world!

Billy Mills had a good deal of experience with such ironies—with victories that gave the victor nothing, or less than nothing. When he was at the University of Kansas in Lawrence, he had seen a museum display of a stuffed horse named Comanche, identified as The Sole Survivor of the Battle of Little Bighorn. Mills wondered about the thousands of Lakota and Oglala Sioux and their Cheyenne allies who had destroyed Custer's force that day. Maybe it was true that they hadn't survived. It had been one of those victories where the victors were run down and killed or herded back onto the reservation.

The Comanche display had special resonance for Mills because he was himself a seven-sixteenths Lakota Sioux, one of a family of 15 on the Oglala reservation at Pine Ridge, South Dakota—a family that had disintegrated early. His mother had died when he was 7, his father when he was 13. The reservation was what Mills later called "a no-philosophy world," where life was lived a day at a time and nobody thought much about a future because there didn't seem to be much of one.

His father—his beloved father—had boxed and wrestled, and he advised Billy to follow some sport. "Compete in sports, take care of your body, believe in a creator, and learn to live with the white society," he told son. He had meant, Billy Mills learned later, that it would make his way easier if he competed with white men and won. Because his father had boxed, Billy tried boxing, and he began running to get fit. His legs became strong enough to bicycle around a ring forever, but he hadn't much of a punch, and he soon tired of being pummeled. He tried basketball too, and rodeo—sooner or later, everybody on the reservation tried rodeo. But in the meantime, his true

sport had begun to spread through his soul. The five-mile training jogs of the aspiring boxer brought Mills an addictive taste of the long-distance runner's exhausted tranquility and clarity of mind. Running became his sport.

When his father died, Mills was sent off to Haskell Indian Institute in Lawrence, Kansas, a boarding school like Carlisle Indian School in Pennsylvania, where Jim Thorpe and other fine Indian athletes had learned their stuff. Mills kept running, so well that 18 track scholarships awaited him on graduation. But the transition from high school into college also entailed a bigger change, the step across the invisible line between a small community of Indians and the white world beyond. Mills stepped cautiously, electing to stay in Lawrence and attend the University of Kansas. Even on that familiar ground, he soon learned what it was to be an Indian in a white society. Fraternities rushed the track star—until they discovered he was an Indian. Parents gathered protectively about their dating-aged daughters. Mills's frustration fueled him on the track. He ran angry. Once he even quit in the middle of a race.

Even so, his university running career showed flashes of something extraordinary hiding inside Billy Mills. He made first-team all-American in cross-country two years in a row and finished third in the Big Eight cross-country. There was enough talent inside, and Mills knew it, that even before his 1962 graduation he was taking aim on Tokyo 1964. In the meantime, he married a classmate, Pat Harris, and entered the U.S. Marines officer candidate program, emerging as a second lieutenant. For a while, he let himself be a full-time Marine; then in 1963, at Pat's urging, he resumed running. Tokyo was not much more than a year away then, and he had a lot to do.

Training under Camp Pendleton's highly regarded coach, 70-year-old Earl Thomson, Mills did poorly at first, even in the relatively

Germany's Willi Holdorf makes his run-up to the bar during the decathlon's high-jump competition. Holdorf became the first German to win the Olympic decathlon.

EVENING THE SCORE

Change was the order of the day at the decathlon competition at Tokyo. For one thing, just before the Games the International Amateur Athletic Federation had revised the point tables, the basis of the event's esoteric scoring system. The changes' main thrust was to even out the scoring values of the 10 events so that an outstanding performance in any one specialty didn't count as much as it had previously. The alterations were prompted in large part by field events, whose athletes were beginning to hit marks the previous tables hadn't envisioned.

Every elite decathlete's score took a dip because of the table revisions, but the least affected was a group of Germans. These men were all coached by Friedel Schirmer, who stressed consistency in every event rather than excellence in one or two. Foremost among his protégés was Willi Holdorf, a balding, 24-year-old physical education student from Leverkusen. Holdorf took the decathlon lead after the first event, the 100-meter dash. He fell back as far as fourth place after the shot put and high jump, while the Soviet Union's Mikhail Storozhenko surged to the front on the strength of a tremendous put. Holdorf regained the lead after the 400 meters and maintained it through the final five events.

The gold medalist's score of 7,887 points was well short of a record; nevertheless, the Tokyo Games validated Schirmer's decathlon philosophy. Germans claimed three of the top six spots, and Schirmer-trained athletes would dominate the event for the rest of the decade.

short 1- and 2-mile races against the competition—such schools as the University of Southern California and the University of Arizona. But he was looking beyond those races to the 1964 Games and to what may be the hardest race of all: the 10,000 meter. This exhausting 6.2-mile contest combines the worst features of the mile and the marathon—it has to be run all the way, and there has to be enough left at the end for a final burst of speed. It would be a terrible race even for horses; it is one of the ultimate tests of the human machine.

For Americans, the 10,000-meter run seemed jinxed. The American Olympic record had been set by Max Truex's sixth-place finish at Rome 1960, and no Yanks had medaled in the event since Stockholm 1912, when Louis Tewanima finished second. On the other hand, that could have been a favorable omen to a young man from the Pine Ridge reservation—Tewanima was a Hopi from Arizona.

Mills had run the 10,000 only once, at an intermilitary meet in Belgium in 1963. He had run the 10-kilometer course in 30 minutes 8 seconds—30 minutes is considered the threshold of ability, like the 10 seconds in the 100-yard dash. In early 1964, Mills began running with a marathoner, Alex Breckenridge, pounding along a 20- or 25-mile course through the rough, hilly country that makes Camp Pendleton a drill instructor's paradise. In late July, Mills placed second in the Culver City marathon, thus qualifying for the marathon in Tokyo. Ten days later he broke the American record in the 6-mile race, and a few weeks after that he ran the 10,000-meter in 29 minutes 10 seconds—below the 30-minute mark. Now he was on the U.S. Olympic team for two events, the marathon and the 10,000-meter. He began training for the latter, although he planned to run in both.

In Tokyo, Mills' plans didn't seem to matter—nobody was watching the 26-year-old Marine. The American hope was Gerry Lindgren, 18, a fragile-looking, 5-foot-5 high schooler from Spokane, Washington. Young as he was, Lindgren had dominated the Olympic trials—Mills had run a poor second to him there—and had beat Soviet runners in a Los Angeles meet. But the hard fact was that, despite Lindgren, America had no real business dreaming of a medal in the 10,000. Australia's Ron Clarke, the world-record holder, would be in Tokyo, as would Murray Halberg from New Zealand and Britain's Ron Hill. There would be Ethiopia's Mamo Wolde, a corporal in Emperor Haile Selassie's imperial bodyguard and a teammate of that nation's legendary marathoner, Abebe Bikila. Mohamed Gammoudi, a Tunisian army sergeant, would be there, along with defending Olympic champion Pyotr Bolotnikov from the Soviet Union. The field was the best of the best.

But in the two weeks before the October 14 contest, Mills trained better than he ever had in his life. The Marines had given him a confidence he had thus far lacked, and his focus was now consuming and complete. He was running more than a hundred miles a week, covering the ground in long, effortless strides. He had felt his legs grow supple, elastic; and the terrible fatigue that comes to every runner now and then had vanished. Now he had a powerful kick left in him at the end. Two days before his Olympic race he ran the 220 in 23.4 seconds—a strong sprint for anybody, but especially for a distance runner.

A drenching rain had swept Tokyo the night before the race and had continued into morning. But as Mills and the other runners jogged around the rust-colored track in their sweatshirts, the sky cleared and the sun swiftly dried the course. Mills could just make out his wife, Pat, up in the stands of the National Stadium. She was probably the only other person on the planet who thought he was going to win.

Now the starter summoned the 29 runners and got them milling nervously as wild horses at the line, where they would start from a standing position. When the gun went off, the runners stampeded down the track, the herd swiftly stretching out into a long, thin, diamond shape, with Mamo Wolde suddenly at the point, Ron Clarke a close second. Mills moved in behind Clarke, following the only strategy he thought would let him win: Stay with the leaders through all 25 laps, then use that powerful kick in the stretch. Mohamed Gammoudi, the Tunisian, ran at his side. Behind him drummed the other 50 legs in the race, beating out a steady rhythm on the track.

The lozenge of runners stretched into a line that lapped the track, and by the 15th circuit the leaders had begun to overtake stragglers. Mills stayed with the front runners—Clarke, Wolde, Gammoudi—conscious that the Soviet, Bolotnikov, was on his shoulder. Lindgren was running on an injured ankle, well back and out of contention. Lap by lap, the number of stragglers increased, so that the runners had to buck traffic as well as run their race. By lap 20, Mills could feel the long-distance fires burning in his lungs, a familiar pain flowing up his legs. Somewhere he had developed a blister on his left foot, and it jabbed him every time that foot hit the reddish grit of the track.

Now some strong contenders began to fade. Bolotnikov and Wolde dropped back. Clarke, Gammoudi, and Mills went into the final lap knowing they would share the medals among them. But how?

Clarke accelerated in the backstretch. Mills, wondering how much the Australian had left, kept with him, passing Gammoudi. Clarke

slowed, and he and Mills pounded around the track like a high-stepping team in an invisible harness, the Tunisian two steps behind them.

A knot of stragglers loomed ahead, some of them several laps behind the leaders, wobbling, their balance skewed by fatigue, their arms waving like gyros to keep them upright. Clarke and Mills had to move outside to pass them. As Clarke swept past one, the straggler tumbled into him, knocking the Australian off stride—and into Billy Mills, who was pushed to the outside of the track. Desperately close to crashing, Mills managed to stay on his feet and regain his stride. Clarke looked toward him and Mills read his lips: "I'm sorry." Mills moved back alongside him.

Suddenly, there was Gammoudi again. He had come up behind the two leaders, intent on pushing his way through the narrow space between them. Instead, he ran into them. Unaware that Gammoudi was anywhere nearby, Mills was surprised when the man's shoulder hit his own, and a powerful push sent him stumbling, almost falling, toward the outside lanes. Something— perhaps a surge of his old anger—washed through Mills then and swept away the fatigue, the fuzzy vision, the pain. The world righted itself. Off to his left he could see Clarke staggering, evidently bumped off stride by Gammoudi, who now led Mills by a good three steps. The tape, the finish line, the end of this eternity of running, lay some 200 meters down the track.

The track. Mills realized that running on the little-used outer lanes was giving him better traction. Whatever Gammoudi's intentions, his push had been a tremendous favor. Mills' spirits rose; the sprint to the finish began uncoiling in him like a great spring.

They were in the homestretch.

Clarke had already turned it on. He caught Gammoudi, and the two thundered toward the tape shoulder to shoulder, nearly 10 yards ahead of Mills. A great roar seemed to fill the world, but it wasn't coming from his heart and lungs,

Australia's Ron Clarke leads the pack of 10,000-meter runners at the start of the race. The field for the 10,000 didn't have to qualify in heats. The 29 competitors from 17 countries—a comparatively small group—all ran in the final.

An exultant Billy Mills (*No. 722*) breaks the tape at the finish of the 10,000. His surprising victory overshadowed the milestone of the second-place finisher, Mohamed Gammoudi (*No. 615*), who became Tunisia's first Olympic medalist. Gammoudi would become his country's first Olympic champion by winning the 5,000 at Mexico City 1968.

people were on their feet, shouting crazily to help the two runners along.

Mills let the coil unwind. He passed Clarke and Gammoudi 20 yards from the tape and crossed the finish line 3 yards ahead of them. He had run the 10,000-meter in 28:24.4—46 seconds faster than he ever had before. Thirty years later, editors would rate Billy Mills' gold medal the biggest upset in sports history—bigger than the New York Jets beating the Baltimore Colts in Superbowl III, bigger than Cassius Clay's defeat of Sonny Liston. The upset evidently ignited Clarke. The Australian may have thought about retiring after Tokyo, but instead he would go on to break a dozen world records in Europe the following summer, beating Mills every time they raced—five times in all. There would be a movie, *Running Brave*, about Mills and his impossible victory.

But at the moment of that victory on October 14, 1964, there was just the 26-year-old Marine lieutenant, and his wife hurrying down from the

stands, and a Japanese official running up to ask, "Excuse me, but what is your name?"

No one had ever heard of Billy Mills.

Everybody had heard of Dawn Fraser. The 27-year-old Australian had swept into Tokyo like a film star, trim and pretty behind the dark glasses, trailing a reputation that cut two ways. Some people thought her nothing but temperament and trouble. But for the past half-dozen years or so, most had believed Dawn Fraser was the world's best woman swimmer. She had come out of the seedy suburb of Balmain near the Sydney docks—her father had been a shipwright over on Cockatoo Island—and her family shared an old, metal-roofed semidetached house on Birchgrove Road. Dawn had been a cheeky kid, asthmatic and allergic to chlorine, among other things, living in the big shadow cast by four older brothers. At the Elkington Park Baths, however, she had learned that the disciplined breathing of the swimmer eased her asthma, and the water soothed her and brought her a profound peace. She had become a swimmer—then *the* swimmer in a nation of them.

Not that Fraser's life had been anything like easy. Her parents had their share of illnesses—the father, like the daughter, suffered from asthma finally teased into lung cancer by years of cigarette smoking; the mother had heart trouble. Dawn's strapping big brother Don had died in 1951 of leukemia. Indeed, the swimmer's successes sometimes seemed to grow from a bed of tragedy.

During the austral summer of 1955-56, Fraser had won every South Australian freestyle championship—110, 220, 440, 880 yards. On Saturday, December 1, 1956, she had won her first Olympic gold medal, in Melbourne, in the 100-meter freestyle. She had won the gold in the 100-meter at Rome 1960—where she also began acquiring a reputation for trouble that would cling to her like a barnacle. She refused to swim in a medley relay, causing her teammates to give

her the silent treatment. She was censured for wearing a nonregulation swimsuit. Officials of Australia's amateur swimming union hinted that there had been other, unspeakable offenses—all denied. For a time, there had been some doubt whether she would compete internationally again, or that she would go to Tokyo at all. The simple

Cycling was a fun way for Dawn Fraser to get around Tokyo, but it wasn't her sport. She was a swimmer attempting to win her third consecutive gold medal in the 100-meter freestyle.

NEW HEIGHTS

World records usually increase incrementally, but from 1960 to 1964, the pole vault standard changed 17 times. The revolution was clear at the Tokyo Games, where the top nine finishers all bested the Olympic record of 15 feet 5 inches (4.69 meters). America's Fred Hansen won the event with a vault of 16 feet 8 ¾ inches (5.09 meters). The big difference wasn't better athletes, but better equipment: The era of the fiberglass vaulting pole had begun.

The pole vault dates back some 200 years. The earliest vaulters planted hickory poles on the ground, climbed to the top of them, and swung themselves over a bar. Around the beginning of the 20th century, Americans developed the basic fixed-hand style of vaulting that persists today. Hickory gave way to the more resilient bamboo (*right, top*) that remained the material of choice until World War II, when bamboo from Japan, the world's biggest supplier, became scarce. Manufacturers responded by developing poles of alloyed aluminum and steel (*right, center*). These were adequate, but they didn't improve performance.

Fiberglass poles made their first Olympic appearance at Helsinki 1952. America's Bob Mathias, defending decathlon champion, complained to his high-school coach that his metal pole was too heavy. The coach, who worked summers at a factory that made fiberglass fishing poles, fashioned some fiberglass into a lightweight pole—one that helped Mathias win his second consecutive decathlon.

A more durable commercial fiberglass pole (*right, bottom*) reached the market in 1961, and within two years it was revolutionizing the sport. The flexible pole stores the athlete's energy, releasing it as the pole straightens at the top of the leap's arc and propelling the jumper to new heights. In 1963 the 16-foot (4.87-meter) barrier in the pole vault was cracked, and within two years the once-unthinkable 17-foot mark would fall.

America's Fred Hansen vaults 16 feet 8 ¾ inches (5.09 meters) on his final try. Hansen set three world records during the 1964 track season. His performance at Tokyo was good enough to win, but well short of his best.

Decathlete Dramane Sereme of Mali rests comfortably on landing pads. Early pole-vaulters jumped into sand or sawdust. The new highs in the event wouldn't have been possible without better cushioning in the pits.

or that she would go to Tokyo at all. The simple fact was, however, she was too good to exclude.

Fraser's father succumbed to lung cancer in 1962, the same year that she swam the 100-meter in less than a minute—the swimmer's equivalent then of the runner's 4-minute mile. Her mother died in an auto accident in February 1964, a collision that injured Dawn enough to cast doubt on whether she would ever swim again, especially in Tokyo: The Olympic sojourn was to have been her mum's first overseas trip. But then October had arrived, and here Fraser was, like a film star, the great swimmer everyone remembered from Melbourne and Rome and points in-between. She was celebrated, but few thought she had a chance at a third gold medal in her event. Life had slapped her too hard, spiritually and physically; no one could bounce back so quickly. Besides, she was so old, at 27, that her 14 Australian women teammates called her Granny.

With or without Fraser, Australia had lost its preeminence in swimming to the United States. The women's swimming sprints in Tokyo were expected to be dominated by a 15-year-old California girl named Sharon Stouder. Confounding the Aussies further, Fraser—the rebel as always—started out on a sour note, ignoring a team rule forbidding any swimmer scheduled for an event within three days from marching in the opening ceremonies. The rule was meant to keep the swimmers fresh, but Fraser, miffed at being excluded from the opening rites in Melbourne and Rome, resolved not to be thwarted again. So march she did. "Good on you, Dawnie," one manager said. But other team members were angry and resentful. Gold medalists, they asserted, should behave the same as anybody else.

Fraser, however, was not inclined to behave. In a second heresy, she refused to wear the team's regulation swimsuit, claiming it constricted her breathing. She got away with wearing her own suit for a while, but team managers forced her back into the proscribed costume for the final heat in the 100-meter competition.

The race was set for 8 p.m. on Tuesday, October 13, a rainy night in Tokyo. Fraser arrived at the National Gymnasium's vaulting natatorium at about ·7:20 and took a slow quarter-mile warm-up swim, then two hard 25-yard sprints. Then she changed into a dry suit, had a trainer give her a rubdown, and did some exercises. She was nervous, knowing that Sharon Stouder would be in the race—the only female there who might outswim her. She was also wrung out from the swimsuit debate, and her breathing was tattered by a bad spell of asthma and a cold, not to mention the tight regulation garb she now wore. Her spirits dragged.

In the water, Stouder gave Fraser no quarter. They pounded along, the young Californian matching the Australian Granny stroke for stroke. Worried about her own condition, Fraser chose to do a slow, conventional open turn rather than her usual quick tumble, and peering underwater, she saw Stouder take advantage of the moment's slack. Heading back, the two were even. Then, 25 meters from the finish, Fraser put all her experience and power into the race and pulled ahead to win by what one reporter called a touch. Her time: 59.5 seconds. Stouder finished just 0.4 of a second behind her to become only the second woman to break the minute barrier. For the third time in a row, Fraser had taken the 100-meter Olympic gold medal, an unprecedented achievement. The brash kid from Balmain stood on the dais and cried with pride.

Still, Fraser continued to encounter more turbulence out of the water than in it. On Wednesday the 21st she moved out of the Olympic Village and into the Imperial Hotel to work with a film vérité team shooting *The Dawn Fraser Story* for Australian television. Two days later she was arrested by Japanese police for helping to pilfer an Olympic flag flying near the moat of the imperial palace. She wasn't charged for the prank—indeed, the

Finalists in the women's 100-meter freestyle take their marks. Dawn Fraser (lane 4) was the first woman to break one minute in the 100, but her age and injuries turned America's Sharon Stouder (lane 3) into the prerace favorite.

police ended up giving her the flag in question—and on Saturday, October 24, she was honored as the first woman ever to carry her own nation's flag in the closing ceremony of any Olympic Games.

But the incident at the emperor's palace, taken with her other iconoclasms, had set an official fuse sputtering. In March 1965 the Australian national governing body for swimming suspended her from all forms of competitive swimming for 10 years. The harsh penalty was never quite explained, and after a lawsuit it would be shortened to four years. Still, the ban would spell the end of Dawn Fraser's Olympic career and forever moot the question of whether yet another

gold medal—another impossible victory—would have waited for her at the end of the 100-meter swim at Mexico City 1968.

Like two sides of a coin, the lives of two very unlike Australian athletes had been linked since the glory days of the 1956 Melbourne Olympics. On one side was etched the mischievous profile of Dawn Fraser, a self-acknowledged magnet for misbehavior. On the obverse was a likeness of Fraser's veritable opposite. Betty Cuthbert was Australia's golden girl, devoutly religious, team minded; she had been the much-liked captain of the Australian squad that went to Rome in 1960. The slender sprinter had garnered a pocketful of world records, and in her homeland she was a grand celebrity, her face instantly recognizable to millions of compatriots. Fame was not the only thing she shared with Fraser in the autumn of 1964, however. Dogged by injuries, Cuthbert also seemed to have no chance of winning in Tokyo.

The fleet-footed girl next door had come to international attention by winning three gold medals in Melbourne, and she had been expected to sweep the sprints in Rome as well. But a few weeks before those Games she had ripped a hamstring muscle in her right leg. The injury held her to a painful fourth place and sent her limping from the finish of the 100 meters.

After Rome, Cuthbert had put away her running spikes. People said the Games had ruined both her leg and her competitive spirit. She might always be fast, they said, but she would never again be the fastest. In fact, though, the blonde girl from the Sydney suburbs wasn't leaving because of injuries or a poor showing: The former would heal, the latter could be improved. She had another motive altogether. "I hated being a public figure," she explained. She wanted privacy, an ordinary life, a chance "to wear a dress more than a tracksuit." She went to work

in her father's plant nursery and slowly faded into a background of normalcy.

But running was at the core of her existence, and within a year Cuthbert felt her life had lost its center. "A voice was telling me that I had to run again," she would tell an interviewer nearly three decades later. "I knew it was God, and even though I tried to resist I finally just had to give in." In 1962, only 18 months after her decision to retire, Betty Cuthbert was back in training, this time for the 1962 Commonwealth Games in Perth—and for that greater contest just beginning to show on the horizon: Tokyo 1964.

Cuthbert ran badly in Perth in the 100 yards and the 220. But on the last day of the meet, she ran the final leg of the 4 x 110-yard relay and rediscovered, in a remarkable spurt of speed that won what had seemed an unwinnable event, the form she thought she had lost. Firmly out of retirement, she started rethinking the kind of runner she ought to be. It now seemed to her that her true destiny lay not in the shorter sprints, but in the 440-yard, or 400-meter run. She had never been beaten in that quarter-mile lap.

It was, in its singular way, a killing kind of race, a hard gallop as draining and demanding as the 100-meter sprint, but four times as long. "After

Windmilling through the water, Sharon Stouder is in the clear in the 100-meter butterfly. Stouder recovered from her loss in the freestyle sprint to win the butterfly in world-record time.

Percy Cerutty puts Australia's Betty Cuthbert through a drill at his training camp in Portsea. The controversial coach helped Cuthbert rebuild her stamina at the start of her comeback attempt in 1962.

my races I'd feel sick, my legs would go to jelly and feel like they were going to cramp up," Cuthbert said of the 440. "I'd become light-headed and often my eyes would go all blurry." Moreover, by the spring of 1963 she felt the return of a persistent ache in her right foot. Any weight on the ball of the foot sent out knives of pain.

Cuthbert's name was on Australia's 31-person Olympic track team, but her injury seemed incurable, despite trips to one physiotherapist after another. Finally, a chiropodist in Bondi Beach, John Nolan, found the problem: a dislocated bone under her second toe. She had been running on it, pain permitting, for about six months, with each run exacerbating the injury. By July 1964, Nolan's therapy had her back on the track for the southern winter training for Tokyo. She did well, with unexpectedly good times in the 100- and 200-meter races; but her right calf muscle strained, hobbling her yet again. Further osteopathic therapy put her back in training, but the pain wouldn't go away; she decided to forgo running the shorter races and did a weekly 400-meter run instead. Finally, annoyed at her own fluttering performance, Cuthbert went out to the track at night, determined either to run the trouble out of her body or render herself immobile with pain. Six 200-meter sprints did the trick. By October she was ready.

In Tokyo the press had little interest in Cuthbert. With her history of leg trouble and the questionable karma of making a comeback at the age of 26, she would be lucky to win the bronze. Reporters were more interested in the people tipped to win, among them Maria Itkina of the Soviet Union and Cuthbert's teammate, Judy Amoore. The holder of the world record in the women's 400-meter, North Korea's Dan Shingeum, had been banned from the competition, Cuthbert remembered, "for some political disturbance." Even the so-called Happy Games in Tokyo bowed a little to the Cold War.

The first heats were run on Thursday, October 15, in the National Stadium, and Cuthbert won an easy third place in hers, putting her in the next day's semifinals, where she again found a place without running flat out. She began to think she might be able to take the gold on Saturday.

Certainly the day's first omens were favorable. One of the Australian coaches reported that Cuthbert would be in lane 2, on the inside. It

Wyomia Tyus leans into the tape an instant before Edith McGuire (No. 216) in the 100-meter dash. Both women were members of the Tennessee State Tigerbelles, a team that would dominate women's sprinting in the United States and the Olympic Games throughout the 1960s.

went against a recurring nightmare of Cuthbert's, in which she had drawn lane 8, the worst of them all. Not this time. Holland's Mathilda van der Zwaard ran in lane 1, on Cuthbert's blind side. Then, staggered ahead of her to compensate for the greater circumference of their lanes, were teammate Judy Amoore, Hungary's Antonia Munkácsi, Maria Itkina, Britain's Ann Packer, Gertrude Schmidt from the German Democratic Republic; Evelyne Lebret of France had drawn lane 8.

Out on the track, a cold wind was blowing into their faces at the start, and it would be against them in the finish at the end of the lap. On the far side of the track, they would fly before it. Cuthbert, jittery until now, felt suddenly calm; the race stretched before her with tranquil clarity. The runners were called to their marks, they set their spikes against the starting blocks—then came the *crack* of the starter's pistol. Amoore, always quick off the blocks, shot forward with Cuthbert right behind. Cuthbert then caught her compatriot going into the turn and soon passed her. Ahead of Cuthbert ran the Briton, Ann Packer, moving well but perhaps not well enough, if the golden girl could ignore the terrible weight of her legs, the flame of fatigue flickering inside. She caught and passed the English runner coming out of the turn, and they pounded along the downwind side, barely a yard apart. Recalling the event in 1992, Cuthbert would explain, "It wasn't really me running. It was as if my body had been taken over. And I felt at great peace afterwards. I asked God, 'Have I done enough?'"

She had. Cuthbert flashed across the finish line in 52 seconds, 0.1 of a second off the world record held by Dan Shin-geum of North Korea, and just 0.2 of a second ahead of Packer. The first women's 400-meter race ever run in the Olympics had been taken by Australia's golden girl—who never raced again.

Sizing up the competition in Tokyo in her insightful way, Betty Cuthbert had easily fixed on the runner she regarded as the woman to beat: 22-year-old Ann Packer of Great Britain. Cuthbert observed warily the attractive Briton's terrific speed in the quarter-mile, along with the psychological ploys in Packer's arsenal. Walking out to that final 400-meter contest, Cuthbert noted, Packer had started singing, perhaps to cope with her own nervousness—perhaps to distract her competitors. At the starting line Packer had been very slow to set herself in lane 6, inducing tensions in those who waited, already doubled over, their spikes pushed against the blocks. On the other hand, such stuff could have been entirely innocent: Packer had seemed ingenuous enough, confiding to her Aussie rival after a semifinal that the only way she knew how to race was flat out. And Cuthbert, who had just cruised past Packer in the heat in question, deduced that the British runner might be beaten after all.

The fact that Packer lost to Cuthbert by only the briefest blink of an eye was little comfort to the younger woman, who had been pretty confident of winning: She had been running at maximum throttle and to good effect since her childhood in Berkshire. In 1959 the 17-year-old runner was English schools champion in the 100-yard dash, and she also flourished in the long jump and the 80-meter hurdles. Her abundant athletic gifts had taken awhile to sort through, but by 1963 she had found the heart of her sport: the 400-meter. She had also found her man, Robbie Brightwell, the finest 400-meter man in Britain, and they had gotten engaged.

In 1964 the couple had come to Tokyo figuring to take home two gold medals, and indeed, their performance against European athletes had made them favorites to win their respective 400-meter races in Japan. Brightwell was the British team captain, the cheerful spring from which flowed a remarkable spirit. Packer was delighted by the teeming city, the boisterous camaraderie of fellow athletes. Then, abruptly, the ebullient pair found themselves outsiders looking in.

First came Packer's bitter loss to Cuthbert in the 400-meter. "I had hoped for the gold and I was favorite for the gold," she said afterward. "I

just wasn't good enough on the day, and I shall always be disappointed about it." Worse news: Robbie Brightwell hadn't even placed, finishing in fourth place in his 400-meter run. The gold medals so recently a stride's length away seemed suddenly beyond the reach of either runner.

Without much heart in it, Packer now turned to her second-choice event, the 800-meter—two laps totaling a half-mile. She had run this contest only twice before, and besides, the field in Tokyo was daunting. The brightest prospect, here in the 800 as in the 400 meters, had been the absent Dan Shin-geum. Dixie Willis, the world-record holder, was also missing, too ill to compete. Packer thought she could run with most of the remaining field—still among the best runners on the planet in this event—but she gave herself scant chance to beat such giants as Maryvonne Dupureur of France, the Lille housewife who had set an Olympic record of 2:04.1 in the semifinals, or New Zealand's Ann Chamberlain. Nevertheless, Packer improvised a plan. She could use her 400-meter speed to stay with the leaders for that first lap and perhaps hold the pace to the 600-meter mark. After that, she would just have to see what kind of sprint she had left.

Betty Cuthbert reaches the tape inches ahead of Great Britain's Ann Packer *(No. 55)* at the finish of the 400 meters. Between 1962 and 1964, Cuthbert, originally a 100- and 200-meter specialist, would set three world records in the 400.

A logotype pin from the Tokyo 1964 Games *(left)*, a collector's pin from Hungary showing a water polo player *(center)*, and a Soviet team pin *(right)*.

x 400-meter relays—Britain would later take a silver medal there—and he and his teammates waited on the field while his fiancée ran her final 800-meter contest. For a lap and a half, Dupureur set the pace, and turning the last bend she led Packer by more than 4 meters. The British runner had begun to flag, as if the pain and exhaustion of the run were proving more than she could handle. Unable to keep step with Dupureur and others, Packer dropped back until she seemed to have abandoned serious contention. Then, as though shaking herself clear of her fatigue, she suddenly accelerated. The astonishing final kick shot her ahead, and with about 60 meters to go, she flashed past a shocked Dupureur, who had thought the race was hers.

Ann Packer won by more than 4 meters. She stumbled across the finish and into her fiancé's arms, uncertain whether to laugh or cry at her win. Improbable it had been, but there was nothing indecisive about it. Packer set a new world mark of 2:01.1 for the half-mile.

The unlikely gold medalist ran only once more after Tokyo, at a meet in Osaka. Then she and Brightwell headed toward retirement, marriage, and a family life in Cheshire. "There was nothing very special about me, except that I really wanted to do it," Packer told a reporter years later, describing her victory in Tokyo. "At that time in my life, I wanted it more than anything else."

One thing the United States wanted more than anything else in 1964 was entry into an exclusive Olympic preserve, that of successful long-distance runners. In the first week of the Tokyo Games, Billy Mills had dazzled the world with his improbable victory in the 10,000-meter. But more was needed to ratify American ascendancy in a sport where victory had proved so elusive for U.S. competitors. The opportunity was the 5,000-meter—3.1 miles with the same grueling provenance as the 10,000, straddling the endurance of the marathon and the speed of the sprint. History went as powerfully against the United States here as it had in the 10,000-meter. The last American medal in an Olympic 5,000 had been taken by Ralph Hill in 1932. Yet, for the first time in decades, it looked as if there might be a strong American contender in Robert Keyser Schul.

Schul was a tall, skeletal 27-year-old Ohioan who had grown up on a 100-acre farm near West Milton, asthmatic and something of a recluse during the long midwestern seasons of pollen and ragweed, waiting, as he put it, "until the first heavy frost would allow me to be active again." Asthma almost killed Schul on several occasions. Nevertheless, despite doctors' warnings, his parents let him begin running. "They decided they couldn't keep me indoors forever," Schul said. And when he ran, he discovered that no one could match him over any distance. He may also have discovered, as Dawn Fraser had, that the breathing discipline of lung-straining aerobic sport can sometimes offer relief from asthma. Schul went out for track in seventh grade and stayed with it through high school, but on graduation he had not yet shown his real stuff. No college recruiters pursued him.

The budding runner worked for a year, then enrolled at Miami of Ohio in the autumn of 1956. Two years later, with poor grades and little money, Schul left Miami for a stint in the Air Force. It was in 1961, while he was stationed at Oxnard, north of Los Angeles, that he came under the powerful wing of Mihaly Igloi, the legendary run-

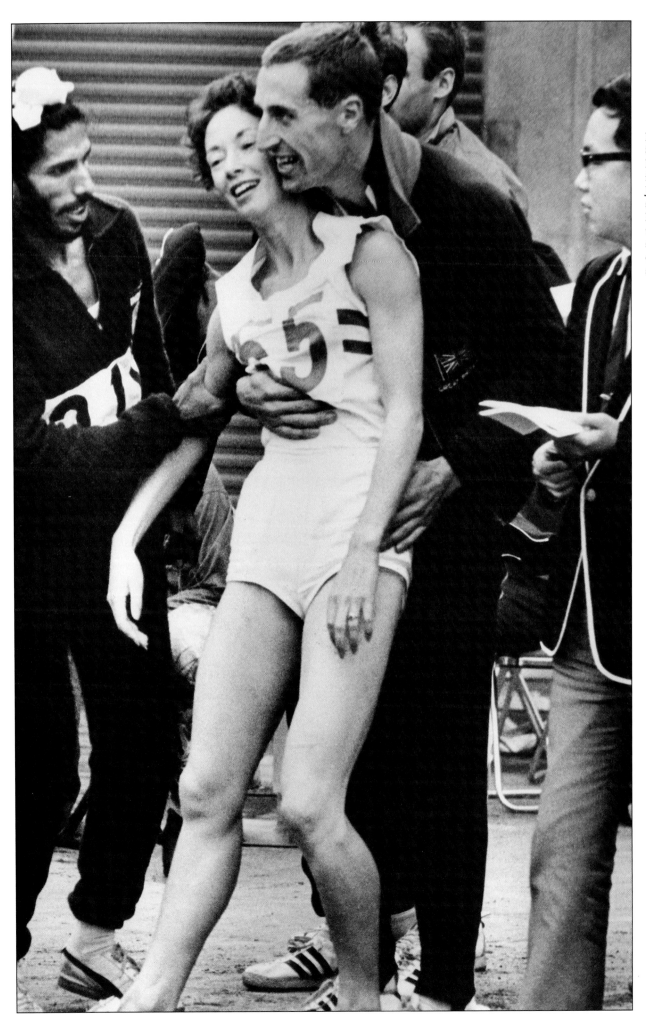

Exhausted after the 800 meters, Ann Packer needs help from teammate John Cooper to stay on her feet. Packer had covered that distance only six times in her career before the start of the heats.

The water jump is a simple hurdle for Belgium's Gaston Roelants. The dominant steeplechaser of his generation, Roelants once won 45 consecutive finals.

ning coach who had defected from Hungary in 1956 after fielding a generation of world champions. "I couldn't believe what he had his runners doing," Schul recalled later. "I didn't think the human body could take that kind of strain, and I surely had serious doubts whether mine could." The young runner had joined the 30 or so athletes training with Igloi. When Schul returned to Miami of Ohio in 1963, he had a modest sort of scholarship—his $100 tuition was paid and he had access to the athletic department's pool of used textbooks. But the school couldn't offer coaches of the caliber of Igloi, so Schul trained alone, eschewing college meets and fixing his eye on the middle distance: Tokyo 1964.

On the winter indoor circuit of 1963-64, Schul

had shown what conditioning could do. At his first race in Boston, he had broken the American record in the 3-mile, and he had won all his races after that, including a couple against Ron Clarke, the Australian who had set the world record for the 10,000-meter. Then, in the spring of 1964, Schul had taken the 5,000-meter in the Compton Relays—promoted as the best 5,000-meter race ever run in the United States.

All in all, 1964 was shaping up as a good year for American middle-distance runners. The United States beat the Soviets in a dual meet—the one in which young Gerry Lindgren had become famous by winning the 10,000-meter. Schul also won in the U.S. nationals and set a world record in the 2-mile, and he began to look like a serious contender for the gold at Tokyo. Indeed, the splendidly conditioned youth had no doubt that he could win the Olympic 5,000; he had told reporters as much before leaving for the Games. It seemed the only negative was a cosmic one, a karmic edict that Billy Mills' upset victory had absorbed all the luck that the Americans were entitled to. A second victory in the distance races, history muttered, was quite impossible.

As the day of the 5,000 dawned, Schul himself seemed mindful of the long odds. He had awakened nervous and jittery, fretting about a pain in his Achilles tendon, fretting about everything, keeping to himself. About an hour and a half before the race, he took the 20-minute bus ride from the Olympic Village to the National Stadium. Cold rain pounded down outside the bus, and a stiff wind drummed through the narrow streets.

In the American dressing room, Schul heard a bad omen: America's Willie Davenport, the best hurdler on earth, had slipped on a muddy track and was out of the finals. Brooding on that, the runner warmed up briefly under the stadium with his competitors, then joined them in the strained silence of the starting room for some 20 minutes before all the contestants were turned out into the wind and wet. "When the cold rain

out into the wind and wet. "When the cold rain hit us," Schul would write, "we just froze." It was 52 degrees Fahrenheit, and there was time for just a single run up the track before the runners were called to the line. Schul's case of nerves seemed to dissolve in the miserable rain; his jitters vanished, and the highly conditioned machine took over—that and a sudden certitude that he could win.

The race started slowly, as cold-knotted muscles gradually warmed and relaxed. Clarke took the lead in the third lap, and France's Michel Jazy stayed with him. Schul kept well back, sixth or seventh. A British runner caught American teammate Bill Dellinger's heel and went down on the slick cinders; Schul hopped over him, careful not to lose his own footing, and stalked Clarke. The Australian was running a race calculated to weed out runners who lacked his powerful kick. He would rev up suddenly to a 4-minute-mile speed, then slow down, then accelerate again. Schul

watched the tactic with the detachment of an astronomer, knowing that it was a strategy no runner could sustain.

Jazy stayed with Clarke, as did a German star, Harald Norpoth, pounding along in the sodden chill. All the runners were splattered with mud from head to spikes, and still the rain fell and the wind blew. With two laps to go, the racers began their kick. Clarke had little sprint left in him, however, and drifted back into the pack. Jazy led, then Norpoth; Schul accelerated easily into third place. Suddenly, Dellinger pounded past them all and took the lead, still with a lap and a half to go.

Just after the bell signaled the final lap, Jazy once again took the lead, trailed by Norpoth and, in third place, Bob Schul. Jazy speeded up for the final 400 meters and Schul tried to pursue him, only to be boxed in by Kenya's Kip Keino. After an eternity that covered nearly 100 crucial meters, the Kenyan lagged. Schul burst forward in the backstretch, convinced that he

An awkward landing ends a terrific effort by Poland's Jczef Schmidt, the triple-jump champion at Tokyo. Only two months removed from knee surgery, Schmidt had recovered enough to register the four longest jumps in the finals. A two-time Olympic gold medalist, he held the triple-jump record of 55 feet 10 ½ inches (17.03 meters) from 1960 until 1968.

The leading 5,000-meter runners slog through a sloppy final at Tokyo. Hard rain kept the pace slow, leaving victory to runners with the best kick.

could now do no better than second even if he ran flat out. He was closing, but Jazy stayed out of range some 10 meters ahead. At the middle of the turn, Schul passed Norpoth and zeroed in on the Frenchman. The gap slowly narrowed; Jazy had begun to seize. Schul could see the leader's shoulders tighten, and with 130 meters left, Jazy slowly ran out of steam. At the 60-meter mark, Schul took the lead, still at full tilt, uncertain who was sprinting up behind him. In fact, no one was within 6 meters of him at the finish, not even Jazy: The American's final burst had so dismayed the Frenchman that he dropped to fourth place, after Norpoth, who took the silver, and Dellinger, who took the bronze. Schul had run the final 300 meters in 38.7 seconds—an average speed of just over 17 miles per hour.

Between them, Mills and Schul had put America securely into the select company of long-distance gold medalists—for a single, glittering moment. From 1964 through Barcelona 1992, no U.S. runner won so much as a bronze medal in the 5,000- or 10,000-meter races.

Distance runners may hate the rain, but not all athletes do. Welsh athletes, like Welsh poets, do best in the heavy weather of their homeland, where a stiff wind beats forever off the crashing sea, and clouds the color of mercury spread sheets of icy rain across the land. Thus on Sunday, October 18, 22-year-old Lynn Davies, a miner's son from the Welsh village of Nanty-moel, peered out his window and felt his spirits lift. "The Welsh gods must have been looking down on Tokyo that day," he would say, "because it was pouring with rain."

Davies was a long jumper who had picked his way up the ladder of his sport, excelling, but not always at the top. He was like a horse that always runs half a length out of the money. Still, he had done well enough to attract some attention at the schools championships in Cardiff early in the 1960s, where he jumped 21 feet in his first time out. Track wasn't much of a sport at his school in the Ogmore Valley; rugby and soccer were what a young man followed. But Davies' long jump had interested Ron Pickering, the newly appointed national coach for Wales and a man of grand enthusiasms. "If you're prepared to concentrate on athletics," Pickering had told Davies, "I'd say you could be one of the best athletes this country's ever seen."

The coach and his protégé worked together after Davies enrolled in Cardiff's local college. "I'd been used to drinking eight pints with the rugby team on a Tuesday night and turning out without training," Davies would recall. "Suddenly I started working with Ron and I discovered the meaning of discipline."

The discipline had fine raw material to work

Even if his long jumps lengthened steadily, however, an Olympic berth for Tokyo 1964 remained unimaginable; he just wasn't that good. Yet there he went, level by level: from collegiate victories to the Welsh championships, Britain's Commonwealth Games, and the European championships. Pickering began to hint that the Olympics were not, after all, an impossibility. Davies began to believe him.

In 1964 Davies opened powerfully, setting a Commonwealth record of 26 feet 3 ⅛ inches (8.01 meters) in May; in July he increased that to 26 feet 3 ¾ inches (8.02 meters). But his athletic life had to be shaped around a budding teaching career, and the split attention took its toll. Davies had made the United Kingdom's Olympic team, but anything better than a bronze still seemed irretrievably beyond his grasp. America's Ralph Boston, the 1960 gold medalist in the long jump, would be waiting for him in Tokyo; so would the Soviet Union's Igor Ter-Ovanesyan. Both men had jumped a full foot farther than Davies' best, the 26 feet 4 inches (8.03 meters) that had got him to Tokyo.

Once there, Davies had seemed to fizzle altogether. Entered in the 100-meter dash, he failed to qualify in his heat, running a poor 10.7. The long jump promised to be little better—until he had looked out the window and seen the wind and rain.

The long-jump competition begins with a qualifying round, where athletes must meet some minimum standard to go forward. In Tokyo the opening standard was 24 feet 11 ½ inches (7.60 meters), which finally declined to 24 feet 5 ¾ inches (7.46 meters). In the final, the contestants are allowed three jumps, and the best eight competitors each get three more.

Davies narrowly advanced, jumping only 24 feet 3 inches (7.39 meters) in his first effort, fouling his second, then making it into the finals with a jump of 25 feet 6 ½ inches (7.78 meters). Meanwhile, the chilling wind and rain took their toll on many of the leading contenders. Of the dozen men who had exceeded 26 feet in 1960, only three went on to the finals.

As expected, Ralph Boston took the lead and held it, followed closely by Ter-Ovanesyan. Davies squeaked into third place with a mediocre 24 feet 10 ¾ inches (7.59 meters). On their

A mud-splattered Bob Schul acknowledges the crowd's cheers after his 5,000-meter victory. Schul had boasted to the press that he was the man to beat at Tokyo, even though America's lackluster record in the event at previous Games suggested otherwise.

A damp sandpit waits to absorb the landing of Great Britain's Lynn Davies. The ugly weather didn't bother the Welshman as much as it did America's Ralph Boston, the long-jump favorite, who'd fared poorly in his four previous track meets in strong winds and rain.

24 feet 10 ¾ inches (7.59 meters). On their fourth jumps, all three men improved, although their order didn't change. Boston had grumped about the weather and had protested the decision not to reverse the direction of the jump so that the contestants would be jumping with the stiff wind, not against it. Davies was pleased. "What did encourage me," he said after the contest, "was Boston's persistent grumbling about the weather conditions. Because you regard a man like Boston as infallible, and as soon as you see a weak chink in his armor, you're glad."

Still in third place, Davies walked out through the puddled track and took up his position. He remembered Pickering's advice: "Look at the flag at the top of the stadium. If it drops, it's a fair indication that the wind could be about to drop inside the stadium." Davies glanced at the flag. It dropped. Off he went down the runway, sprinting like a 100-meter man. He hit the takeoff board and soared, writhing, over the sandpit. He landed, his powerful arms spread downward like pinions—and immediately realized he had done something spectacular. The jump had carried 26 feet 5 ¾ inches (8.07 meters), more than 7 inches better than Boston and more than 10 inches ahead of Ter-Ovanesyan. But both men still had one more jump coming.

The Welshman watched in the pouring rain, pacing nervously in the mud. Boston, like Davies, knew to watch the flag, and he took off when it sagged; but the wind revived just as he rose into it. He landed an inch and a half—less than 4 centimeters—short of Davies' mark. Boston walked over to Davies to shake hands with the new champion, both men forgetting momentarily that Ter-Ovanesyan had a final jump to go.

They watched the Russian rumble down the runway and hurl himself into the air. It was his second-best jump of the competition—but about 10 inches short. For the first time in Olympic history, a Welshman had won a gold medal.

Back home, Davies would find his life transformed. There would be a reception at Buckingham Palace and another at Paddington Station. In Cardiff, 4,000 compatriots would meet his train, and a motorcade would take him the 30 miles to Nanty-moel, where the children would have a holiday from school, the homes would drip with bunting, and the entire town would celebrate its prodigy.

But the highest honor may have come in Tokyo the day after Davies' win, when he had sat at breakfast with Pickering. A fiftyish African-American gentleman had crossed to their table and held out his powerful hand. "Hello, Mr. Davies," he said. "I saw you compete yesterday. It was a great performance." High praise from Jesse Owens, the legend who had won four gold medals at Berlin 1936. His winning long jump of 26 feet 5 ½ inches (8.06 meters) all those years before was just a quarter-inch under Davies' remarkable achievement that rainy autumn day in 1964. It was a record that had stood for more than a quarter of a century.

A collector's pin from Tokyo 1964

Perhaps from some atavistic Viking link, javelin throwing has been predominantly a Scandinavian sport. If there were any doubt of this as the Tokyo Games approached, Norway's big, blond Terje Pedersen dispelled it. On September 2, 1964, he had thrown the javelin an incredible 300 feet 11 inches (91.72 meters), 15 feet 1 inch beyond his own world record. It made him the man to beat in Tokyo, the apparent best in a stellar field that included 15 of the 16 men on earth who had hurled the javelin farther than 260 feet (79.25 meters). Low in this pack of contenders was 23-year-old Pauli Nevala of Finland, who had set off for Tokyo

Dueling Americans Blaine Lindgren (*top lane*) **and Hayes Jones** (*third lane from bottom*) **are the first two over a barrier in the 110-meter hurdles. The pair was dead even by the seventh hurdle, but a tactical error by Lindgren, leaning for the tape too soon, handed the race to Jones.**

pense. Nevala had distinguished himself in 1963 with a throw of 283 feet 2 ½ inches (86.32 meters), but he had declined since, even losing his Finnish national title to Jorma Kinnunen. There were people back in Finland who wondered why money should be spent to send a washed-up champion all the way to Japan.

The qualifying rounds got under way in the National Stadium on Wednesday, October 14, with the skies as gloomy and rain-whipped as

they would be for Lynn Davies. For men intent on throwing a light, metal-tipped shaft through the air, conditions could hardly have been worse.

To qualify at Tokyo, throwers had to send their javelins at least 252 feet 7 ½ inches (77 meters) through the turbulent atmosphere. That failing, the best dozen, whatever distances they scored, would move to the finals. As the competition unfolded, it became clear that qualifying distances on the windswept field would be under

distances on the windswept field would be under the 70-meter mark. The paradigm of Scandinavian superiority in the event, Terje Pedersen, set the day's negative pace; his first throw dropped nearly 100 feet short of the record he had set only six weeks earlier, and his best for the day was a poor 236 feet 6 inches (72.10 meters). He didn't even qualify.

The rain stopped before the finals began, but the wind still blew restlessly, whirling unpredictably in the bowl of the National Stadium. Poland's Janusz Sidlo took the lead in the first round of the final with a throw of 263 feet (80.16 meters). Urs von Wartburg of Switzerland took second, breaking his country's record with his qualifying throw of 262 feet 2 ½ inches (79.92 meters). Pauli Nevala came in third. The contenders vied for position through two more rounds, the lead passing to the Soviets' Jānis Lūsis. Then, in the fourth round, everything changed.

Hungary's Gergely Kulcsár moved into first place with a great heave that carried his javelin a full 2 meters beyond his competitors'—270 feet 1 inch (82.32 meters), a lifetime best for him and a record for Hungary. It looked likely to win the gold, for none of the favorites came within 10 feet of Kulcsár's challenge.

Then Pauli Nevala took his turn. He cantered easily down the runway, twisted backward, raised the javelin, and in a finely coordinated looping release, sent the shaft sailing into the leaden Tokyo sky. Its metal point bit the turf 271 feet 2 inches (82.66 meters) away, 13 ½ inches (34 centimeters) beyond Kulcsár's mark.

The only challenger to Nevala after that was von Wartburg. His final throw traveled about 271 feet (82.60 meters), very close—but according to officials, the spear landed badly; the red flags came out, disqualifying the mark. Thus the gold medal in the event went to someone who wasn't expected to win—as it had in every Olympic javelin contest since Los Angeles 1932.

Pauli Nevala, the erstwhile waste of Finnish travel funds, would take the coveted medal back to Helsinki, becoming the fifth Finn, and the 10th Scandinavian, to win the gold in the 13 opportunities since 1906.

The year of the Tokyo Games was also the year that Elvira Ozolina, the melancholy Soviet athlete who had won the women's javelin competition at Rome 1960, hurled the spear beyond the 200-foot mark. Among the young women gathered in the autumn sunshine

Finland's Pauli Nevala releases the javelin in his bid for an upset. Nevala took command of the event in the fourth round of the finals with a throw of 271 feet 2 inches (82.66 meters).

Mihaela Peneş prepares to hurl her javelin during the finals. The teenaged Peneş won the championship at Tokyo as an unknown. She would finish second as the favorite four years later at Mexico City.

October 17, there seemed to be no one capable of exceeding Ozolina. She was the best, and she knew it.

As soon as the qualifying rounds began, however, her competitors began to prove her wrong. Her 31-year-old Soviet teammate, Yelena Gorchakova, set a world record with a throw of 204 feet 9 inches (62.40 meters). In the finals, Ozolina's best was a poor throw of 179 feet 9 inches (54.79 meters), only enough for fifth place.

But by then attention had shifted away from the Russian javelin queen to a young woman few had ever heard of, one of those brilliant athletes who kept coming out of nowhere to win in Tokyo. Mihaela Peneş, a powerfully built 17-year-old from Romania, threw the javelin 17 feet farther than she ever had before, to 198 feet 7 inches (60.53 meters)—enough to stun the crowd and to take the gold back to Bucharest. Her runner-up was Márta Rudas of Hungary, followed by Yelena Gorchakova, who in the end

couldn't touch her qualifying world record and threw her javelin only 187 feet 2 inches (57.05 meters) for the bronze.

Ozolina may not have won a medal, but she had, in her dour way, the last word. That same afternoon, a statuesque woman with beautiful shoulder-length chestnut hair entered the Olympic Village beauty parlor and, mostly through hand signals, communicated to the stylist her desire to have all her hair chopped off. Minutes later, with both barber and barbered streaming tears, the woman strode defiantly back into the sunlight, her head as bald as a javelin point. The word was that the mystery athlete was Elvira Ozolina, although the Soviets denounced the reports as bad journalism.

Whatever the truth of the matter, Ozolina's shaved head entered Olympic history, as had the shaved heads of the Japanese wrestlers who had made a poor showing in Rome. Journalists amused their readers with such headlines as

amused their readers with such headlines as "Mystery Girl Commits Hair-a-kiri"—forgetting, perhaps, how ashamed an athlete must be when he or she fails to meet that secret inner standard of excellence. Indeed, some reporters would come to regret their puns on suicide.

Death has shadowed the marathon ever since the legendary run of a Greek soldier from Marathon to Athens in 490 BC. That first marathoner died at the end of his 26-mile ordeal, and anyone who has tasted that race's modern Olympic counterpart will attest to its being a potentially killing contest. It also defines, as few other contests can, the physical and spiritual discipline that are the essence of sport.

One embodiment of such discipline, Ethiopia's Abebe Bikila, had spent the years since his first Olympics as he had always spent his time—testing his body against the red clay and thin air of the Ethiopian foothills, where he had run since childhood. Bikila, a sergeant in Emperor Haile Selassie's imperial bodyguard, had captured a gold medal and the world's heart at Rome in 1960 with his barefoot marathon run down the Appian Way. His gold was the first ever for Ethiopia or for a black African athlete.

Since then, with his colleague, Corporal Mamo Wolde, Bikila had trotted past the lush fields of his nation's high country, staying fit, but also staying quiet, a man so intact as to seem mysterious. Indeed, Bikila didn't regard his running as especially exceptional; most of his fellow Ethiopians ran long distances as a matter of course. Running was often the only means of travel available to them, and even at the oxygen-poor elevation of 6,000 feet, they were used to it.

Running may thus have been Bikila's birthright, but that didn't necessarily mean that he was still the best marathoner in the world. In Tokyo there would be more than a dozen serious contenders for the gold, including several who had already bettered the Ethiopian's Rome time. If the

daunting competition weren't enough to make the odds for Bikila seem long, there was also his own dubious physical condition. Just over a month before the Games, he was felled by appendicitis. Although he was training again 10 days after the operation, it simply didn't seem within human parameters to run a championship marathon a few weeks after major surgery. And finally, there was history to contend with: No man had ever won back-to-back Olympic marathons.

If Bikila worried about the odds, he didn't show it. He merely trained—steadily and relentlessly. That was the way of this quiet family man, whose central realities differed from those of most long-distance runners. Bikila was first an Ethiopian, with great pride in his country, and then he was a soldier—and only then he was a runner. For casual observers, who inevitably overlooked the steel at the core of his character, he was easy to underrate.

The host country for the 1964 Games had its own hope for the marathon, embodied in Kokichi Tsuburaya, a 23-year-old member of the Training School of the Japanese Ground Self-Defense Force. Tsuburaya had run only three marathons before Tokyo, but he seemed to have the requisite stamina and discipline. He would need it, for he carried quite a burden: It had been 28 years since Japan had taken a medal in an Olympic track and field event. Because the marathon loomed so large in prestige, a gold medal here would be hugely symbolic of Japan's recovered greatness.

Tokyo's marathon route led from the National Stadium out along the Koshukaido highway to a turning point—and halfway mark—at Tobitakyu-machi in the northwestern suburb of Chofu. By six o'clock on the morning of the race, Wednesday, October 21, the first of some 1.1 million spectators had already gathered along the highway, most of them hoping to see a Japanese victory.

At one in the afternoon, 68 racers broke from

Bikila, starting from well back in the pack, had made one concession to this particular marathon; instead of running barefoot, as was his custom, he was wearing white running shoes and socks.

Like a flock of flightless birds, the runners swarmed around the stadium track once, then completed another half-lap before streaming out into the city. Tunisia's Hedhili Ben Boubaker was leading at that point. He would not be among the 58 who finished the race. Bikila, the picture of effortless equanimity, kept to the middle of the pack. Australia's Ron Clarke, who was running his fourth long race in a week, took the lead at the 5-kilometer mark, a bit over 15 minutes into the contest, followed by Ireland's Jim

Hogan. Bikila positioned himself to overtake them. Although he still seemed to be in no hurry, by the 10-kilometer mark he had eased past both Clarke and Hogan, who managed to stay close behind him through 15 kilometers. So easily was Bikila running that he took a moment's pause for glucose and orange juice before continuing his untroubled transit of western Tokyo.

At the Chofu turning point, Bikila was still dogged by Hogan, but Clarke had dropped some 200 meters back. Bikila seemed to have no serious challengers, but in his wake the contest continued to play out. Hogan faltered after the 25-kilometer mark; at 37 kilometers he paid for running at Bikila's pace by being reduced to a wobbly, ex-

A turn at the halfway point in the marathon shows Ethiopia's Demissie Wolde leading Japan's Kokichi Tsuburaya, the eventual third-place finisher. Wolde would fade to 10th.

hausted walk that could not carry him to the finish.

Bikila cantered into the National Stadium shortly after three o'clock. He broke the tape at 2 hours 12 minutes 11.2 seconds—more than 3 minutes better than his time at Rome 1960 and nearly 2 minutes faster than the previous world record, that of Britain's Basil Heatley. The Ethiopian sergeant had averaged almost 12 miles per hour over the 26-mile course. As no other runners appeared, the droll champion amused the roaring crowd by doing calisthenics. "I could run another 10 kilometers," he told reporters.

Four minutes after Bikila's finish, the first of the other runners trotted into the stadium, and the crowd went wild. It was Kokichi Tsuburaya, very tired but nevertheless in second place. Heartened by the cheers, his spirits seemed to lift. He raised his head, and his pace accelerated slightly. Then, as Tsuburaya entered the first turn, Heatley burst into the stadium. The Briton had just overtaken Hungary's József Sütö to guarantee himself a bronze; now he began to stalk the depleted Japanese runner. Tsuburaya had given the race everything he had; there were no reserves left for fighting off this final challenge. Heatley sprinted past him to finish second, some 20 yards in front of Tsuburaya, who crossed the line in third place.

The gold and bronze medalists couldn't have known it, but tragedy had been running with them on this epic marathon, although it wouldn't show its face for a while. Kokichi Tsuburaya had won Japan its first Olympic medal in track and field in a generation, and he would become a hero to his people and dream of greater glory four years later in Mexico City. But his effort had cost him his talent; operations for hernia and Achilles tendon problems would kill his dreams. His final marathon in 1966 would rate him only 131st in the world, destroying any possibility of his winning in Mexico.

In Tokyo on January 9, 1967, two months after leaving the hospital, Tsuburaya wrote a letter that included the words: "Cannot run any more."

Then he sliced his right carotid artery with a razor and bled to death.

Abebe Bikila would confront calamity and death as he had faced the ordeal of his sport and his astonishing success. He would leave Tokyo convinced that at Mexico City 1968 he would win his third consecutive Olympic marathon; after all, it would be run at the same elevation as his homeland training ground. "I hope to win easily," he said. In fact, he would be forced out of contention in the 1968 race. A bone would crack in his leg, generating pain not even he could bear. A year later, Bikila would break his neck and injure his spinal cord in the Volkswagen his grateful government had given him. The accident would put the world's grandest runner into a wheelchair, from which, on October 25, 1973, a brain hemorrhage would finally free him.

Agony in the endgame of his life did nothing to ruffle Bikila's imperturbable dignity. Success and tragedy were both part of life, he told those who asked how he bore his misfortune, and one must learn to accept both. Life was long and had many twists and turns, he might have added. Life was a marathon.

Abebe Bikila crosses the finish line first in the marathon for the second time in consecutive Games. Before accepting congratulations, Bikila performed some exercises to work out his sore muscles. Observers took this to mean he was ready to race some more.

UNDER THE VOLCANO

Fans liked to come up and touch the heavily muscled legs that had propelled New Zealand's Peter Snell through every temporal barrier of middle-distance running. At Rome 1960, the then-obscure New Zealander had defeated a host of fast favorites in the 800-meter run, giving his country its first taste of Olympic gold since the Berlin Games of 1936. At home, Snell was the cinder-track counterpart to Sir Edmund Hillary, the New Zealand beekeeper who in 1953 had conquered Mt. Everest. Those machinelike legs had brought Snell the kind of fame formerly enjoyed by Britain's Roger Bannister—later Sir Roger—who had shattered the 4-minute barrier running the mile for Oxford in 1954, and whose best times were a good 2 seconds behind Snell's. Indeed, the newcomer's successes had set all New Zealand jogging around the rough, rolling terrain of the two islands; he had created a nation of runners.

Snell had come to Tokyo as the world's premier middle-distance man, holder of world records for the mile, half-mile, and 800 meters, along with indoor half-mile and 1,000-yard events. The question was less whether he would win a gold medal than how many, for he was inclined to enter both the 800- and 1,500-meter events.

Like many great athletes, Snell had always felt a restless excess of energy, and sports had been a way of draining some of that away. Sports had also been the lingua franca of the household of George and Margaret Snell. George was chief engineer at the Electric Power Board of Opunake, a small town on the North Island's west coast, when Peter was born there in December of 1938. The boy had spent his first decade in a spectacular natural architecture. The dark lava beach at Opunake was hugged by a semicircle of hundred-foot cliffs and constantly pounded by giant waves spun up across the vast fetch of ocean to the west, all in the shadow of Mt. Egmont, a towering extinct volcano just to the east. Volcanoes—some forever quiet now, some

New Zealand's Peter Snell, Olympic Gold Medalist, Rome 1960, Tokyo 1964

merely sleeping—honeycombed this rough, beautiful homeland, imparting a peculiar uncertainty to it. Beneath the tranquil landscape lived a potential for grand destruction. Ferocious mountain rivers drained the mountains' flanks, and everywhere around young Peter Snell there swirled an exotic mixture of native and imported languages: He lived in the Taranaki, as the Maori called the region, but only a few kilometers to the north was the very English-sounding town of New Plymouth.

Among the undulating hills and old volcanoes and crescent beaches of the Taranaki, Peter had tagged after his dad to cricket matches and followed his mother to her tennis. By the time he was five he had grasped the rudiments of both sports; at eight, like most of his compatriots, he entered rugby, then discovered badminton, then golf, then field hockey. Sports were about all that really interested young Snell, and he went at each of them with the tenacity that would eventually bring him fame. In 1947, Snell's father moved the family north to Te Aroha, near Auckland. Peter continued to excel in sports. He was his primary school's tennis champ, a regional rugby halfback, singles and doubles tennis champion in the Thames Valley. Soon it seemed to him and to his parents that he must inevitably make his way as a champion athlete. Nothing else had ever held the slightest gravitation for him.

As for running, Snell had treated that initially as just a way of venting his simmering excess of energy. In Opunake he had run every morning along the glittering sea, under the frown of Mt. Egmont. At Te Aroha, having no bicycle or bus, he ran the several miles between home and school each day, mainly to save time for playing lunch-break rugby or cricket, depending on the season. He ran his first real races at 12; two years later he ran his first mile, setting a school record with an unexceptional 5 minutes 21 seconds. His future, Snell was certain, lay in tennis. Of course, he was dead wrong: Those legs were meant for running.

In a 1957 meet Snell ran the half-mile in 1:54.1, and as he wrote later, "I tossed tennis and everything else away." He was no longer a promising athlete of all work; he was a track man. His parents wondered what their stellar son could possibly have in mind; no one could make a living doing track, and he was dropping out of school to do it.

But Snell pursued his new goal with characteristic single-mindedness. He placed himself under the care of Arthur Lydiard, a small, charismatic man whose theories—and unshakeable certitude—made him one of the world's great track coaches. Putting Snell with Lydiard was like handing a Ford Mustang to Carroll Shelby, for it was at Lydiard's that a fine running machine was transformed into a formidable racing one.

Lydiard had eschewed the interval training used to such good effect by Roger Bannister. "They're trying to develop stamina through speed," he told one reporter dismissively, referring to the technique of having runners sprint, then coast, then sprint. The way to build stamina, Lydiard believed, was controlled speed, applied over a long course of undulating terrain. "You must exhaust yourself systematically and sensibly," he explained. "Not go ahead and kill yourself. You must train and not strain." The regimen was a triad of workouts, one over distance, one over hills, one on a track. There was no weight lifting or calisthenics or special diet—the techniques used by most of the running world. His method, Lydiard said, would work for any athlete.

Perhaps, but at first it seemed not to work for Peter Snell. In 1958, Snell had begun running the long races Lydiard used for training, but the results were uneven. "Two good 15-mile runs," Snell wrote afterward, "would be followed by a feeble 4-miler as I struggled to recover." He felt he couldn't take on New Zealand's grueling Waiatarua, a spirit-cracking 22-mile run through the steep-sloped wilderness of the Waitakere

Ranges south of Auckland. Lydiard had said that when Snell could do a good Waiatarua and at the end feel like going around again, he would be ready. Snell ran the Waiatarua, but he was anything but ready. He finished in a weaving zombie stumble, then flopped down and cried with shame.

That was the oddity about Peter Snell, the man who had made the mile—the one race that truly separated the merely fast from the indomitable—inseparably his event. Standing on those steel-spring legs, he was plagued by a peculiar frailty threading through the rest of him. Like his volcanic homeland, he had a webbing of subterranean flaws: Doing poorly could make him cry. His upper body was so little trained that a couple of laps in a pool could wear him out. He got carsick. He cramped easily and was a magnet for colds and flu and gastroenteritis. And he had nothing much on his mind but running well. His friends were running friends, his life the runner's life, which meant that beyond running was a void. Even his job carried irony: The celebrity athlete was a spokesperson for a New Zealand cigarette company.

Where Arthur Lydiard was all certitude, Snell was all doubt. Success could hit the athlete like a quart of British gin. "After he broke the world records," his coach told one reporter before Tokyo, "he went haywire—racing and racing, wearing his condition down, looking jaded. He became confused." Intense, alone, calculating, rather humorlessly intent on winning, filled with self-doubt—Snell was the victim of faults that, like the cracks in subterranean New Zealand, like those that wrinkled the earth around Japan, tensed with a potential for failure. It was strange equipment to bring to Tokyo, to the race of his life. But it was Snell's secret; only he questioned his ability to win in the National Stadium that October of 1964. He was everyone else's favorite.

Spinnakers catch breezes for the 5.5-meter yachts at the Olympic regatta. At the time Tokyo bid for the Games, Japan didn't have a suitable venue for yachting. Organizers built the Enoshima Yacht Harbor, a 22-acre complex on the shores of Sagami Bay, creating an Olympic legacy for Japanese boating enthusiasts.

THE OLD MAN AND THE SEA

The opening ceremony of the Melbourne Olympic Games in 1956 was an inspiration for Australia's Bill Northam. He vowed then and there that he would become part of an Australian Olympic team, an audacious pledge for a 51-year-old man. Fortunately, he'd recently taken up sailing, and he set his sights on qualifying for Australia in the 5.5-meter yachts.

A corporate executive for Johnson & Johnson, Northam had the time and money to work at his quest. No dilettante, he was a natural yachtsman with a great feel for steering a boat, a skill he attributed to a brief, early career as a race-car driver. In his first race he left little doubt that he was a novice—he objected that the starter's boat was anchored in his way, not realizing it was needed as a marker—but within a year he and his two-man crew started to win. Soon they were collecting the most prestigious yachting trophies in Australia. Even so, it was a shock to his country's sailing fraternity when Northam won at the Australian Olympic trials.

Now 59, Northam took his boat *Barrenjoey* to Tokyo, where America's John McNamara, piloting *Bingo*, was the acknowledged favorite. The two helmsmen waged a spirited battle of words as well as seamanship throughout the seven-day Olympic regatta. The decisive clash came in the last race. Northam led on points, so McNamara needed to win if he was to have any chance for the gold. During the race, however, the American cut off a Swedish boat, an infraction that resulted in his disqualification. Northam, who cruised in fourth, came away with a golden victory, far exceeding his ambition merely to make the team.

That same potential for failure—the same sense that something was about to yield catastrophically—had followed other favorites to the Games. Snell had his physical frailty, his aloneness, his disconnection—curious traits in a national celebrity. But others had fault systems of their own. In some, it was an immaturity that left the moral core not quite hardened, so that the Games became a portal to early success, followed by terrible letdown. Still others brought a species of recklessness and a tragic certainty that they would win—not knowing that the glint of gold would illuminate their descent into anomie. Ambiguities of gender and body chemistry offered other blends of victory and doom. For many athletes, Tokyo was the opportunity of a lifetime, but it would also be the brink beyond which lay a life emptied of the sport that once filled it.

Indeed, Olympism itself had come to one of those pivotal junctures. Outside the calm center of Tokyo 1964, a Cold War between East and West deepened, now and then igniting in regional conflicts between competing ideologies. The commodity of trust, in surplus when these Games began, would be in relatively short supply

before the XVIII Olympiad ended in the 1968 Winter Games in the French mountains near Grenoble. And a disturbing commercial reality was abroad in the world. Tokyo's were the first Games available on television virtually worldwide, some venues in color, and the first to hint at the vastness of the money to be mined from future Olympic contests; after Tokyo there could be no going back to a simple kind of amateur athletics. Observers would remember Tokyo not just as the Happy Games but, bittersweetly, as the end of innocence.

Peter Snell was not worried about fate, but still he fretted over the possibility of failure. He had decided to compete in both the 800- and 1,500-meter events—to go for the double victory that can happen only a few times a century. But the night before his first qualifying heat in the 800-meter, Snell brooded about his decision. "I felt I could produce a really good performance over 1,500 meters," he wrote later. "But if I ran in the 800 meters first, there was a strong possibility that not only could I run out of a place in that event—or even fail to qualify at all—I could find myself too tired for the 1,500. I could, through tackling both, miss out on both."

Nerves jumping, Snell mustered at the Tokyo Metropolitan Gymnasium track for the first heat of the 800-meter, relieved to note that only one world-class half-miler opposed him: America's Jerry Siebert. By the time he began his warm-up, Snell's jitters had evaporated; the famous legs were taking over. His world records gave Snell the status of an alpha male in a wolf pack, and his doubts melted into the certainty of victory. He won his first heat easily, then relaxed to watch the others. Afterward, he watched the 10,000-meter, which was supposed to go to Australia's Ron Clarke or to Murray Halberg, a fellow New Zealander. Billy Mills' upset victory shook Snell and the other athletes from Down Under—Americans were kings of the short

Journalists at the Tokyo press center watch the progress of the Games on television. Japanese organizers had hoped that NBC would make extensive live broadcasts to the United States, but that didn't happen. Although a new satellite made it possible, the drastic time difference from East to West undermined the effort. NBC opted to show only the opening ceremony. The rest of the Games were broadcast to American audiences on tape.

track, not the long race, and yet here they were.

The next day Snell ran his 800-meter semifi-nal, again winning easily. But this time, watching the other heats, he saw two runners—Jamaica's George Kerr and Kenya's Wilson Kiprugut—improve on his qualifying time by almost a sec-ond. Snell thought, or perhaps hoped, that this speed in a semifinal would doom the runners in the finals the following day. But he knew it might also portend a dizzyingly fast field.

Going into the finals, the New Zealand run-ning machine mapped out a strategy. He would trail the little Kenyan, who tended to explode from the start, run at his shoulder most of the way, then pass him in the last 250 meters. As soon as the race began, however, Snell watched reality nibble away at his plan. By the time he heard the bell signaling the final lap, he had moved into what seemed to be an impossible po-sition. He was running second after Kiprugut, but he was boxed in against the rail by America's Thomas Farrell and being passed by three other

runners, including Kerr. Snell's solution was to drop back, then circle around the pack in a kind of horizontal leapfrog. He accelerated from the rear to fourth place, running wide until he reached a point where he could fight it out with Kerr, Kiprugut, and Canada's William Crothers. It was a fight that, in the end, had no strategy beyond a sprint for the finish.

Snell broke the tape in 1:45.1, the fastest time in history except for his own world-record 1:44.3. Crothers was just half a second behind him, and Kiprugut and Kerr both finished in 1:45.9. (Kiprugut's bronze was the first medal ever won by a Kenyan—but four years later there would be more.) "With four under 1:46.0," Snell wrote, "that final rated as the greatest 800 of all time." More to the point, per-haps, it was his first good 800-meter time in two and a half years. And, in two consecutive Games, Snell had won the 800. As soon as he had the Tokyo medal in hand, he vaulted into the stands to give it to his young wife, Sally.

Although excellent, the field for the 800 meters lags well behind Peter Snell as he crosses the tape. Snell's speed and stamina should have surprised no one, coming as a result of weeks where he averaged 100 miles of roadwork.

While delicious, the victory had a faint undertaste. Snell had barely a day between this moment of triumph and the opening heats for the 1,500. The 1,500 meters was something over a football field shorter than a mile, but it was still the grail for middle-distance runners. Snell ran two qualifying heats in two days.

The finals were on the same day as Tokyo's epic marathon. The weather was perfect, and large, excited crowds had gathered around the stadium, although not to watch the 1,500. The warm-up area was almost deserted. "I got the feeling," Snell said, "that we were just filling in time for the crowds until the return of the marathon kings."

The 1,500 meters was Snell's sixth race in eight days, and he began it aware that his time would probably not be record-breaking. No matter, as long as it was fast enough to win. France's Michel Bernard led the field for the first lap, with America's Dyrol Burleson a close second. The rest of the pack bulged behind the leaders, with Snell floating along at the tail. Burleson overtook Bernard, then New Zealand's John Davies moved up, seduced by an indecisive eddying of the field into accelerating a full lap before he ordinarily would have. Snell trotted into second place behind his compatriot, running well, but preoccupied with staying clear of traffic. "I was so determined not to be boxed in," he recalled afterward, "I was quite often running a lane wide."

With something over a lap left to go, the deck of runners shuffled for position—and Snell found himself back in the box. The elaborate leapfrogging he had used to escape this kind of trap in the 800 wasn't an option here, so Snell took the direct route. "I merely glanced back to see who was behind me as we rounded the bottom bend and then extended my arm, rather like a motorist's hand signal, to show my intention." Britain's John Whetton, running at Snell's shoulder, saw the signal and, "with the manners of a true Englishman," Snell noted, gave way. Snell was free, and breaking into a powerful drive.

Observers have described what followed as a bifurcation of the race into two separate events. In one, five contenders fought it out for second place, which finally went to Czechoslovakia's Josef Odložil, followed by John Davies. The other event was entirely Peter Snell's. After pouring it on to move into the lead, he opened up a comfortable 12-yard gap between himself and the nearest contender. His time was not earthshaking; at 3:38.1 it was 2.5 seconds behind the world record set by Australia's Herb Elliott at Rome 1960. But Snell had won the elusive double. The last man to win the gold in both the 800 and 1,500 had been Britain's Albert Hill at Antwerp 1920.

Peter and Sally Snell celebrated far into the night in Tokyo. For a glimmering moment it must have seemed that they stood at a way point on the road to greater glory. Mexico City would want those legs in 1968, and who knew?—perhaps there would be other great races beyond those. Meanwhile, there was a world tour to do, the job of a celebrity runner who could draw a crowd no matter how well, or badly, he ran.

The illusion of new worlds at the threshold persisted into November. Just weeks after the Tokyo triumph, Snell reduced the world-record time for the mile to 3:54.1. And yet, by the summer of 1965, the three-time gold medalist would be running for oblivion, finishing dead last in a mile race in Vancouver. A bout of intestinal flu—that odd frailty again—would do its bit, but he would also begin to sense some loss of momentum in Vancouver. Snell told the disappointed crowd over the public-address system: "Because I have performed like this, it will no doubt take a long time to get over the shame of having run last."

Although he would continue his world tour, Snell had discovered that some ineffable impetus fueling his mighty legs had vanished. He wondered whether a change of attitude had made him "mentally geared to giving up," and why his friendships had vanished into the glare of athletic fame, and how one lived without a profession. Then, just 26, Peter Snell retired. The door that had opened in Tokyo closed forever.

As Peter Snell's powerful legs produced velocity, the muscular pins supporting Valery Nikolayevich Brumel produced lift. Speed was of little interest to the 22-year-old from Moscow; he preferred to toil against gravity, now and then escaping that universal force for an exhilarating second. His sport was the high jump, one of humanity's paradigms of challenge. Jumpers speak of raising the bar—precariously

suspended so that it falls at the slightest bump—in the same way test pilots talk about pushing the envelope: It's a vocabulary of steadily increasing risk and difficulty.

At Rome 1960, Brumel had finished a close second to his countryman, Robert Shavlakadze, and ahead of America's John Thomas, a rangy Bostonian who was never far from being the world's best high jumper. Still, Brumel, the handsome, gregarious Siberia-born Muscovite, remained the man to beat. In 1961 he had set the world record at 7 feet 4 inches (2.24 meters), a mark that only Thomas had managed to match. Later Brumel raised the record bar another couple of inches. He belonged to the

Traffic in the middle section of the 1,500-meter race gives Peter Snell (No. 466) some temporary worries. Nevertheless, his conquest at the finish line made him the first Olympain in 44 years to take the difficult double victory in the 800- and 1,500-meter races.

generation of high jumpers who could fly past the 7-foot (2.13-meter) mark, once a seemingly impossible achievement. Earlier conventional wisdom had held that no jumper could leap much higher than he was tall, although jumpers were discrediting that axiom with regularity when Brumel set his world record.

The event itself had changed considerably since the early days of competition, evolving from a nearly upright vault over the bar to a variety of horizontal techniques. At the heart of Brumel's special brand of high jumping was a sequence of carefully orchestrated moves that Nijinsky might have envied. A big, powerfully assembled man, Brumel made his run-up with an awkward-looking sprint as he shifted his elbows forward to compensate for his upper body's gradual backward lean as he approached the bar. He had trained with weights, so that his takeoff was like the explosive uncoiling of a spring: Then, for a moment, he was flying. To clear the bar, every extremity had to be under the fine, split-second control of a bird's primary feathers. First the folded right leg went over, then the head, the big, friendly mouth extended in a white grimace of maximum effort. The right arm flipped back, adding thrust to bring the rest of his large body over the bar. Once the left arm cleared, the left leg kicked upward, adding dynamic balance. Americans called it the spin-roll; to the Russians it was "pouring the body over the bar like a cascade of clear water."

Brumel had poured his body over the world's high bars with a reckless abandon that could bring crowds to their feet anywhere in the world. They loved Russia's jumping bear, his impressive tranquility as the bar went up and up past the 7-foot mark, into the stratosphere of the sport. They liked the power and control of his leaps. By 1964, however, Brumel had begun to feel the same malaise that afflicted Peter Snell, the deepening fatigue that comes from driving the machine too hard, too long. Earlier that year

he lost his Soviet championship to Shavlakadze; Brumel had come to Tokyo with his world record intact, but with his prestige in tatters.

By contrast, America's John Thomas, the bronze medalist in Rome, had come to Tokyo relaxed, unencumbered by the expectations of others. Since Rome, Brumel and Thomas had competed, but they had also become fast friends, training together before meets in Moscow, sharing barbecue at Brumel's dacha, exchanging birthday gifts. Now, once again competing for the gold, Thomas found himself with none of his old friend's physical and emotional baggage. This gave Thomas an enormous psychological advantage—had he only known it.

But Brumel's distress was one of Tokyo 1964's best-kept secrets. Once the Russian had greeted

Comrades in sport, the Soviet Union's Valery Brumel and America's John Thomas hold medals won during a February 17, 1961, New York Athletic Club track meet. The Soviet Union and the United States had started dual meets in 1958, a practice that spawned many friendships among athletes despite political differences between the two countries.

Yukio Endo of Japan lofts upward on one arm during an exercise on the parallel bars. Endo had the highest scores on three apparatus during the all-around competition to earn the first of his three gold medals at Tokyo .

RIVALRY REDUX

The men's gymnastics competition at Tokyo was a near repeat of the Olympic meet at Rome 1960: Russians and Japanese fighting for top honors. Ukrainian Boris Shakhlin was back to defend his all-around title, though his foil at Rome, Takashi Ono, had retired, giving way to Yukio Endo. At 33, Shakhlin was a bit past his prime, and while he remained tops in the high bar, he was not up to the challenge of the younger Endo, who took the individual all-around title. Shakhlin was part of a three-way tie for second with teammate Viktor Lisitsky and Japan's Shuji Tsurumi. Team honors went to Japan for the second Games in a row; the Soviet Union, as in Rome, won the silver.

It was a swan song of sorts in the women's events. The Soviet Union's two-time Olympic champion Larissa Latynina was back to defend her all-around crown. But as in the men's competition, age gave way to youth. The challenger was Czechoslovakia's 21-year-old Vera Čáslavská, whose acrobatic skills in the vault and on the balance beam and uneven bars were adjudged more appealing than the balletic grace of Latynina. Čáslavská won the all-around title, along with two individual event gold medals, but the Czech's singular greatness was not enough to deny the Russian women the team title.

Larissa Latynina flattens into her approach during the vaulting competition at Tokyo. Latynina would claim two golds, two silvers, and two bronzes at Tokyo to raise her career Olympic medal total to a record 18.

Japan's Haruhiro Yamashita comes out of a handspring from the pike position off the vault, a maneuver that now carries his name. He used it to win gold in the long horse vault.

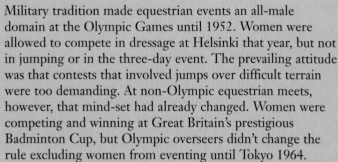

America's Lana duPont leads Mr. Wister over a jump in the cross-country leg of the three-day equestrian event at Karuizawa. DuPont's entry in the contest was a milestone for Olympic equestrians.

BREAKING TRADITION

Military tradition made equestrian events an all-male domain at the Olympic Games until 1952. Women were allowed to compete in dressage at Helsinki that year, but not in jumping or in the three-day event. The prevailing attitude was that contests that involved jumps over difficult terrain were too demanding. At non-Olympic equestrian meets, however, that mind-set had already changed. Women were competing and winning at Great Britain's prestigious Badminton Cup, but Olympic overseers didn't change the rule excluding women from eventing until Tokyo 1964.

It was a timely decision for America's Lana duPont, heiress to the DuPont chemical fortune and a determined equestrian. She'd been riding since her youth, joining her family in fox hunts, but focusing on eventing only after she won a competition at her local club in Delaware. Her goal became to ride at Badminton, an aim she achieved in 1961 on a Thoroughbred named Mr. Wister. Her success with the horse over the next three years won her the fourth spot on the American equestrian team.

The three-day event began on October 17. DuPont turned in an average ride in dressage, but the real test came in cross-country, where rain had transformed an easy course into a difficult one. DuPont miscalculated a jump, prompting a hard fall that broke her mount's jaw, but she finished the ride. Rider and horse were sound enough to complete the jumping course the next day, finishing in 33rd—place no fairy-tale ending for the first female Olympic eventer, but a ground-breaking ride all the same.

Thomas and signed some autographs at the National Stadium, he was spirited away in an embassy limousine to train in a remote corner of Meiji Park, where no one would see what kind of shape he was in. Thus protected, he remained the favorite, and reporters followed him like foraging bees. When photographers burst upon his private training ground, team director Gavriil Korobkov quickly struck the crossbar and uprights. No one from the media saw Brumel deliver his miserable best, 6 feet 7 ⅛ inches (2.01 meters). The champion was shut up in a room to play chess with his masseur. The next morning, in an abandoned school stadium guarded by embassy personnel, Brumel jumped 6 feet 10 ⅔ inches (2.10 meters). He decided he must be regaining his form, although it took a tumbler of vodka to make him sleep that night.

In the high jump, each athlete has three chances at each height of the bar; the winner has the fewest failures at a given height. Brumel's best in the next day's qualifying jumps was a poor 6 feet 9 ⅛ inches (2.06 meters), and it took him all three tries to do it. "I appealed to God," Brumel said later. "'Jesus,' I said, 'why are you doing this to me? I've never done anyone any harm!'" He narrowly qualified, but so did almost everybody else; only seven jumpers were eliminated in the trials, which meant that 20 would compete in the next day's finals.

On his way back to the Olympic Village,

Brumel saw the Soviet team director watching him, and, filled with shame, he ran off—and bounded headlong into an iron gate. He thought the impact must have cleared his head, for that evening he jumped 6 feet 10 ¼ inches (2.09 meters). He also received another jarring, although this time there was no iron gate to shake him up. Sweden's Stig Pettersson reported Brumel for using shoes with thicker soles than regulations permitted. Brumel duly reported to officials with his much-repaired lucky spikes; the soles were according to spec. But the incident ignited the Russian's anger.

Wednesday, October 21, was damp and chilly under pewter skies. Activity was high in the National Stadium that day. It was the day when Peter Snell completed his remarkable double and also the day of the marathon. Just after 2 p.m. the high-jump finalists, all 20 of them, began taking their turns at the bar, placed at 6 feet 2 ⅞ inches

(1.90 meters). It was the opening of a long afternoon for the jumpers. Abebe Bikila ran and won the marathon in the time it took to eliminate one finalist, and another half hour went by before others started falling. The contenders included Brumel and Thomas, Rome gold medalist Shavlakadze, Stig Pettersson, and America's John Rambo, a long-limbed Californian. By 4:23 the bar had been raised not quite 9 inches (22.9 centimeters), and a few finalists began to miss. The stadium lights had come on before the jumpers had passed the crucial 7-foot mark by a quarter of an inch. Now the field had dwindled to Brumel, Rambo, Pettersson, Thomas, and Shavlakadze.

Brumel made his clumsy run and simply failed to take off; his hand knocked away the bar. Jumping second, Thomas also failed. Then Stig Pettersson, after barely missing with his first effort, swept over the bar, matching his lifetime best. Rambo's first attempt cleared the bar so effortlessly that the

Japanese dancers perform *Koma Odori* (*Dance of the Horse*), before the medal presentation ceremony for champion equestrians. The ancient dance originated in the Aomori prefecture in northern Japan, a renowned horse-breeding region. It was originally performed during harvest season in homage to Shinto gods.

A straddling leap gets Valery Brumel over the bar in the high-jump competition at Tokyo. Brumel would become the last Olympic champion to win the high jump who didn't use the flop technique, introduced at Mexico City 1968 by Dick Fosbury.

crowd, now reduced to about half the stadium's capacity, murmured attentively, its appetite for drama aroused. Shavlakadze missed narrowly on his first two attempts. Brumel missed badly on his second attempt. Thomas looked to be over on his second but brushed the bar hard enough for it fall. Then Shavlakadze, the old man of the group, took a long, contemplative look at the bar, made his run, and just cleared it: From the pit he watched the bar he had brushed trembling on its frail supports, but it didn't fall. As if some barrier had been swept away, Brumel now soared over the bar, showing form so perfect that the crowd roared. Thomas followed suit.

The bar was raised to 7 feet 1 inch (2.16 meters). Brumel flew over it on his first attempt. Thomas followed on his second effort. As he exited the pit, his Russian friend came over and shook his hand. Of the others, only Rambo survived this altitude, clearing the bar on his third try. The medal winners had been decided. It remained now to slug it out for the gold.

With the bar at 7 feet 1 ¾ inches (2.18 meters), Rambo made the first jump and failed; his two other attempts were no better. Brumel, jumping second, cleared the bar to break the Olympic record. Thomas was right behind him with a tying

jump. By now the jumpers had been on the field more than five hours. "By the time they set the bar at 7 feet 2 ⅜ inches," recalled Brumel, "I was wiped out. I just knew I couldn't handle the jump. I looked at Thomas and he looked back at me. He seemed up for it, but it was clear that he had had it, too. Right away I knew he couldn't make the height either, that he'd settle for second." As if by tacit agreement, the two champions made their three assaults on the bar—and fell short. They had tied at 7 feet 1 ¼ inches, but Brumel, with fewer failed attempts, took the gold.

In a sense, the Tokyo victory redeemed the great Soviet jumper, who returned to Moscow and the life of a celebrity. A year after the Games he trounced the competition in the annual French-Russian meet without missing a day's training at the Institute of Physical Culture. On October 4, 1965, Brumel hitched a ride home from the institute with his friend Tamara Golikova, a champion motorcycle racer. The pair flashed along Iauzkaia Embankment, speeding into the shadows below Dvortsovyi Bridge. Coming out, Golikova skidded, and the bike slammed into the stone ramps along the shoulder. "As I came to," Brumel recalled, "I tried to move my arms; they were OK. I touched my head; it was all right, too.

My takeoff leg seemed fine. Then I glanced at my other leg. A stark white piece of bone was sticking out from under the knee. And my foot? All I saw was an empty shoe lying 15 feet away."

Over the next four years, Brumel endured more than 20 operations. The first rounds left him limping, leaning on a cane, his right leg shorter by an inch and a half. His marriage came apart—"The whole miserable thing began after that damned rendezvous with Tamara," said the beautiful Valentina Brumel. His friends and the media dispersed. He came to view the world through a haze of vodka. "The man who seemed to defy gravity," wrote one journalist, "is only too aware of its grip now."

But, gradually, Brumel rallied. He learned of Gavriil Ilizarov, a Siberian doctor who had performed seeming miracles of reconstruction—

while being branded a charlatan by the medical establishment. Brumel flew off to Siberia, and Ilizarov put him back together. The Nijinsky of Russian track and field would never fly over the 7 ½-foot mark again, but he could return to Moscow with both legs the same length, and without a cane. In May of 1969 he was able to soar higher than most men ever do—6 feet 9 ½ inches (2.07 meters). Twenty years earlier, that would have been more than enough for a gold medal. Not even gravity can keep a good man down.

If gravity was the law defied by the jumpers, conservation of energy was the law that Bob Hayes, a 21-year-old sprinter from Jacksonville, Florida, chose to ignore. He ran pigeon-toed and knock-kneed, with a peculiar yawing motion that seemed a profligate waste of

TOUCHED

The Soviet Union's Grigory Kriss falls to the ground during an épée bout with Italy's Gianluigi Saccaro but keeps up his defense. Resourceful maneuvers such as this helped Kriss to the gold medal.

The stocky physique of America's Bob Hayes *(leading)* was an anomaly in the sprinting world of his day, a time when lean, angular frames were the rule. Hayes seemed built more for football, a sport he would play professionally from 1965 through 1974.

energy as he galloped up the track, ungainly and strangely ill configured. "I looked out of place," he would write, "because of my muscular build and my big butt, which I carried high coming out of the starting blocks, instead of low, the way sprinters are supposed to." His powerful legs ran down to size-eight spikes, tiny for a 190-pound six-footer. He had none of the grace of most sprinters, but he bounded along, according to one California coach, like somebody pounding grapes into wine. *Sports Illustrated's* John Underwood said it best: "Hayes does not run a race so much as he appears to beat it to death."

To some, Hayes looked like a boxer who had inexplicably entered the wrong event. "I might not have had the correct arm pump, the right body lean, or the proper stance," he explained, "but I won my races. I'm built funny, different from other athletes, so what, I did get the job done." In fact, he was built exactly like what he was: a football player. But, against the improbable

physics of his technique, he was also very quick on his feet: For 100 meters, he was the fastest man alive.

Hayes had come into the world in December of 1942. His mother's husband, a builder named Joseph Hayes, was at war in the Pacific when Robert was fathered by a man named George Sanders. Sanders would give his son little, other than the notion that it was all right to cut corners where money or morality was involved. Sanders himself owned and operated a small shoeshine parlor, but he made his real money and reputation running numbers in a Jacksonville neighborhood called Hell's Hole by locals. Bobby was a hyperactive kid without a great attention span, but he was a natural athlete, good at everything, especially football. When he entered Matthew Gilbert School, he knew he wouldn't have to study. He was a star jock, and his father was a big shot, of sorts.

In fact, most of what the young athlete learned

in those days he acquired outside school. One of his father's many girlfriends introduced him to sex when he was 12. By the time he matriculated at Florida A. & M. in the autumn of 1960, he had already fathered three children that he knew of. By that November he had also been implicated as an accessory in a robbery that had netted exactly 11 cents and two sticks of chewing gum. In Tallahassee, Florida's closely segregated capital near the Georgia line, that petty offense was more than enough to threaten the future of a black 17-year-old: In April of 1961, Hayes drew a sentence of 10 years' probation as an alternative to going to prison. He brushed it off and focused on sports. In all, he spent five years at Florida A. & M. without earning a degree. There never seemed time to study, and he felt no incentive. Football was going to spring him from Hell's Hole.

Hayes had started 1964—his Olympic year—like a champion. He had tied his own world-record 9.1 seconds in the 100 yards at the Orange Bowl Invitational in Miami, though with a favoring wind. In Miami, Bob had stayed with relatives who took him to the famous black club, Nightbeat. Standing by the door were two of the young athlete's idols, legendary running back Jim Brown and a young heavyweight named Cassius Clay. Brown told Clay, "Cassius, here's the world's fastest human right here. He's a Florida boy." According to Hayes, Clay—later Muhammad Ali—hugged him. Then, as others walked by, Clay would introduce himself and his friends, in a vernacular where "bad" meant "awesome," as the baddest trio in the world: the best boxer, the best football player, and the fastest runner. Days later, the best boxer thrashed Sonny Liston for the heavyweight title. The fastest runner went to Tokyo.

There was pressure at the 1964 Games for the United States to reclaim some of the ground ceded to other nations at Rome 1960, where Americans had not fared as well as expected. Particularly,

they had taken only silver medals in the 100- and 200-meter sprints, events they traditionally won. Seventy-five sprinters were entered in the 100 meters in Tokyo, but Hayes worried about only a couple of them: Canada's Harry Jerome, and Enrique Figuerola of Cuba. Hayes began his qualifying heats in a windy rain and on the next day easily made the semifinals. Even on the still-damp track he turned in a spectacular 9.9—another world record discarded as wind aided.

The finals came an hour and a half later. Hayes drew the inside lane, where the 20-kilometer walkers had badly plowed up the cinders. While the lane was swept into better order, Hayes eyed Jerome and Figuerola warily and wondered about the others: Wieslaw Maniak of Poland, Germany's Heinz Schumann, Gaoussou Kone of the Ivory Coast, Thomas Robinson from the Bahamas, and Hayes' teammate Melvin Pender.

As it turned out, the others hardly mattered. Moments after the gun, Hayes was in his top, energy-expensive form, and about 20 meters into the race he let everything out. He boomed through the tape 7 feet ahead of Figuerola, his time 10 seconds flat, setting an Olympic record and tying the world record of Armin Hary of Germany, the 1960 gold medalist. Most observers rated it as one of the best 100-meter races ever run. Hayes climbed into the stands and handed his gold medal to his mother, thinking that he had done what he came to Tokyo to do. In fact, his best race was still to come.

Several days later, Hayes was back on the track, this time anchoring the American team in the 4 x 100-meter relay. The race had been a traditional winner for the United States, but in 1960 the baton passing had been so bad that the team, which finished first, was disqualified. Recalling that debacle, the men who mustered in Tokyo were as jittery as a string of ponies, fearing they would somehow bungle the race a second time. In the first baton pass of the second qualifying heat, it looked as if they would, for Germany picked up

Ulis Williams *(No. 710)* stumbles in a clumsy handoff to Henry Carr, jeopardizing America's chances in the 4 x 400-meter relay. Carr was unfazed by the mishap, though, easily completing the exchange and anchoring his team to a world record and a gold medal.

2 meters while the Americans were passing their baton. With Hayes as the final runner of the quartet, however, the Americans managed a 39.8-second victory—but more than a full second slower than the Italians had done earlier. In the semifinals the U.S. team ran to a 39.5 victory, but France, Jamaica, Italy, Poland, and Venezuela were all just 0.1 of a second slower.

In the final the Americans again appeared headed for a baton-bobbling disaster. They lost a couple of meters as Paul Drayton passed to Gerald Ashworth, who about broke even in passing the baton to Richard Stebbins. By the time Stebbins handed to Hayes, the American team was trailing Poland, the Soviet Union, France, and Jamaica. "It seemed like I would never get the baton," Hayes wrote later, "and when I finally did I saw all the other runners ahead of me, led by the French, who were at least 5 yards ahead. The runners in front of me were kicking up cinders off their spikes, and the

cinders were burning my eyes. I was trying to get out of that traffic just so I could see clearly, which gave me more incentive to run fast."

To observers, what felt like incentive to Hayes looked like nearly superhuman acceleration. Gasped one reporter, "The man just exploded, he was absolutely fantastic, just like a clenched fist traveling along the track." The crowd began to roar its excitement. "I knew I was moving faster in the first 50 meters than I had ever moved before," Hayes recalled. "How could I be running this fast?"

Hayes burst past the tape with room to spare, winning a contest that, moments earlier, had seemed beyond reach. He hurled the baton skyward, losing it forever to a souvenir hunter. As for his time: No official record was kept of the race's segments, but observers estimated that Hayes might have covered his 100 meters in as little as 9.4 seconds—9.6 at the most.

The fastest man on earth would not run again

as a track and field amateur. A contract with the Dallas Cowboys waited for him at home, and in the 1965 season he would begin nearly a decade of dazzling broken-field running with that club. Also waiting for him on the far side of this Tokyo watershed was a good deal of personal trouble—not least, problems with alcohol and jail time for a drug conviction. The two best moments of his life, he wrote later, were spent atop the victory platform in the National Stadium; that was the top of the world for Bobby Hayes.

There was nothing psychologically subtle or subterranean about the flaws that Al Oerter brought to Tokyo. They were clearly delineated, mapped in a crippling radiation of pain. A year earlier he had slipped a cervical disk; unless he moved cautiously, he could pinch a spinal nerve that, in an explosion of agony, would paralyze his left arm. Then, about a week before the Tokyo Games began, Oerter slipped on wet ground during practice and tore the cartilage in his rib cage. Had he been a runner or jumper, the injury would have been bad enough. But Oerter's sport was the emblematic one of the Olympics: the discus throw. It should have been an impossible sport for a man with his injuries.

So anciently affixed to Greek culture that he recurs through Homer, the discus thrower has personified the Olympic track and field athlete from the fifth century BC, when the Athenian sculptor Myron created his splendid bronze statue, *Discobolos*. In that famous figure, which survives today as marble copies in European museums, the muscular thrower looks intently down on a disk dynamically suspended between his four fingertips and centrifugal force, as he begins the transition between the spin and the throw. In another split second his cocked body will release the discus for its whirring

Two diplomas, one for officials and one for winning athletes, were created by Japanese artist Hiromu Hara. Japan's rising sun was the primary decoration. The Olympic rings and the words Tokyo 1964 were printed in gold.

The commemorative medal, presented to all the Olympic athletes, was made of copper with a dark green finish. The front, which depicts stylized runners and swimmers and an olive branch, was designed by artist Taro Okamoto. The obverse bears the Olympiad designation and the intertwined Olympic rings.

Summoning all his energy for the release, a badly injured Al Oerter defies pain as he swings into his discus-throwing motion. Oerter wasn't favored to win the discus in his two previous Games, yet he was able to outmuscle his rivals. He was second choice once again at Tokyo, this time to Czechoslovakia's world-record holder Ludvik Daněk.

flight. The statue demonstrates the central truth of the sport: The discus is not just thrown; it's hurled like a projectile from a sling, and the sling is the athlete's body, spun into coiled momentum until the instant of release. To achieve that instant caused Oerter intolerable pain—and still he achieved it.

The 28-year-old New Yorker might have been Myron's model, had he competed 25 centuries ago. Oerter had followed sports in high school —as a sprinter and football player—and had trained as a weight lifter to drape ropes of muscle on his spare frame. But his taking up the discus had been purely serendipitous. One day, playing at track and field, he had picked up the tapered 4.4-pound (2-kilogram) disk and sent it flying farther than any of his classmates had. Oerter had discovered his sport, and he never looked back. The discus had won him an athletic scholarship to the University of Kansas at Lawrence, and a gold medal in both the 1956 and 1960 Olympic Games. In 1961 he became the first man to throw the discus more than 60 meters, to a world record of 61.10 meters—200 feet 5 ⅜ inches. Early in 1964, protected by a dose of cortisone, he raised that to 206 feet 6 inches (62.90 meters). And yet in Tokyo, few expected him to win. For one thing, his injuries were too severe to be borne. For another, Ludvik Daněk, a 27-year-old Czechoslovakian, had

thrown the discus almost 6 feet farther than Oerter's world record. That was in August, and Daněk had performed at that high level since.

Confronting such competition in Tokyo, Oerter worked to compensate for his slipped spinal disk. He devised a kind of harness that permitted his body to be the sling for the discus while controlling the pain that otherwise dropped him to his knees. He wore an improvised surgical collar made of a leather strap wrapped in toweling, providing support for his head and back. The truss kept his nonthrowing left arm from whipping around in the reverse segment of the throw—at least enough so its motion wouldn't pinch the nerve and paralyze the arm.

Then, six days before the competition began, Oerter had taken his fall while practicing in the 8 ½-foot-diameter throwing ring. "I just tripped and went down," he recalled. "I thought I'd hurt myself. I felt it—but I did it again and this time I tore a tremendous part of my rib cage." Doctors told Oerter to forget the Olympics; he should rest for six weeks. But at his urging they reconsidered. They scheduled him for a course of heat treatment, ultrasonic massage, and enzymes to clear away the blood leaking into his rib cage. Surgical tape wrapped him like a mummy from chest to bottom, and his damaged right side was kept packed in ice. When he started practicing again, his first throw went nowhere and doubled him up with pain.

But Oerter was on the field when the discus competition—three throws to qualify, three more to win or lose—began in the National Stadium. At first, Daněk and 11 other throwers weren't much concerned about the American; trussed up in an ice pack and shot full of painkillers, he was obviously crippled and out of contention. Then Oerter threw 198 feet 7 ½ inches (60.54 meters) to qualify, and the rest of the contenders took another look. But Oerter's next four throws were inadequate. He seemed, predictably, to be succumbing at last to the ballooning agony in his

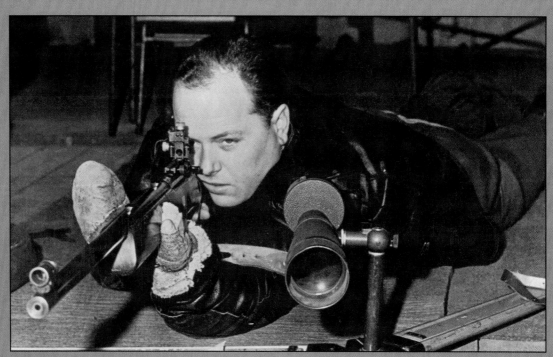

BORING IN

Hungary's László Hammerl lines up a shot during the small-bore rifle event. Hammerl dueled with America's Lones Wigger in matches in three positions and in the prone position. The two marksmen tied with world-record scores in the prone match, with Hammerl winning on a tiebreaker. Wigger shot for another world record and a gold medal in the three-positions contest. Hammerl finished third.

body. By the end of the fourth round, Daněk looked like the winner.

That was when Oerter altered his style. "I was using a slow spin and trying to stretch the tendons to get a little higher," he explained later. "I had been throwing too low and I was trying a very easy turn to correct the problem." On the fifth throw of the final round he threw the discus 200 feet 1 ½ inches (61 meters). "It felt like somebody was trying to tear my ribs out." Then he added, famously, "These are the Olympics—you die for them."

His fifth throw was enough to win, and it brought Oerter an unprecedented third gold medal in the same event in three consecutive Games. And his "you die for them" comment achieved a kind of independent life that caused him to elaborate later. "I know something about pain," he explained. "You can see from the scars on my face that I've been in a couple of bad car crashes. Yet I've never before, or since, felt such pain as I had in Tokyo. I guess I was a little crazy to compete—maybe my remark about dying for the Games wasn't so exaggerated after all."

There would be more for Al Oerter. Mexico City would make him the only athlete up to that time to win four gold medals in a single event in consecutive Olympics. Although his pain trailed him like a shadow, he persevered. An "aging" 32-year-old athlete by the time of the 1968 Games, Oerter would keep throwing a world-class discus until the 1980s—like Myron's ancient bronze, fated to be eternally the discus thrower.

A lithe, pretty brunette from Great Britain had also seemed fated to spend her life in the relative warmth of competitive sports, eternally the versatile track and field athlete. As Mary Bignal, she had gone to Rome in 1960 favored to win the gold in the women's long jump. Just the year before, she had become the first British woman to clear 20 feet in the long jump, and in Rome she had seemed to cinch first place by leading her qualifying round with a personal best of 20 feet 9 ¼ inches (6.33 meters). But, while the 20-year-old golden girl

of British track and field radiated charm and confidence, something had ultimately failed within—something temperamental. "Everything," she said of those Games, "had gone wrong." Misjudging her run-ups, she had stumbled through two attempts and had finally leaped a mediocre 19 feet 8 ½ inches (6 meters), finishing ninth. The next day she battled to fourth place in her other event, the 80-meter hurdles. The stress of dealing with formidable competition had unnerved her, and her shredded nerves had intruded on her performance.

In Tokyo four years later, Mary—now Mary Bignal Rand, having married Olympic sculler Sidney Rand—was still charming and still favored to win. She had done well in the 1962 European championships, taking bronze medals in the long jump and the 400-meter relay, and she had come to Japan as what one journalist called "the finest all-round woman athlete Britain has produced." Still, observers couldn't quite put away their memories of the 1960 disappointment, noting that Mary was now not only a wife, but the mother of a two-year-old. Almost certainly, domesticity had dulled her former edge.

It had not.

As Mary Bignal had been unable to do anything right in Rome, Mary Rand could do nothing wrong in Tokyo. She began powerfully, setting an Olympic record of 21 feet 7 ¼ inches (6.58 meters) in the qualifying rounds. When the finals began, her first jump bettered her own record by another quarter-inch; her fourth jump took her an inch and a half farther; and in the fifth round she went an astonishing 22 feet 2 ¼ inches (6.76 meters). It was the first time a woman had cleared 22 feet, and it put Rand 6 inches ahead of Poland's Irena Kirszenstein, her nearest competitor. The gold medal was the first ever earned by a British woman in track and field.

Competing in the women's pentathlon, Rand led the eight-woman field in the high jump, long jump, and 200-meter dash, running second in

The Soviet Union's Irina Press (left) breeches a hurdle in synch with Germany's Karin Balzer. Balzer would win the race in a wind-aided and therefore unofficial world-record time, while Press would fade to fourth. Press would fare better in the women's pentathlon, making its Olympic debut at Tokyo.

the 80-meter hurdles and finishing seventh in the shot put. She took a silver medal in this extremely demanding medley of events and then picked up a bronze in the 4 x 100-meter relay: The British team ran just 0.1 of a second behind the American team and 0.4 behind the Polish team that won the gold.

Rand had redeemed the 1960 failure, and a good deal more. She had found in the world of competitive sports—the same one that had unnerved her four years earlier—a cocoonlike comfort that she was loath to leave. And there was celebrity as well. Back in her hometown of Wells, Somerset, the dimensions of her record-breaking long jump in Tokyo were written in gold letters on the sidewalk, and the January following the Games, Mary Rand was awarded an MBE—Member of the British Empire.

But Britain's preeminent woman athlete-of-all-work would not go to Mexico City, except as a

paid BBC commentator. On August 30, 1968, warming up for a pentathlon fitness test at London's Crystal Palace, she fell and injured herself. Perhaps she knew that the injury was enough to end her athletic career; perhaps she sensed, as some others did, that she had stayed on too long. "Let me have some prints, boys," she joshed the photographers present on that same, final evening. "It may be the last ones you want to take of me."

The woman who outpointed Mary Rand in the pentathlon was Irina Press, a 25-year-old champion who, with her elder sister, Tamara, had dominated international track and field for almost a decade by the time of the Tokyo Games. Born in Leningrad—Tamara in 1937, Irina in 1939—they had been forced by the Great Patriotic War to a small town near Moscow while their father, a professional driver with a zest for motorcycle racing, went off to fight the Germans. Eventually, the girls and their widowed young mother went to live in Samarkand, where the sisters studied engineering.

Tamara was the first to be drawn by sports. After experimenting with several track and field events, she decided, at 17, to concentrate on the shot and the discus. By the mid-1950s the tall, muscular blonde had become a national Soviet sports figure, unbeatable in the shot put. She was the first woman to put the metal shot past the 60-foot mark, and she took a gold medal at Rome 1960 with an Olympic record of 56 feet 10 inches (17.32 meters).

Watching her big sister, Irina had considered herself puny and awkward by comparison, and she had been diffident about trying sports herself. But Tamara's gravitation had proved irresistible, and Irina had gone into training. She won her first gold medal in the 80-meter hurdles at Rome and was widely viewed as the best woman hurdler in the world.

Both sisters were powerfully built, and their times and distances sometimes seemed closer to the parameters of men's events than women's. In a Cold War atmosphere where diabolical conspiracies were considered the norm, it was not much of a jump to imagine Soviet Frankensteins using hormones and other sinister chemicals to create women athletes with the strength and endurance of men. Irina, it was said, had to shave regularly to avoid sprouting a beard, and Tamara was assembled along the lines of a male weight lifter or wrestler. Irina dated men and had a husband, but Tamara traveled with a pretty blonde girlfriend. Some began to wonder if the sisters were not really brothers after all.

By the time of the Tokyo Games, such suspicions had just begun to harden into policy, but too late to inflict gender testing on the Happy Games. Irina won a gold medal in the pentathlon—the first women's pentathlon to be included in the Olympics—on the strength of her

performance in the 80-meter hurdles and on a shot put of 56 feet 2 ½ inches (17.10 meters). Tamara took two golds, one for a narrow fifth-round victory in the discus over the German Democratic Republic's Ingrid Lotz, and one for putting the shot 59 feet 6 ¼ inches (18.14 meters). Between them, the Press sisters had amassed a career total of five Olympic gold medals and one silver and had set 26 world records.

The year after Tokyo, Tamara Press won in the shot put at the U.S. national indoor championships with a toss of 57 feet 2 ½ inches (17.40

The Soviet Union's Tamara Press watches her shot soar after a forceful put. A champion with the discus as well as the shot, Press set six world records in each event during her career.

Japan's Masamitsu Ichiguchi uses overpowering upper body strength to force Czechoslovakia's Jiři Švec headfirst into the mat during a bout in the bantamweight Greco-Roman wrestling tournament at Tokyo. Ichiguchi didn't lose a single match in his march to the gold medal.

meters). Officials remembered more than her performance; of all the athletes competing, only Tamara had gone over to them to shake hands and thank them. Weeks later, she set a world record of 61 feet (18.60 meters) at the European championships.

Both Press sisters would retire before the 1968 Games in Mexico City, where chromosomal "femininity control" tests were waiting to screen all female contenders. Their retirement just ahead of such testing would be viewed in some quarters as an admission of sexual duplicity. In fact, the two young women, at 29 and 27, were nearing the upper limit of any athlete's career; it would have been time to put their advanced academic degrees to work and to leave the field to younger competitors. Tamara and Irina took up quiet lives in Moscow and pursued successful administrative careers linked to Soviet sports.

They would never quite escape a cloud of suspicion, however. Some believed that they were men who had competed as women, the vile creations of mad sports scientists. More sympathetic observers saw in the Press sisters, as in other big, strong women champions of the day, the tragic possibility of individuals stranded between sexes—women in most obvious respects, but with the musculature and strength of men.

The Press sisters were not the only women suspected of excessive maleness at Tokyo 1964. Romania's Iolanda Balaş, who had won the Olympic high jump in 1960, setting a record that stood until 1971, quietly left the sports scene before chromosome testing began. But gold medalist Ewa Klobukowska, who had run for Poland in the 4 x 100-meter relay in 1964, was less fortunate. In 1967 a chromosome test would indicate that she was what one doctor called a genetic mosaic, with one too many chromosomes. Not male, but not sufficiently female either, Klobukowska was allowed to keep her Olympic medals but was barred from future amateur competition. "It's a dirty and stupid thing to do to me," said an angry, devastated Klobukowska. "I

A muscular thigh and a firm arm hold help American featherweight freestyle wrestler Robert Douglas momentarily subdue Nodar Khokhashvili of the Soviet Union. Khokhashvili would turn the tables on Douglas by the end of the match. The Soviet won the bronze medal; Douglas placed fourth.

know what I am and how I feel." It may be that the Press sisters also knew what they were and how they felt, and retired to keep their degree of femininity to themselves.

Although they were by no means ordinary, the Press sisters were not the oddest couple sent to Tokyo by the Soviet Union. That distinction belonged to two weight lifters in the heavyweight category, Yuri Vlasov and Leonid Zhabotinsky.

Vlasov was the son of a Soviet military advisor to Mao Tse-tung; the father was later killed in one of Stalin's purges. A tall, good-looking man, Vlasov had taken up weight lifting while in the Soviet Air Force, seeing it, perhaps, as a way of confronting and defeating all that was rough and vulgar in his life. In 1958 he had won the national championship, and in 1960 he had taken the gold medal in Rome. The victory had been his cue to abandon the sports world for what he considered his real career, that of a man of letters. The 275-pound champion had an openness and vulnerability that had inspired a film director to

WRESTLING WITH RULES

Almost every culture in the world has developed some form of wrestling, and the myriad styles were a dilemma for officials looking to include wrestling in the Games. Two popular styles had an edge. Europeans favored the French classical style, or Greco-Roman, which bans attacks below the waist and outlaws any hold involving the legs. Americans, however, had developed a less restrictive sport that allowed leg holds. Known as Catch-as-Catch-Can, or freestyle, the American version was popular only in English-speaking countries. The International Olympic Committee set no mandate, so organizing committees were free to choose the style they preferred.

The first modern Games, Athens 1896, held a Greco-Roman tournament without weight classes. The talent level was thin, and the surprise winner was Germany's Karl Schuhmann, normally a gymnast. Organizers left wrestling off the program at Paris 1900, but it was back at London 1908, with weight classes and with both Greco-Roman and freestyle bouts. Contests were timed in rounds only to keep the program moving. Greco-Roman was the sole style at Stockholm 1912, and bouts didn't have rounds. One contest lasted 11 hours, prompting a cry for international standards.

Steps toward standardization didn't begin until a wrestling forum was held during the 1921 Olympic Congress at Lausanne, where the Fédération Internationale de Lutte Amateur (FILA) was formed. This governing body decided that Olympic tournaments would include both freestyle and Greco-Roman and would have weight categories and timed rounds. Rules and holds were codified—upsetting the Americans, whose freestyle form differed slightly from the one adopted at the Congress. Nevertheless, from Paris 1924 onward, there have always been competitions in both styles at every Games.

Yuri Vlasov *(right)* gets an assist from his mighty legs in jerking a barbell over his head. Vlasov, the defending Olympic heavyweight champion, faced a challenge from countryman Leonid Zhabotinsky *(above)*. The two strongmen represented the first generation of great USSR weight lifters: Soviets would win the heavyweight and super heavyweight titles from Rome 1960 to Moscow 1980.

offer him the role of the bemused and philosophical Pierre Bezukhov in a film version of *War and Peace.* In fact, this resemblance to the brooding Pierre would prove to be Vlasov's undoing. The motion picture project hadn't worked out—the director took the role himself—and success continued to elude Vlasov the writer. What was needed, he decided, was the celebrity of another gold medal. He began training in his customary hard-driving style for Tokyo.

A 341-pound, red-haired Ukrainian from Kharkov, Zhabotinsky seemed to be Vlasov's virtual opposite. He was nicknamed Zhaba, which is Russian for "toad," and his manners explained why. Loud and flatulent, he seemed not just unintellectual but unintelligent, and he was

a lazy athlete with a keen eye for the paths of least resistance. Still, in 1963, Zhabotinsky had broken the world record with a 363-pound two-hand snatch. Although his dreadful reputation made him seem shaky as a contender, his world record set him up for a journey to Tokyo.

Some six months before the Games, the Soviet Sports Committee arranged for the two heavyweight lifters to be closeted in the village of Dubny, where the national team was training. Vlasov found himself sharing his table with a man whose personal habits would have embarrassed Genghis Khan. As demanding as a child and a good deal louder, Zhabotinsky had steadily depressed the contemplative Vlasov, while attracting support from coaches of the national team who were put off by Vlasov's aloofness. Finally Vlasov had fled to Moscow to train alone in the Central Army Club gym. The solitary regimen appeared to be effective: A month before the Tokyo Games began, he broke three world records, lifting an astonishing aggregate of 1,278 pounds (580 kilograms). Back at Dubny, Zhabotinsky fretted, painfully aware that his chances of victory had diminished nearly to zero.

That was how the competition seemed in Tokyo on October 18. Vlasov was ahead of Zhabotinsky (none of the other six finalists would come within 60 pounds of the two Russians) by 11 pounds and had just set two more world marks in the press and the clean and jerk. No one had the slightest doubt that Vlasov would win his second gold medal—least of all Zhabotinsky, who appeared to have trouble even with lesser weights. Later, the contender cornered Vlasov in the warm-up room. "Let's call it off, Yura," he urged. "I've had it with competing. The gold is obviously yours. Why wreck ourselves?"

Perhaps heartened by this voice of sloth, Vlasov declined. He had spent a life in a sport that seemed to him to be all integrity, cleanly and purely one of strength. Now he was about to retire. This was to be his last day lifting iron, and he wanted it to be perfect. Vlasov asked for 463 pounds (210 kilograms), and he lifted it easily in a single, graceful movement.

In what appeared to be a desperate bid to move ahead of the champion, Zhabotinsky called for 479 ½ pounds (217.5 kilograms), but he couldn't raise it past his knees. He dropped the bar and walked out, his aura that of a broken man. He hugged Vlasov in congratulations for winning the gold.

Lulled and pleased by Zhabotinsky's evident collapse, Vlasov decided to go for more. A 474-pound (215-kilogram) lift was enough for him to win. But to excel, to shatter every record on the final lift of his career, he decided to try the 479 ½-pound bar recently dropped by his failed competitor. Gripping the bar, Vlasov raised the weight smoothly enough; but once over his head on his outstretched arms, the enormous mass began to tremble. Vlasov was not holding it. Suddenly he found himself chasing the balance point, and he realized that in another moment he would feel his spine begin to yield. He threw down the weight.

Then, miraculously revived, Zhabotinsky leaped back on the platform, gave his coach a mischievous wink, and lifted the same bar that had been too much for him only minutes earlier. It was enough to give him a total of 1,262 pounds (572.5 kilograms) lifted, surpassing Vlasov's 1,256 ½ pounds (570 kilograms). The gold medal that had poised, ready to fall into Vlasov's powerful hands, had dropped neatly into Zhabotinsky's.

That night, brooding over his failure, Vlasov realized that he had been defeated not by strength but by guile. The street-smart Zhabotinsky had gulled him with a venerably transparent psychological ploy. "I was choked with tears," the sensitive strongman would write much later. "I flung the silver medal through the window. Damned, miserable mockery of an award! Was that it, the return for all the years of frenzied study, self-mastery, struggle, unyielding self-sacrifice? A silver disk on a colored ribbon? Inwardly I renounced the trophy, wanted nothing to do with it. I had always revered the purity, the impartiality of contests of strength. That night I understood that there is a kind of strength that has nothing to do with justice."

Vlasov would go on to a distinguished literary career, and he would never put down his figurative white plume of intellectual independence. In 1989, with Soviet Communism balanced as precariously as a barbell too heavy to lift, Vlasov would stand up in the Council of People's Deputies and denounce the KGB in a nationally broadcast speech. Tokyo had cost him a gold medal, but it hadn't diminished his courage.

As for the rough diamond who became in Tokyo the world's strongest man, Zhabotinsky would remain immutably Zhabotinsky, ever heavier, ever more opportunistic, ever lazier. His winning lift at Mexico City in 1968 would not advance the Tokyo mark by an ounce, however, and by 1969, obsessed with an elusive pain, he abandoned a competition, fearing that he might die in midlift. The big, loud trickster retired into bitter solitude.

As the Soviet weight lifters had no one to fear but one another, the American swimmers and divers brought an almost hubristic confidence to Tokyo. So sure were they of victory that, in the relays, a second team swam the qualifying heats, leaving the first team fresh for the finals. Gilled athletes from the legendary Atlantis would have been less certain of victory. Young, eager, their bodies trained to perfection by the swimming factories of California, this broad-shouldered, lean-hipped aquatic species was so predisposed to triumph that taking home fewer than half of the 22 swimming and diving gold medals on offer would have been a calamity. In the end, the Americans took 16 gold medals, 9 of 12 in the men's events, 7 of 10 in the women's. But even in this brilliant field, one star shone brighter than the others: an 18-year-old Yale freshman from Oregon, Donald Arthur Schollander.

Scandinavian blond, open-faced, and always ready with a boyish grin, Don Schollander exuded all the qualities of the natural champion—but with something bitter at the core. Born in Charlotte, North Carolina, in 1946, he spent his boyhood in Lake Oswego, a suburb of Portland, Oregon. There, beneath the looming volcanic prominence of Mt. Hood, Schollander had begun a search for his sport. He was propelled, to a degree, by his parents' expectations and experience. Wendell, his father, had played football at his Fargo, North Dakota, high school, but he couldn't go against his own father in the matter of choosing a college. Instead of heading for the Big Ten and the pros, Wendell Schollander had played well but obscurely for North Dakota State. His son would not endure such frustration.

Don had thought that football might be his calling as well, although he was never really big enough—in Tokyo he was 5 feet 11 and 175 pounds—to make much of a mark. In any case, he seemed destined for swimming. His mother, Martha Dent Schollander, was herself an accomplished swimmer. She had been the movie swimming double for Maureen O'Sullivan, the comely Jane to the aquatic Tarzan created by Johnny Weissmuller, himself a winner of three gold medals at Paris 1924. Martha Schollander kept her hand in by arranging water ballets for Lake Oswegans, sometimes employing Donny to fill out the show. The boy had settled into the odd, isolating, three-dimensional environment that cuts through the atmospheres of air and water,

that suspends gravity; for the unaided human, it is the only analogue of flight.

Late in 1961, after some family soul-searching, it was decided that Don should move to a more elevated level of swimming. The 15-year-old left home for George Haines' famous swimming school at Santa Clara, California. Living as a roomer in a widow's house, the young swimmer began the Haines schedule: At the pool by 6:30 a.m., a 500-meter warm-up, another 500-meter "pulling"—using nothing but the arms—followed by ten 50-meter repeats, 500 meters with the kickboard to strengthen the legs, then five 100-meter repeats. After that, a final long swim and work on starts, turns, and breathing. In the evening the series was repeated. "At the peak of training," Schollander wrote, "we were swimming about eight miles a day."

Like many serious swimmers, the young man felt cut off from normal high-school life. When his classmates were at play, he was doing laps. Swimmers hung out with swimmers. But it was in Santa Clara that Schollander the natural swimmer evolved into an athlete who could swim the crawl, as one reporter put it, "with the driving, pulsating grace of a porpoise." And not just the crawl. He could swim anything—breast, butterfly, back, anything—and win. But his specialty was in the middle distances of 200 and 400 meters, in which, by the time he came to Tokyo, he was on his way to being the world's best.

For the Olympics, Schollander had extended his portfolio to include one of the most daunting races of all, the 100-meter freestyle—a 2-lap sprint in which first and eighth place can be barely one second apart, and where strategy is as vital as ability. Races, Schollander believed, were won in the mind. Accordingly, he began stressing that he was really a middle-distance guy, long on endurance but short on speed, a slow starter who tried to catch up on the second lap. He did this the way any hustler bumbles into any game he plans to win. Then—perhaps for aerodynamics,

HIT AND MISS

Parallel with the water, Germany's Ingrid Engel-Krämer swings into her dive from the springboard. Engel-Krämer, the defending Olympic champion, was trying at Tokyo to win both the springboard and platform diving titles in back-to-back Games. While she was successful in the springboard, America's Lesley Bush edged her out for the platform crown.

Sunlight shines through the roof of the National Gymnasium, giving the pool a warm glow. Swimming's popularity in Japan made organizers plan for a stadium to house 25,000 spectators. Seating was scaled back to 11,112 after studies showed a larger facility wasn't feasible. Perhaps it was just as well: The home team captured only one swimming medal.

perhaps for effect—he shaved his head and body.

Schollander also sized up the field, especially the current owner of the world record, Alain Gottvalles of France, who had begun to annoy the Americans with his contemptuous ragging of their training rules. The Frenchman drank a bottle of wine and smoked a pack of cigarettes a day, he boasted, and still he was world champion. He referred to the Americans as machines. Schollander struck back by moving close to Gottvalles on the night of the semifinals, then following him around, silently, psyching him out until the French champion nearly fled. Both men made the finals, along with Hans-Joachim Klein and Uwe Jacobsen of Germany, Gary Ilman and Michael Austin of the United States,

Gyula Dobai of Hungary, and—perhaps the strongest threat to American prominence here— Britain's Bobby McGregor.

As soon as the gun sounded for the final race— the race for gold—Schollander abandoned all pretense of being a catch-up sprinter. He stayed with the field, moving over the first 50 meters 0.6 of a second faster than his qualifying times— an eternity in the 100-meter swim. For a while, Ilman looked like the swimmer to beat, but as he came off the turn he ran into turbulence stirred up by eight pairs of thrashing arms and legs and was caught by a bit of chop just as he turned his head to breathe. "He was a little ahead of me," Schollander wrote. "As he turned his head he hit a wave and just bounced—and dropped almost a foot behind me." Breathing to his right, Schollander could see that he led the field on that side, but McGregor swam the lane to his left, out of view. Although Schollander didn't know it, the Briton was still ahead of him. But McGregor was running out of steam, and Schollander was accelerating. They came in as one. "I just touched him out," said Schollander. "I just touched him out—by one-tenth of a second."

The 100-meter gold medal was the high point of Schollander's fantastically successful Olympic competition. Before the week was out, he had won three more golds: for the 4 x 100 and 4 x 200 relays and the 400-meter freestyle, where he set a 4:12.2 world record. In all, he set three world records and four Olympic ones. The unprecedented harvest brought him enormous popularity and fame.

But there remained that kernel of bitterness at his center, where the inner man felt disillusioned at the intrusion of ideology and big money into supposedly amateur sports. "I left home at 15 and went to Santa Clara, California," he would write later, "to become a professional amateur. Seven years later I retired. If a professional football player retires at 35 and says he's glad not to have to go in there every week and get clobbered—he's tired—you can understand it. If a professional fighter retires at 30 and says he's been taking too many punches for too many years—he's had it—you can understand that, too. When I retired I was 22. A swimmer does not get punched or clobbered—no cuts, no bruises, no broken bones—and I was an 'amateur,' not a 'professional'; but I had had it. I was tired. And I had been tired for three years."

Schollander also wondered whether perhaps the Frenchman Gottvalles had been right: Maybe swimmers who trained at his level were machines. "I won medals, but I don't want to become one myself," Schollander told reporters. Whatever his own wants, Olympic competition itself took care of that. He went to Mexico City

four years after his Tokyo triumph and qualified for only two events, the 800-meter freestyle relay and the 200-meter freestyle. They earned him his last Olympic medals, a fifth gold in the relay, and a silver in the 200-meter—the race that once had been his own.

For the Japanese hosts of the 1964 Games, there were many foreign favorites. They celebrated Don Schollander, they stood up when Billy Mills made his fabulous 10,000-meter run, and they waited into the night for Valery Brumel to cinch his victory. In a sense, each gold medal ratified the enormous time and treasure spent in transforming poor old Tokyo into one of history's finest Olympic venues. Still, watching in the shadow of Mt. Fuji, even these courteous holders of the Happy Games waited anxiously to learn how their own compatriots were doing. And, in fact, the homeland heroes were doing

Two thumbs-up for another great race by America's Don Schollander, the first swimmer to win four gold medals at a Games. American natators captured more than half the medals on offer at Tokyo.

Ecstatic countrymen toss
Yojiro Uetake in to the air
during a wild victory celebration. The bantamweight
freestyler was one of five
wrestling champions for
Japan, none of whom
weighed more than 136 ½
pounds (62 kilograms).

quite well: Japanese men had swept four gymnas-
tic events and had won the gold in combined team
gymnastics. Featherweight Yoshinobu Miyake, a
24-year-old lieutenant in the National Self-Defense Force and son of poor northern farmers,
had earned a gold medal in weight lifting; Takao
Sakurai had boxed his way to the bantamweight
gold; and three gold medals—flyweight, featherweight, and bantamweight—had been won by
Japanese freestyle wrestlers.

But there were events that could be won, and
events that had to be won, and the Japanese people waited with quiet anxiety for results from that
latter category. Judo, making its Olympic debut,
looked especially promising for the host country.
The Japanese had invented judo, the art of using
leverage, momentum, and an opponent's own
strength to defeat him. To mark the arrival of
their sport, they had also erected an elaborately
traditional lodge, Nippon Budokan Hall, as a
kind of temple for an event they had been refining since 1882.

The Japanese were the unquestioned leaders in
the three weight-class divisions. But there was
also an open-weight division, and there the out-

come was less certain. The Japanese champion,
27-year-old Akio Kaminaga, would certainly
give a good account of himself. At almost 5 feet
11 and 216 pounds, he was their biggest judo
warrior—but nowhere near as big as his most
formidable opponent, world champion Anton
Geesink of Holland. The 30-year-old Geesink
was 6 feet 5 and weighed 264 pounds, and he
was one of those enormous men who are unexpectedly quick and aggressive in a fight.

The prospect of this matchup was so troubling
to officials that they had modified the rules of
play at the last minute. Ordinarily, the nine
fighters in the division would have ascended
through competitions within their three 3-man
pools, with the losers weeded out along the way.
But the Tokyo rules created a fourth pool of
three losers, the best of whom would have a second chance at the gold medal. This disturbed
some observers, who saw it as a ploy to ensure
Akio Kaminaga two chances to win.

The contest, beginning on the afternoon of
Friday, October 23, was one of the last events of
the Games, and a crowd of 15,000 packed the
Nippon Budokan Hall to see it. After the fighters

made their bow on the mat, Geesink quickly attacked, defeating England's Alan Petherbridge in the first minute with a *sasae tsurikomi ashi* (left-hand foot-stop). The Dutchman then took on Japanese champ Kaminaga and won a decision with the same foot-stop. In the playoff, Kaminaga and Petherbridge fought hard for a few minutes, until Kaminaga scored a full point with a *tai otoshi* (left-hand body-drop), his favorite throw.

In the second pool, Australia's Theodore Boronovskis beat both John Ryan of Ireland and Tunisia's Ali Hachicha with the *harai goshi* (right-hand leg-spin). Third-pool fighter Ben Campbell of California defeated Thomas Ong of the Philippines, then turned to fight German Klaus Glahn, but a knee injury forced the American's withdrawal. Then, while the three pool winners—Geesink, Boronovskis, and Glahn—took a break, the fourth pool of losers fought it out for the second chance. To no one's surprise, Kaminaga defeated Ong and then Ryan.

As the semifinals began, Geesink stopped Boronovskis, while Kaminaga, with some difficulty, overcame Glahn. Now all Tokyo waited for the judo contest of the epoch, their national champion against the champion of the world.

A Tokyo citizen shades himself from the sun as he walks past the Nippon Budokan Hall, still under construction in this 1964 photograph. The hall was the venue for judo, Japan's gift to world sport. Judo's antecedents date back centuries, although rules and throws of the modern form were only codified in 1882, by Jigoro Kano, a Japanese educator.

Geesink, infuriated that he was fighting Kaminaga for a second time, immediately took the offensive, keeping his opponent drifting warily near the edge of the mat—so much so, in fact, that the Dutchman had to reach over Kaminaga, grab his belt, and tug him back within easier orbit. Geesink made perhaps eight attacks, using his left-side foot-block, and each time he nearly brought Kaminaga down. Then, not five minutes into the match, Geesink caught a left foot-block to pick up half a point, following with a side-holding that seemed the end of Kaminaga—who, to everyone's astonishment, wriggled free.

Now the Japanese champion took the offensive with a blistering attack of fast body-drops and *o-soto-gari* (rear tripping throws). His foot snaked in for an inner reap, then flashed out for a left-side body-drop. But the crowd had lost its voice. Large as he was, Kaminaga might as well have been a man fighting a great tree.

Having taken what Kaminaga had to offer, Geesink drove his opponent to his knees, then flipped him on his back with a rolling bear hug. A perfect *kesa gatame* (left-side arm-holding), and Geesink's great bulk completely immobilized Kaminaga for the required 30 seconds. The gold went to the Hollander.

On the eve of the closing ceremonies, the Japanese had won three gold medals in judo, but they had lost the crucial one; the champion of the world remained a huge Dutchman, not one of their own. In the one sport they had invented, the one they added especially for their Games, they had gone down to defeat. For a time that

Dutch giant Anton Geesink throws Japan's Akio Kaminaga during the final of the open judo competition. The Tokyo judo tournament was for men only; current Games feature a women's division. Judo is the only Olympic hand-to-hand fighting sport open to women.

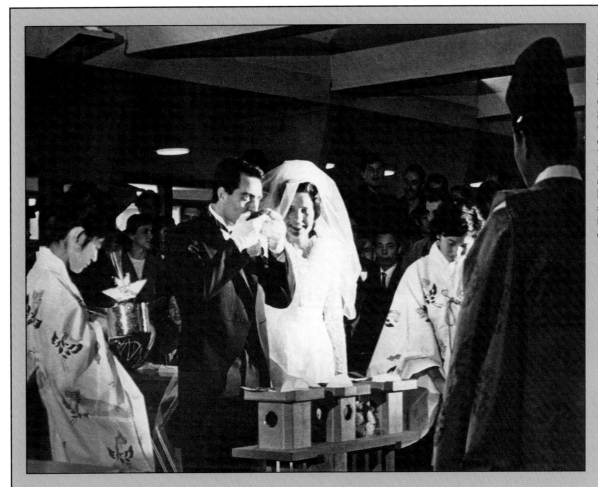

TAKING THE LEAP

Bulgarian teammates Dimitrov Prodanov, a gymnast, and Diana Yorgova, a long jumper, exchange vows in a Shinto-inspired rite at the International Club of the Tokyo Olympic Village. They were the first Olympians to wed at a Games. The couple had a brief honeymoon at Kyoto before returning to Tokyo for the closing ceremony.

Friday evening, a spiritual pall as dense as the eternal veil of smog hung over Tokyo.

Indeed, on that final night of the 1964 Olympic Games, Tokyo was transformed into a veritable ghost town. The public bathhouses, normally teeming on Friday night, were almost empty, and the noisy bustle of the Ginza descended into relative silence. Even the telephone company's toll switchboard switched off. The reason for this lull had nothing to do with the collective disappointment that a foreigner had made off with the key gold medal in judo: That pall had lifted before sundown, giving way to an atmosphere of anxious expectation. Huddled around millions of television sets, jammed into the bleachers at the Komozawa indoor court, the Japanese gathered to watch a final moment of glory—or terrible ignominy. For, at seven that evening, the women's volleyball tournament began its final sets, pitting the Japanese team against its archrival, the hard-hitting spikers of the Soviet Union.

Unlike judo, volleyball was not a Japanese invention, nor did it begin in Russia. In 1895, William G. Morgan, who directed the YMCA gym in Holyoke, Massachusetts, finished refining a rudimentary sport that dated from medieval times into what he called mintonette. The name was changed when a visitor called attention to the volleying exchanges that formed the heart of the game. Whatever the name, volleyball was intended to be a game that anyone could play, anywhere, with the barest minimum of equipment, in a space no larger than a tennis court. Six players rotated the serve on each side of a net, and teams could score only when serving; the first to reach 15 points—or to have a two-point lead in case of a tie—won.

Small wonder, then, that volleyball flourished in all the world's cramped and underequipped corners, in school and prison yards, on the fantails of warships and the landing decks of aircraft carriers. And it was a game that could be played by men, or women, or both. The sport traveled easily, carried by refugees, students,

Stern-faced Hirofumi Daimatsu, Japan's women's volleyball coach, watches his charges during play. Often criticized as a despot, Daimatsu remained unrepentant, saying his drills tested "the spirit as well as the body."

soldiers—it was a game you could take anywhere, even to war.

Volleyball also traveled to the Soviet Union, where its egalitarian aura and scant equipment endeared it to that nation's political system, and to postwar Japan, where it also found broad appeal. Over the years those two nations more or less expropriated the sport, the Soviets developing it into an aggressive, Cossack-like charge, the Japanese evolving a more refined defense backed by tough offensive play. By 1961 the game had won Olympic status, and a men's tournament was duly scheduled for Tokyo. In 1963 a women's tournament was added.

So, on the final Friday night of their first homeland Olympics, the Japanese people waited for the climax of the women's tournament. Earlier in the day they had watched their men's team go down to third place, the gold won by the Soviet Union, the silver by Brazil. But the

men's team had been merely a collection of splendid athletes. The women's team was a myth unfolding. To see whether the legend would end happily or in tragedy, all Japan gathered in the pale cathode-ray light of television screens.

The world had already heard of the Nichibo Kaizuka team—the Kaizuka Amazons, as some journalists called them. Few Japanese had not heard of the team captain, Masae Kasai, or her five teammates. Emiko Miyamoto, Kinuko Tanida, Yuriko Handa, Yoshiko Matsumura, and Sata Isobe were household names by now. But it was their coach, a powerfully compact, almost expressionless volleyball fanatic named Hirofumi Daimatsu, who had created the legend of the Kaizuka Amazons. His players all worked for a spinning mill in the town of Kaizuka, about two hours from Tokyo; the mill owners sponsored the team, which attracted promising players the way film studios draw starlets. Those who showed aptitude for the sport got a $50 monthly stipend, room, board, a tryout, and training—training of the toughest kind, designed to build or break; Daimatsu offered no middle ground. Those who couldn't sustain his pace would fall by the wayside, often with their spirits broken, often in tears. "If you can endure this," he would tell the survivors, "I promise you a gold medal."

What they had to endure was a regimen that outsiders found not merely difficult, but downright cruel. The women would go to their mill jobs at 8 a.m. and work until 3:30. But their day really began at 4, with the seven-hour hell of drill. As the players hurled themselves past him in mock rolling dives and blocks, Daimatsu fired the ball ahead of each runner, making her reach—training her to make saves that, for most players, would be unthinkable. Now and then a woman would sink to the wooden gym floor, exhausted, then resume the drill a few minutes later.

After three hours, if all had gone well, the first team was permitted to eat a rice and meat dinner while the second team drilled. In the final session,

The Japanese women's volleyball team fends off an attack by the Soviet Union. At four consecutive Games, Japanese and Soviet women vied for the volleyball gold medal, each winning two championships. Japan's boycott of Moscow 1980 ended the duel.

Japanese students wave torches while encircling the National
Stadium infield during the Tokyo closing ceremony. Athletes
marched in a chaotic throng, and spectators sang "Auld Lang
Syne"—in Japanese and English—as the stadium scoreboard
bade competitors and visitors farewell.

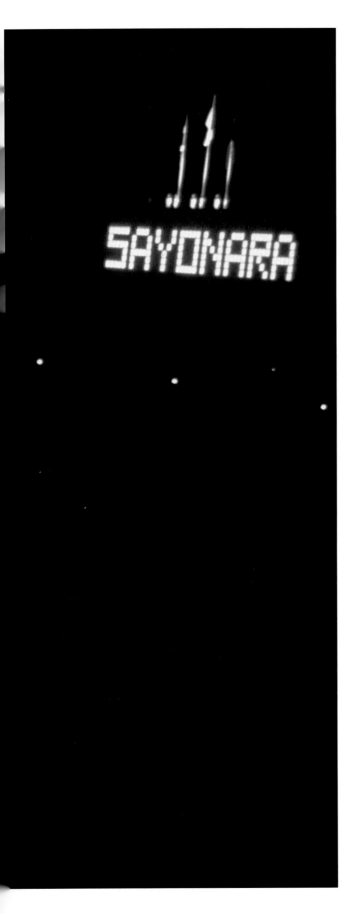

Daimatsu would hurl balls at each player—always just out of reach, or at an awkward angle, or cannonballing right at her. These killer drills had been going on from afternoon to midnight, six days a week, 51 weeks a year, for four years; Sundays were reserved for practice that was only slightly less harrowing than the drills. And thus far, Daimatsu's technique had worked supremely well. In 1963 his Amazons had won the women's volleyball world championship, and they had come to their homeland's first Olympic finals undefeated in 157 straight games.

In the first set, the Soviets took an early lead, but they couldn't sustain it against a Japanese series of quick attacks that soon took the home team to a 14-9 advantage; the Amazons won the set 15-11. The second set was brief and terrible for the Russians, ending in favor of the Japanese women, 15-8. In the third set, the Japanese marched to a strong advantage, only to lose it as the Soviet women squeezed the lead to one point, 14-13. Japan served for the match-winning 15th point five times, to no avail. Then, as play continued—and the island nation held its breath—one of the Soviet women let a hand intrude into Japan's side of the net. The foul gave the Amazons the gold, the first for Japanese women since Hideko Maehata's breaststroke victory at Berlin 1936.

Three more Olympiads would pass before Japan's women volleyballers would defeat a Soviet team again in an Olympic contest. But for the moment, on that final Friday night of the 1964 Games, the Amazons had seen a promise kept. "If you can endure this," their coach had told them, "I promise you a gold medal." His words evoked that larger promise, implicit in all that Japan had done to make its first Olympics a celebration of athletic performance the world would never forget. Orimpikku made ni—by the time of the Olympics—Tokyo would have endured. By the end of the Games, all that had been promised had come true.

A SHADE OF
DIFFERENCE

THE XVIII OLYMPIAD

Few cities seem so well protected from the world's harsh realities as Lausanne, the beautiful old Swiss town that clings to the steep, vineyard-contoured slopes falling toward Lake Leman, the long kidney of blue water that curves southwest to the beginnings of the Rhône. An ordered, peaceful place, it must have seemed the ideal sanctuary when the International Olympic Committee installed its headquarters there—the perfect urban repository for the high principles of the Olympic movement. Strolling the well-kept grounds of Mon Repos, the estate that housed the IOC headquarters, one might truly believe that here, as in the ancient vale of Olympia, the ideal might persist of athletes striving for nothing more than an olive wreath. It was an illusion, of course, and like all illusions, it was inherently frail. A mirage can vanish in a puff of breeze, and by the 1960s, reality was blowing a gale that could be felt even in the Olympic corridors of Lausanne.

The world had always been full of opposites: young and old, East and West, large and small, rich and poor. Now the opposites were hardening into polarities. The antagonistic ideologies of capitalism and communism had divided the world into two armed camps, each with its structure of superpower and satellites—each eager to include sport among its tools for demonstrating superiority. And in each camp, sport was paving an ever widening pathway to wealth—not just for athletes but also for the IOC and other organizations that controlled the apparatus of athletics.

In this grimly competitive and increasingly materialistic world, it was perhaps inevitable that athletes began exploring every possible road to supremacy. Some followed drugs; a few exploited ambiguities of gender to compete as men in women's contests. Olympic officialdom countered by deciding in the mid-1960s to probe gender and body chemistry with simple—critics said too simple—biochemical tests.

But issues such as these were nothing

Giulio Onesti, IOC member in Italy 1964-81, with his wife, Gabrielle

White South African Harry Finlay *(left)* and his black compatriot Lucas Matseke congratulate each other for victories at an Amateur Athletic Union boxing championship held March 9, 1963, at Utica, New York. Finlay was a potential Olympian for South Africa, but rules excluding black countrymen such as Matseke got South Africa barred from Tokyo 1964.

compared with the problem of money—not its dearth, but its sudden, amazing abundance. A tsunami of money—big money by the standards of Olympic organizations that, like ancient athletes, had made a virtue of poverty—was about to break over the shore of amateur sports. It seemed that soon the legendary olive wreath would bear a sponsor's logo, and the genteel penury of the Olympic movement and its young athletes would curdle into celebrity and wealth. Worse, like a family suddenly awash in funds, the Olympic movement's organizations—not just the IOC but also the lesser bureaucracies associated with it— began to fret that some were more equal than others where this new wealth was concerned. Mutinies bloomed within the Olympic community, threatening at times to rip the movement apart.

However serene its facade, then, the IOC's home at Lausanne was in the 1960s what it had been all along: the microcosm reflecting the macrocosm, the small world mirroring the strife that divided and beset the greater one. And in both worlds, yet another seeming polarity—one based on human differences that are really rather superficial—was looming ever larger as a source of contention: black and white.

Even over Tokyo's Happy Games, the politics of race had spread a light mist of poison. Since 1958, when the Norwegian Olympic Committee urged the exclusion of South Africa from the 1960 Winter Games at Squaw Valley, the IOC had known that at some point it would have to confront the ugly business of apartheid—state-sanctioned racial segregation. From the inception of the modern Games, the Olympic Charter had forbidden discriminatory racial policies, and the fact that South Africa's black athletes had suffered many years' discrimination was understood by all concerned. Yet the IOC had managed to evade confronting this reality, always reluctant to let politics steer Olympic policy.

As the 1960s began, the South African National Olympic Committee (SANOC) clashed repeatedly with its counterparts in other nations, particularly in the Soviet camp, where racial injustice was viewed as an inevitable consequence of capitalism. The USSR's NOC and its allies railed against South Africa's bigotry. SANOC usually responded that as soon as black athletes were good enough to compete at the Olympic level, they would be welcome on the South African team. That position seemed to hint faintly at reform; however, unsaid but implicit was the notion that black Africans simply lacked the Olympic right stuff—a patently absurd point of view that should not have survived Ethiopian marathoner Abebe Bikila's stellar performances at Rome 1960 and Tokyo 1964.

East Germany's Ingrid Engel-Krämer carries the unified German team's Olympic banner into Tokyo's National Stadium during the Games' opening ceremony. Tokyo 1964 marked the last appearance of an artificially unified German team, whose unity since Helsinki 1952 was more fiction than reality.

Members of North Korea's Olympic team force their way through the crowded Tokyo train station. All 144 members of the 1964 team were ordered home from Japan on the eve of the Games in an eligibility dispute. Continued arguments with the IOC kept North Korea out of Olympic competition until Munich 1972.

In any case, South Africa's real policies had never been ambiguous in the slightest. In a pugnacious counterpoint to SANOC's more conciliatory when-they're-ready-they-can-play ruse, government officials made it clear that athletes would always be racially separate and unequal in the white-ruled nation. "Government policy," affirmed Interior Minister Jan de Klerk, "is that no mixed teams should take part in sports inside or outside the country." His chilling message merely reiterated South Africa's long-standing rule: White athletes and black must be separately organized; no racially mixed teams allowed; nonwhites from other nations must play only nonwhites in South Africa; government visa policy would enforce the segregation.

In 1963, pressed by the growing number of new black African nations in its ranks and by other member countries appalled by South African racism, the IOC finally took a stand. It suspended SANOC, effectively banishing South Africa to a sort of Olympic limbo, with reprieve available only if the nation showed real progress toward integrating its sports facilities and athletic teams. Meanwhile, South Africa could send none of its athletes to Tokyo.

The suspension was an early salvo in what would prove to be a long war: SANOC would once again promise reform, vowing to send an integrated team if South Africa were allowed to take part at Mexico City 1968. Hopeful in spite of the evidence—the South Africans were holding segregated Olympic trials—the IOC readmitted SANOC. The outraged response from black African nations and their allies, including some black athletes in America, was a threatened boycott that promised to gut the 1968 Games. The IOC backed down. South Africans were barred from Mexico City, and in 1970 SANOC was expelled from the IOC. South African athletes would not return to the Games until 1992, when a racially mixed team would take part at Barcelona.

As a kind of aside, the ouster of South Africa from the Tokyo Games made it easier to suspend white Africa's other racial bad actor: Rhodesia. In 1965, when white-ruled Rhodesia declared independence from the United Kingdom, it encountered such strong British opposition—in the world at large and also within the IOC—that it was easily blocked from participating at Mexico City. Subsequent efforts to include Rhodesians as British subjects were deflected by Kenya and other black African nations, so that Rhodesia remained out of Olympic competition until the Moscow Games in 1980—the year it metamorphosed into the new nation of Zimbabwe.

Retrospectively, one can discern the eventually fatal sickening of apartheid in the consequences it occasioned within the Olympic movement. The IOC's ouster of South Africa and Rhodesia had its lineal descendants in the economic boycotts that, 30 years later, would force white South Africa to choose racial integration over financial ruin. But such upheavals cut two ways. On the one hand, they demonstrated that the Olympic movement could be a lever for equity; on the other, they showed once again the fragility of the Olympic illusion that sport could exist in a vacuum, immune from political realities.

That illusion, seamed with faults through two world wars, was moving further toward fracture. Over the decades, the fates of nations had become linked to the performance of their young athletes, and with that linkage the pressure on the athletes to win mounted exponentially. Athletic excellence meant glory for the athlete's homeland. It also meant a share of the good life for the athlete himself: Old distinctions between amateur and professional in the sports world had frayed steadily over the years. In the capitalist West, it was becoming increasingly clear that Olympic gold could translate into legal tender; and even in the Communist Eastern bloc, Olympic champions could expect privileges far beyond the reach of less gifted mortals. The stakes were rising like the bar on a cosmic high jump. As that bar ascended, many athletes took the hard decision to do whatever was necessary to clear it.

Competition on the playing field determines not just who is very good, but who is best; and for many of the world's most talented young athletes, it is not just performing but performing and winning that counts. One must exploit every weakness in the opponent, seize any improving innovation in training or technique in order to win.

That arcane chemistry might hold the key to victory was evident to athletes very early on: In the second century AD, according to the Greek physician Galen, athletes experimented with various herbs in hopes of enhancing performance.

Streaking down the Bung Karno stadium track in Jakarta, Dan Shin-geum of North Korea is on her way to smashing her own world record in the 800-meter run. Dan set records in both the 400 and 800 meters but never competed at an Olympic Games.

An undated engraving depicts the Greek physician Galen, whose theories on vital humors helped lay the foundation for modern medicine. Active during the second century AD, Galen recorded the doping practices of ancient Olympians.

ture, and concoctions that featured strychnine—an alkaloid poison that acts on the central nervous system—became popular for jump-starting one's sports machinery.

Indeed, the search by athletes for a performance-boosting drug has been as relentless as the quest of impotent potentates for aphrodisiacs, and sometimes as silly: Gelatin powder in orange juice enjoyed a vogue, as did sugar cubes dunked in ether or nitroglycerin to dilate the arteries near the heart. There was nothing comical about the occasional outcome of such tactics, however. In 1886 a British cyclist literally dropped out of the 600-kilometer Bordeaux-Paris race, killed by an overdose of a stimulant called trimethyl.

The cyclist was the first human victim of a practice long applied to improve or impair the performance of dogs and racehorses—doping. The term derives from a southern African word, *dop*, the name of a stimulating ceremonial beverage brewed by the native Kaffirs. A time-honored way of fixing the outcome of games of chance involving animals, doping enjoyed quite a vogue in the United States, where it appears to have begun. But modern chemistry, which can find alkaloids in saliva, blood, and urine, has virtually eliminated the practice since the end of World War II—at least among dumb beasts. Humans have been less fortunate.

The advances in chemical analysis that brought doping to a halt for animals created a kind of drug cornucopia for athletes. The amphetamines Dexedrine, Benzedrine, and Methedrine—the so-called pep pills employed by soldiers, students, and truckers trying to keep awake—made their way into contests where athletes wanted an edge in alertness and energy. By the 1950s doping had lost its animal connotation; it meant drugging competitors, without regard to species. The practice had also lost some of its stigma, since the world—the young world in particular—was evolving a culture in which mind- and

A millennium or so later, Aztec players got a lift from a strychninelike product of an Andean cactus and chewed coca leaves—from which the crystalline stimulant cocaine is extracted—for its relief of hunger, fatigue, and misery. During the 19th century, when cocaine was regarded more as a tonic than a dangerous drug (Sigmund Freud, for one, praised the "magical substance"), athletes found that it could be a turbocharger in the arena. In France, a blend of cocaine and wine called Vin Mariani became a favorite of cyclists and was known colloquially as wine for athletes. Boxers were fond of a brandy and cocaine mix-

body-altering drugs were seen as a shortcut to greater understanding and power.

Where doping had been anomalous, it now became commonplace among athletes, who turned to cocaine derivatives for the qualities of endurance once extolled by Freud, and to the amphetamines for more revs from their human engines. Cyclists became the most dedicated searchers for chemically improved velocity. In a 1955 race, tests turned up dope in five of 25 urine samples. In 1956, a cyclist found himself at a psychiatric clinic, jangled by amphetamines. On the Tour d'Autriche, some cyclists stuffed more than a dozen amphetamine capsules into their jerseys. French cyclist Jacques Anquetil put it succinctly: "Everyone in cycling dopes himself," he said, adding, "Those who claim they don't are liars." For the many, doping may have meant improved performance. But for the few, it meant death. Tommy Simpson, a 25-year-old cyclist from Great Britain, died after ingesting eight phenylisopropylamine and 15 amphetamine pills with a thermos of coffee. Danish cyclist Knut Jensen collapsed at the 1960 Rome Games after a fatal cocktail of amphetamines and nicotinic acid compounds.

Cycling provided the most egregious examples, but in the 1960s many sports began to take chemical casualties. Dick Howard, who won the bronze in the 400-meter hurdles at Rome 1960, died of a heroin overdose in 1967, as did welterweight boxer Billy Bello in 1963. Football, American and otherwise, proved to be pervaded by performance-boosting drugs.

By the middle of the decade, doping had taken a sinister new turn. Where drugs had previously been used mainly to increase endurance, energy, and tolerance for pain, a new family of compounds was coming into common use, compounds that actually increased strength, adding power to the human machine by mimicking and modulating the body's natural chemistry.

Anabolic steroids, a family of artificial hormones modeled on the male sex hormone testosterone, were developed in the 1930s as a means of correcting hormone imbalances. They also produced a side effect, one soon seized on by athletes: They offered the prospect of bigger muscles. The catch is that steroids work only when injected in massive doses, so that the trace amounts eluding the embrace of blood proteins can migrate into muscle tissue. Once there, the synthetic hormones bond with testosterone receptors and enter the cell itself, linking to certain genes in the coil of DNA, the cell's coded blueprint. In a kind of cascade of cause and effect, the DNA's altered instructions increase

Cocaine, then legal, is a key ingredient publicized in this advertisement for Vin Mariani in an 1893 edition of *Harper's Weekly*. The nostrum was touted as a tonic. Athletes felt it promoted endurance.

99

A weary Tommy Simpson of Great Britain pedals through a leg of the 1967 Tour de France. An overdose of stimulants during the race killed him.

protein production that ultimately enlarges muscle. Athletes found that steroids maximize the effects of strength training, enabling them to bulk up bigger, quicker.

But steroids are as volatile and potent as the natural hormones they imitate. Testosterone is linked to aggression, and athletes doped with steroids sometimes experience what they call roid rages—sudden storms of violent anger triggered by the drugs' links to the brain's testosterone receptors. Women may find that while steroids add muscle, they also masculinize: They can add chest and facial hair, diminish or stop menstruation, and shrink breasts. Obversely, men on steroids may find themselves sprouting breasts. Both sexes may experience liver and heart damage. The drug is a potential killer.

The risks didn't seem to matter to some athletes. "Just prior to the 1964 Olympic Games in Tokyo," wrote American hammer champion Harold Connolly, "all around me it seemed that more and more athletes were using steroids for athletic preparation, and one began to feel that he was placing himself in a decided disadvantage if he did not also get on the sports medicine bandwagon." He told of athletes with "so much scar tissue and so many puncture holes on their backsides that it was difficult to find a fresh spot to give them a new shot." The motive? "The overwhelming majority of the international track and field athletes I know," Connolly said, "would take anything and do anything short of killing themselves to improve their athletic performance." He was optimistic; some didn't stop short of death.

In fact, though, the practice of doping wasn't entirely a matter of choice for athletes. Often the drugs were supplied and administered by sports physicians and trainers whose interest in having their men or women win often made them generous with shady substances. But the toll was too high for the practice to go unchallenged. In 1959 the Association Nationale d'Education

America's Harold Connolly winds into his hammer throw at Tokyo 1964. Connolly was a three-time Olympian and Melbourne gold medalist who, during a 1960s inquiry into doping, was outspoken in his description of drug abuse by athletes.

Physique established a doping commission in France, and that year's Sports Medicine Congresses in Paris and Évian were dedicated to the doping issue.

The caretakers of the Olympics made their move in 1961 by establishing the IOC Medical Commission in Athens. This was short-lived, however, and it was not until 1967 that the IOC's present Medical Commission came into being, led by Belgium's Prince Alexandre de Mérode. This new organization provided guidance to host countries in setting up medical facilities for

Olympic Games and was responsible for controlling doping, among other infractions.

Regulating secret practices is never easy, and the Medical Commission found the matter of doping immensely more complicated than it had first seemed. Drawing up comprehensive lists of forbidden drugs, it turned out, gave an advantage to pharmacologically advanced countries where a substitute substance could be invented and put into use. Banning painkilling narcotics and such psychomotor stimulants as amphetamines proved not to be a problem, for these

An arrow points the way for Grenoble athletes who need to leave a sample for drug testing. Tests were conducted on 86 athletes chosen at random. All came up negative. Los Angeles 1984 holds the high mark for drug disqualifications at a Games with 11 positives.

chemicals have no therapeutic use in sports. But the so-called sympathomimetic amines were less straightforward, since some are used to treat colds, allergies, and asthma. When a champion swimmer, for example, began sucking on an inhaler, was it to alleviate asthma or to expand interior airways for a rush of extra oxygen? The commission got around this dilemma by screening pre-Games requests from physicians for certain therapeutic drugs and approving those with relatively little effect on performance.

Tranquilizers were not included in the ban, and at first, neither were anabolic steroids. Where other drugs could be detected in urine and saliva, steroids hid in the body's hormonal chemistry, and ways of detecting them would not be available until the mid-1970s.

Drug testing of Olympians would begin with the 1968 Winter Games at Grenoble. There, 86 tests yielded not a single trace of banned substances.

No one likes to be singled out and tested like a suspect racehorse, and some athletes try to circumvent any system. Cyclists, for example, have been known to appear for testing with jars of someone else's urine taped to their armpits to supply clean samples. The IOC would conduct its tests after events, selecting athletes for testing randomly, by lot—unless there was some compelling reason for suspicion. Two urine samples would be taken, sealed, and labeled with a code to protect the athlete's anonymity; one sample would be sent forward for a battery of tests, the second kept in reserve. Analyses would be made using thin-layer chromatography, gas-liquid chromatography, and mass spectrometry—techniques requiring a very well-equipped laboratory and highly trained staff. No matter how good the lab and its people, there would always be ample opportunity for error. Nevertheless, the IOC made the stakes quite high: An athlete who tested positive for doping would be excluded from the Games, as would any team with even one member shown to be doped.

Drugs weren't the only path to athletic advantage; there was also the matter of gender. Men competing as women—or, at least, individuals who were not fully female competing as women—was hardly an unknown phenomenon in the Olympics. At Berlin 1936, for instance, a German champion and a Pole purporting to be women would later be revealed as sexually ambiguous—as much male as they were female.

With the rise in the 1960s of a generation of female superathletes from the Communist bloc, there was speculation that these women excelled because they were incompletely women—or even men competing as women. Indeed, as soon as such suspicions began to be bruited about, and there was talk of chromosomal testing for gender, many of the mannish champs vanished into retirement, although they continued to live as women.

Just as drugs had seemed a fairly straightforward matter until the experts probed into the details—what substances should be banned and what permitted—so the issue of gender proved surprisingly complex. Science was finding increasing evidence that, far from being polar opposites, male and female are merely points on a complex and confusing scale, with gradations all along the way. There are female athletes, for instance, who gravitate to sports in the first place because their body chemistry affords them more of the "male" characteristics of greater strength, size, and muscle mass.

In setting up what it called its femininity control standards in 1968, the IOC imposed tests on all who wished to compete as women in the Olympic Games. The first round of evaluations was made on the basis of the presence or absence of organelles called Barr bodies in cell-tissue samples—scrapings from a mucous membrane inside the cheek or in the roots of plucked hairs. Because Barr bodies occur in much higher proportions in the tissue of women than of men, their dearth suggests a lack of femininity. A parallel test looked for Y chromatin, a substance found in about 35 percent of male cells, but in only about 3 percent of female cells. The "true female" would test positively for Barr bodies and negatively for Y chromatin. If the subject flunked these tests, a blood sample would be extracted for a chromosome mapping test. If the subject failed to indicate female here, a final round of examinations would be made—if the athlete allowed it—by a team of gynecologists.

The tests were a good deal more intrusive than urine samplings, and a good deal less reliable as well: The search, after all, was not for a man, but for signs that the examinee was not a "true female." No one knew quite what that meant, except that, to a woman barred from Olympic competition because of a chromosomal irregularity, it would probably mean heartbreak.

As with drug testing, Olympic gender testing would begin at Grenoble. Of the 50 young women tested at random there, all would prove female. In fact, gender testing would turn up not a single ringer over the years. It would eventually appear that steroids, not inborn gender anomalies, would help explain the superiority—and mannishness—of certain women athletes from the Eastern bloc.

Even as the IOC developed ways of testing athletes, some of its members were poised to test the institution itself.

At its inception in 1894, the IOC was hardly a bureaucracy at all; rather, it was Pierre de Coubertin himself, and a few close friends and colleagues, making all the decisions affecting the nascent Olympic movement. Similarly, most sports were themselves relatively disorganized and rudderless in those days. But inevitably, the small, loose structure of international amateur sports would change over the years as the movement and the Games expanded. The parent IOC would spawn national Olympic committees (NOCs) to oversee parochial Olympic affairs in every participating nation and select athletes for the Games. The IOC also had to deal with the international federations (IFs) that regulated individual sports. Two IFs already existed at the time the IOC was founded, and by 1964 there were 22 for Olympic sports. Finally, there were the host cities' organizing committees, or OCs, the ad hoc groups that actually produced the Games.

Traditionally, the IOC's attitude toward the lesser bureaucracies had been one of benevolent paternalism: There was support for their endeavors and concern for their welfare, but there was never any question about where the big decisions about the Olympics were made or where the true power lay. It rested squarely with the IOC, or, more particularly, with the one man at the organization's helm. Now, in the 1960s, change was afoot: An irresistible force—the natural and inexorable tendency of any bureaucracy to spread—was about to meet up with an immovable object—Avery Brundage. It was time for change, for democratization, but not everyone saw it. Like a captain ignoring mutterings from an angry crew, Brundage remained determinedly deaf to a rising clamor among the national committees.

In 1963 the mutiny began. Giulio Onesti, the 51-year-old president of the Comite Olimpico Nazionale d'Italia (CONI), Italy's national Olympic committee, had long urged the IOC to hold annual meetings with the national committees. But Onesti didn't have much luck. Brundage believed that too much contact would inevitably

Romania's Iolanda Balaş exults in having cleared the bar for a gold medal in the high jump at Tokyo. It was her second consecutive Olympic championship.

HIGHEST, LONGEST

As record setters go, few athletes equal Romania's Iolanda Balaş. Rail-thin and just a little over 6 feet tall, she had the perfect body for high jumping. Her long legs and her talent propelled her to her first national title at 14. She set the first of her 14 world records in the summer of 1956 when she cleared 5 feet 5 inches (1.65 meters), making her a favorite at Melbourne. But America's Mildred McDaniel was a sensation at the Games, while Balaş was merely good. The Romanian finished fifth.

Stung by defeat, an inspired Balaş would not lose again until June 11, 1967—a span of nearly 11 years. She matched the world record in 1957 and raised it five times in 1958, the year she became the first woman to break the 6-foot barrier. She was in a league all her own at Rome 1960, outjumping the field by 5 ½ inches. Balaş set four more records in 1961, including a career high of 6 feet 3 ¼ inches, a mark unequaled until 1971. At Tokyo 1964 she beat her closest rival by nearly 4 inches.

But excellence exacted its toll. Injuries forced Balaş to sit out the 1966 season, prompting rumors that she was evading the new mandatory gender tests. A comeback in 1967 put an end to the gossip and, unfortunately, to her career: She lost for the first time after 140 consecutive finals. She retired from competition later that year.

HOMELESS NO MORE

In the first six decades of its existence, the United States Olympic Committee shuttled from place to place like a hapless orphan. It originally met once every four years at the New York Athletic Club. Then, for almost two decades beginning in 1930, the headquarters were the office of USOC president—and later IOC president—Avery Brundage, who worked out of the LaSalle Hotel, a Chicago property that he owned. New York's Biltmore Hotel served as a temporary office after the Brundage era, but growing bureaucracy in the 1950s meant the committee needed something more permanent.

In 1960 the USOC moved into a five-story Victorian home at 57 Park Avenue that became known as Olympic House *(left)*. Famed financier J. P. Morgan had built the opulent mansion around the turn of the century to house his mistress, Maxine Elliott. With Morgan's passing, the building went into decline, becoming a boarding house for a time, slowly decaying until its rescue by the USOC.

With a full-time staff of six, the committee in its new home could handle paperwork more efficiently and establish a library. By the late 1970s the staff had increased to 29, and more room was needed. The solution was a property in Colorado Springs that provided, in addition to more office space, room to build a training center for athletes. The USOC moved west in 1978 and continues to operate there today.

destroy the Olympic movement's political purity, not to mention its effectiveness, and he steadfastly resisted any change in that direction. "We'd have meetings with the national Olympic committees," said American IOC member Douglas Roby, "and Brundage would say, 'We'll take it under advisement.' It was a brush-off. He just wouldn't listen. Let them talk, and then forget it." The IOC, Roby believed, treated the national committees and federations like children.

But Giulio Onesti was no child, nor was he a pushover in a fight. A lawyer from Turin, Onesti had been an enthusiastic rower, fencer, and tennis player in his youth. World War II deprived him of athletic pursuits; a shoulder wound sustained in battle left him unable to maneuver a boat, foil, or racquet very well. But he proved supremely able at maneuvering politically. He fought in the Italian Resistance against Benito Mussolini and his Fascists, establishing close ties with the Socialists who would lead Italy after Il Duce's downfall. Onesti took over the presidency of CONI in 1944, reconstituting Italian sports after the ravages of war. He was utterly tireless, and he was brilliant and charming, with a shark-sized smile and a quick eye for useful innovation. Socialist or not, he pulled off a coup any capitalist would envy: He acquired for CONI the rights to the profits from Italy's national soccer lottery, assuring that the committee would be lavishly funded in perpetuity.

Nevertheless, Onesti's socialism was a philosophical tie to Soviet-led elements within the Olympic movement that had been trying since the 1950s to dent Brundage's autocracy. Elected to the IOC in 1964, the Italian newcomer wasted no time in inviting representatives from other national committees to caucus in advance of the IOC's Session in Tokyo. Clearly, it was a move toward establishing a permanent organization of national committees whose collective power would rival that of the IOC. Such a step, Brundage warned, was "fraught with many dangers." The greatest

peril, to his mind, was the threat that all NOCs would have an equal say in Olympic affairs. Since the Olympic movement began, a few European nations and the United States had dominated IOC decision making, and that, Brundage thought, was as it should be: Nations with older Olympic traditions and more experience in the movement should be trusted to guide it. If Onesti and his allies had their way, a one-man, one-vote arrangement would give the myriad small countries of the Third World a majority voice in Olympic affairs—a model that had proved ineffective, if not chaotic, in the United Nations General Assembly.

Brundage set out to scuttle the national committee movement. In March 1967 he issued a memorandum telling the rebellious members that no new organization was needed—and none was endorsed by the IOC. Onesti countered a month later by convening 64 national committee presidents in Tehran, where they voted to establish a Permanent General Assembly (PGA) at their 1968 meeting in Mexico City.

Onesti's was not the only rebellion in progress. As Brundage busily tried to deflect the national committees—with methods that veered from courtship to threat—the restive international sports federations came forward with their agenda. For years the IFs had lobbied the IOC for a greater say in Olympic business. Now, watching the national committees coalesce into a powerful cooperative, they quickly followed suit: In 1967 they formed their own General Assembly of the International Federations (GAIF). Directed by Berge Phillips of Australia, who represented the Fédération Internationale de Natation Amateur (governing water sports), and France's Roger Coulon of the Fédération Internationale de Lutte Amateur (governing wrestling), the GAIF became a third force jockeying with the IOC and the PGA. Big egos were involved, and considerable power was on the line. It would take five more years—and Brundage's retirement—

for the IOC, PGA, and GAIF to settle into relatively comfortable tripartite cooperation.

In fact, the maneuverings of the 1960s were probably less about power and egos than about money. Until 1964 the IOC had experienced no money problems, for it had possessed almost no money. Its staff comprised only a chancellor and two part-time assistants at the Lausanne headquarters; and thousands of miles to the west, on another, larger lake, two part-time assistants in

Giulio Onesti (*center*) stands among his colleagues in the Permanent General Assembly (PGA) of National Olympic Committees along the shore of the Adriatic after a 1969 meeting at Dubrovnik, Yugoslavia. The PGA became the Association of National Olympic Committees in 1979. NOCs have also banded into continental groups.

Chicago at the IOC's American headquarters— the residence of IOC president Avery Brundage. He had come to office in 1952, and for the first eight years of his tenure, IOC expenditures were incredibly modest: They amounted to about $10,000 a year for the Lausanne office. The Chicago office was supported out of Brundage's pocket. By 1964, however, expenses had increased by a factor of six, and the IOC was busily involved in media relations, political protocols, and such tender issues as race, gender, and drugs. The money to pay for all this was coming from what Brundage saw as the Enemy—the

relatively new medium of color television, broadcast live, worldwide.

Brundage deplored television's intrusion on Olympism's sacred precincts: To him, the cameras merely represented another threat—perhaps the worst one—that commercialism would corrupt what he saw as the purity of the Games. So thinking, he tended to turn a blind eye, or at best a jaundiced one, toward revenues that television might someday produce. But if Brundage couldn't see the cornucopia to come, others could, and they were positioning themselves at its mouth. The NOCs and IFs had also grown up poor. Now, scenting wealth in television fees, they were jockeying to cash in.

There would be several years of squabbling before the affected parties would evolve a formula for distributing this new money. The arrangement, worked out in 1966, called for the IOC, NOCs, and IFs to get equal one-third shares of the first $1 million from broadcast rights. The same parties would get the same split of two-thirds of the next million, with the remaining third going to the organizing committee of a particular Games' host city. Any surplus over $2 million would yield two-thirds to the organizing committee and one-third for equal division among the three Olympic bureaucracies.

This plan was subverted almost immediately when the host city organizing committees for two upcoming Games, Sapporo and Munich, refused to abide by it. Both insisted on taking a cut off the top to supply the television networks with necessary facilities. Sapporo eventually backed off its demand. Munich didn't. In the

An ABC camera gives viewers a close-up view of the ski-jumping action on the Autrans hill at Grenoble. The network's presence at Grenoble 1968 was a trial run for more comprehensive worldwide live coverage of the Games planned for Mexico City later that year.

end, the Olympic bureaucracies agreed to the initial rake-off, and with that the basic distribution formula fell into place.

At first, there wasn't much money to pass around. CBS paid a mere $50,000 to telecast the 1960 Winter Games from Squaw Valley and only $394,000 for rights to the Summer Games in Rome. Parts of the Rome Games were broadcast live to Europe, but they could only be carried by film to the rest of the television-watching world.

Four years later, Syncom III was lofted into geostationary orbit to provide a transpacific communications bridge capable of carrying live television coverage of the Tokyo Games to viewers in the United States. Providing such coverage in America had been worth more than $1.5 million to NBC, although the network would end up broadcasting only the opening ceremonies live; the 14-hour time difference sabotaged prime-time possibilities.

Despite this sluggish beginning, the Games and their new partner were setting out on a golden road. Soon a combination of new, highly mobile video technology and rising public interest would link Olympic athletes with a vast audience around the world. Television would display to those millions of viewers the products favored by the planet's finest athletes. It would sell everything from sunglasses to skis, and it would illuminate the Olympic universe as it had never been lit before.

All of these questions—of global polarities, of chemistry and gender, of autonomy and power and great wealth—were converging, but not on the IOC headquarters in Lausanne. Instead, these issues stalked a venerable city in the Rhône-Alpes region of France: Grenoble, where the 10th Olympic Winter Games were about to begin.

A badge for employees of Radio Television Française

GRANDEUR IN GRENOBLE

Organizers who bid to bring the 1968 Winter Games to Grenoble had wanted merely to produce a great sports festival. Their government wanted more. French president Charles de Gaulle saw the Winter Games as a chance to parade his prosperous country before the world, to show France as a leader in technology and a master of hospitality. Naturally, the opening ceremony would have to be suitably grand. So, in a show that owed more to Hollywood flash than Gallic taste, Grenoble delivered.

  The skies were perfect, the Alps snow-covered, and the 60,000-seat Olympic stadium filled to capacity. A plane flew overhead, disgorging parachutists who drifted down onto the infield, coming neatly to rest within the boundaries of the five interlocking Olympic rings inscribed on the ground. The crowd cheered as 1,293 athletes from 37 countries marched into the stadium. Enthusiasm was merely polite during a brief speech by IOC president Avery Brundage, but it grew as de Gaulle himself declared the Winter Games open. Cheers mounted again when Alain Calmat, a figure-skating star from Innsbruck 1964, appeared with the Olympic flame. He bounded up a ramp at the end of the stadium and lit the fire in the Olympic cauldron to a crescendo of applause. Instantly, cannons boomed, ejecting tiny Olympic flags that soared—sadly off course—over the heads of spectators and out of the stadium. Helicopters swooped overhead and, with better aim, dropped 30,000 scented paper roses, symbolic of the city of Grenoble, onto the crowd. A squadron of skywriting planes followed, tracing the Olympic rings in the heavens. As athletes filed out and the stadium cleared, all conceded that despite a few minor glitches, it was a grand beginning for the Games.

UTMOST GRAVITY

The sheltering walls of the starting ramp kept out the wind that swept the snowy knob of the Croix de Chamrousse, but they also limited skiers to a blinkered view of the terrain they were about to descend as fast as gravity and courage would allow. One had to imagine the course—Casserousse—the long, open turns of the Sun Dial, then peeling off toward the gully and a stand of dark pines where the trail narrowed like a rocket nozzle past the dead tree and across a snowy corrugation of bumps called *le coq*—the rooster; then squirting out onto the Col de la Balme, a steep schuss before the fall toward the narrow valley that wound to the finish just west of Chamrousse.

The course was 1.8 miles long and dropped not quite half a mile, its maximum gradient 65 percent, and it never flattened out to more than 29 percent. For about 1,500 feet after the Col de la Balme there was some relief before the course seized the skier again and dragged him through a final series of humps toward the finish. At best,

Casserousse was tricky, with twisting turns along icy fallaways, big rolls to be jumped, radical variations in terrain, nine sharp changes in direction. Starting at an elevation of only about 7,000 feet, it was almost un-Alpine, and some racers complained that it was less a natural challenge than a contrived and dangerous trap.

Casserousse twisted down out of the Belledonne Mountains east of Grenoble, a place described by one native son, the novelist Stendhal, as "a mediocre town in an exceptional location." Although it was the capital city of the French Alps, Grenoble was no ski resort, but rather a smoggy industrial city of about 180,000 souls, situated in a narrow valley where the rivers Drac and Isère meet, surrounded by wonderfully skiable mountains.

Over a 75-square-mile area around Grenoble, French organizers had distributed nearly a quarter-billion dollars' worth of construction in the form of Olympic villages, a 12,000-seat ice rink, 67 miles of ski trails, nine miles of

Jean-Claude Killy, Olympic Gold Medalist, Grenoble 1968

The modern buildings of the Olympic Village stand within an industrial patchwork of offices in Grenoble. Venues for the Winter Games were as far as 45 miles from the city center, necessitating separate housing areas for athletes. Critics complained that the far-flung quarters diminished Olympic spirit.

ski roads, magnificent 70- and 90-meter ski jumps, and—this being France—a million dollars in abstract sculpture. Since three-fourths of the money came from public funds, there were also some lasting civic improvements: a new airport, a hospital, a convention center, a new town hall, a new police station.

To fit the Olympics into the Isère's narrow valley, venues had to be spread out: Alpine skiers were some 45 miles from their Nordic brethren, the bobsled run about 25 switchbacked miles from the skaters; instead of one enormous family of athletes in a single Olympic village, skiers were grouped by specialty in small hotels and chalets all over the Dauphiné Alps.

This is the region where Europe's northern winter skirmishes with the warmer, wetter winds that patrol northward from the Mediterranean, only 150 miles away, producing legendary cold fogs and heavy snows. Some say that true winter never really arrives here, but there is always cold, dirty weather. The combination of bad terrain and bad weather made the Casserousse a formidable run

on this February Wednesday in 1968. Days earlier, leaden skies had dumped so much snow that skiers had to cancel their practice runs. Today an unnerving wind drummed up the hill, spinning disorienting webs of fog and cloud that caused the course to flicker eerily.

Yet to Jean-Claude Killy, the 24-year-old Frenchman in today's 14th slot, this treacherous place was as familiar as his mountainous backyard in Val-d'Isère. His father, Robert, had tired of the Parisian suburb of St. Cloud and in 1945 had moved his family—his wife, a daughter, and two-year-old Jean-Claude—to the little village about 70 miles east of Grenoble near the Italian frontier. Val-d'Isère had been revived in the 1930s as a ski resort, and Robert Killy had settled into the local economy, opening a ski shop, then a restaurant, then a small hotel.

The elder Killy had hoped the move would improve the fragile health of his shy, quiet son. And, in fact, the boy quickly became more robust in the bracing mountain air. At three Jean-Claude was skiing; by the time he was an adolescent, the

WHERE THE GAMES WERE PLAYED

Alpe d'Huez Bobsled Course

Ice Stadium

Speed-Skating Oval

French figure skater Alain Calmat salutes the crowd with his torch after igniting the fire in the Olympic cauldron. Organizers rigged Calmat's chest with a microphone so that his heartbeat could be heard over loudspeakers as he carried the fire on its final leg of the relay.

sport had become all-important, a pursuit infinitely preferable to days spent in a stuffy classroom. "By the time he was six," Robert Killy said of his son, "he could ski faster than I. I never saw him after that."

Indeed, were Jean-Claude to swing a 100-mile circle from the starting gate above Chamrousse, he would encompass much of what had occurred in his young life, good and bad. His childhood had been shaken in 1950 when his mother ran off with a lover. Following that shock came the boy's cloying incarceration in a school that he hated, then a bout with tuberculosis that put him into a sanatorium for several months at the age of 11. By the time he was 15, however, he was allowed by his father, now happily remarried, to leave school and pursue what he truly loved: Skiing was the core of Jean-Claude's life, perhaps even the sum of it.

"I always believed that skiing was something serious," Killy told a reporter once, "that it was a way of living a whole life. Others didn't. They used it only as a form of play." The young downhiller skied with the instinctive abandon of the perfect natural. His early nickname on the runs: *Casse-cou*—breakneck.

But bad luck plagued him. At 14, after winning local prizes, Killy was selected for a junior competition in Cortina, but there he broke his leg in the downhill. Two seasons after that he dominated the junior national championships in Alpine

events. But later that year the unlicensed 16-year-old, who drove cars the way he skied (he would later race them professionally), rolled a borrowed convertible just south of Lake Leman; his best friend died in the crash. Good luck and bad. His fortunes flickered like the light dappling the slopes that dropped away beneath him now, the rutted snow of Casserousse.

"I took him on the team in 1960-61, and he never finished a race," recalled Honoré Bonnet, the legendary coach who had made French skiers the best in the world, edging out the long-dominant Austrians. "He'd be ahead by 2 seconds halfway down, but he'd fall. I encouraged him. I told him that I selected people not by their finish but by their performance in the gates on the way down. I reminded him that, of course, if he wished ever to win he would have to arrange to also finish."

Killy began to finish, and in style. He won his first international event, the giant slalom, in December 1961 in his own hometown, Val-d'Isère. He was 18. He would have gone to the 1962 world championships in Chamonix, but a bad crash in Cortina broke his leg; he finished the run in good time on one ski, but he missed Chamonix. Then followed a tour with the French army in Algeria, a summer that left him convalescing from dysentery and hepatitis. At Innsbruck 1964, where Killy was expected to become an Olympic star, he did nothing at all:

He fell at the start of the downhill, lost a binding on the slalom, and finished a poor fifth in the giant slalom.

Two years later, though, the young Frenchman began to peak. His earlier frailty repaired by determined conditioning, in 1966 he won the downhill and combined world championships in Portillo, Chile. A year later Killy won 23 of 30 races, among them the five World Cup downhills. He became a national hero. "When he has a sore throat France gargles," wrote Sanche de Gramont in the *New York Times Magazine*. "He is in the same orbit of fame as Brigitte Bardot." Agreeably, he was also almost as photogenic.

Given his glut of World Cups, Killy began pondering the wisdom of retiring while he was on top, but others urged him to wait for the Grenoble Games. Yet as he waited, his performance seemed to wane. His equipment began to fail him, and so did his Algeria-battered stomach. In the six World Cup races leading up to the Olympics, he won only once. He became a potential national calamity.

Now, poised above Chamrousse, Killy was sick with the certainty that the national calamity lay only a few minutes away. He had made a seemingly fatal mistake. When the wind delayed the starts, he used the time for a warm-up run down the side—and crossed a patch of rough ice that rubbed away the perfect hot-wax layer on his racing skis. Nothing could be done about it in the starting ramp, so Killy waited, all bluff, knowing that as the final molecules of wax came off during his run he would go slower and slower. "Nervous?" he wisecracked to reporters. "After 10 years of skiing, it's all I can do to keep from falling asleep." But to a friend he murmured: *"C'est foutu."* "It is lost."

Then it was his turn. He seated his goggles and crabbed his wiry 5-foot-11 frame into position, crouched on the rim of the starting ramp, poles and powerful legs cocked to push him off. At the buzzer he left the gate like a 165-pound

Austrian Olympian Karl Schranz extols the virtues of Kneissl skis in this promotional poster. Commercial endorsements like this one violated the Olympic Charter and would get Schranz ousted from Sapporo 1972 for professionalism.

panther, in the springing start that only he did well. There could be a half-second advantage in that first leap into space, and he would need it—and more.

The 10th Winter Olympics were barely a day old when Killy made that catapulting start above Chamrousse. Tuesday had begun under a pall of winter fog that had lifted by early afternoon when some 38,000 spectators

KNEISSL – der Welt erste Fabrik für Kunststoffski

WELTCUP-SIEGER KARL SCHRANZ

streamed into the cold U of the stadium at the south end of the valley, a stadium that would be used only for this opening ceremony. In the arena were 1,293 athletes from 37 countries, along with more than 3,000 reporters and radio and television people. Luminaries abounded, chief among them French president Charles de Gaulle. And, of course, the president of the International Olympic Committee, Avery Brundage, was there, still trim and fresh-faced at 80.

Picturesque ceremonies got the 10th Winter Games off to a spectacular start. They seemed to announce that these snowbound sports had come of age, that they were a full partner with the Summer Games. The Winter Games that had been born at Chamonix in 1924 had now returned to France as remarkable adults—though some thought them a trifle worldly. And some thought they belonged anywhere but in the Olympic movement.

Arguably, this latter group included Avery Brundage himself. Brundage and others of his vintage had always considered the Winter Games a stepchild, an afterthought lacking the classic legacy of its age-old summer sister. Besides, an old decathlete himself, the IOC president may have perceived a frivolous center in sports that could not be played in a conventional stadium—indeed, that were usually played in lush ski resorts. These athletes neither ran nor jumped, but spent their lives following winter back and forth across the equator, camping at such spas as Portillo and Kitzbühel, Chamonix, and Sun Valley. Where, Brundage may have wondered, was the serious sport in activities that could be reduced to sliding on slick surfaces? Worst of all, to the IOC's hoary leader, were the winter athletes in such hot pursuit of money—the hockey stars linked to the pros, the skiers who were too often photographed with their boldly labeled equipment. Brundage, the self-made millionaire, despised in others the flagrant grasping for gain.

THE GAMES AT A GLANCE

	FEBRUARY 6	FEBRUARY 7	FEBRUARY 8	FEBRUARY 9	FEBRUARY 10	FEBRUARY 11	FEBRUARY 12	FEBRUARY 13	FEBRUARY 14	FEBRUARY 15	FEBRUARY 16	FEBRUARY 17	FEBRUARY 18
OPENING CEREMONY	■												
BIATHLON							■			■			
BOBSLED			■		■						■		
FIGURE SKATING			■	■		■	■		■	■	■		
ICE HOCKEY	■	■	■	■	■	■	■	■	■	■	■	■	
LUGE							■			■			■
SKIING, ALPINE						■	■	■	■	■	■	■	■
SKIING, NORDIC			■			■	■		■	■		■	■
SPEED SKATING						■	■	■	■		■	■	■
SKI JUMPING							■						■
CLOSING CEREMONY													■

At the opening ceremonies, Brundage had given a short speech. It was mild enough, asking for "a less materialistic and happier and more peaceful world." But Olympic observers knew that this innocuous plea was the tip of an iceberg of rancor—one capable of sinking the Winter Games. At issue was amateurism, which had withered in the light of a kind of athletic realpolitik: The men and women who competed had to live, train, eat, clothe themselves, follow their sports across the planet, and contrive to somehow survive their athletic youth when, still young, they could no longer play.

The amateurism question had, of course, bedeviled the Olympic movement for years. Some members of the IOC and other great sport bureaucracies had tacitly acknowledged that the problems of athletic life could be smoothed by subsidies based on the Olympics' commercial value. The easily recognized guns used in shooting competitions, the machines used for time-keeping and computing, the quickest running shoes—all conveyed some added Olympic-derived value to their designers and manufacturers, even if no blatant logos appeared.

But other czars of sport were not so pragmatic. Avery Brundage, in particular, was a purist. Against the ever-swelling flood of commercialism,

Brundage had steadfastly kept his finger in the dike—absurdly, perhaps, but with stubborn passion: Play-for-pay athletics were an abomination in the venerable Summer Games. In the Winter Games, he may well have thought, they were even worse.

The IOC leader's irritation had peaked during the 1964 Games at Innsbruck. Skiers there had flashed their brand-name skis at the finish line and worn ski-makers' logos under the ski tips, where they could be read at every jump and turn. Moreover, everyone who was not hopelessly naive understood that racers accepted help from equipment manufacturers. "When ski racers openly display the trademarks on their skis," Brundage had observed after Innsbruck, "we can guess why they're doing it even if we can't prove it."

Lacking proof of under-the-table payoffs, Brundage at first resorted to going after the manufacturers rather than the offending athletes: He sought to ban advertising on equipment. The IOC pressed one of its own members, Marc Hodler, the Swiss lawyer and ardent skier who was then president of the Fédération Internationale de Ski (FIS), and he evidently promised reform: The FIS, governing body of amateur skiing, approved what it called neutral skis—skis without logos. But nothing really

Laughing as they work, French skiers Jean-Paul Augert *(left)* and Georges Naduit make light of the order to cover the brand names of their skis. Avery Brundage, the IOC president, would later call for obscuring the brand names on athletic shoes as well. Both demands would prove unworkable.

changed. In January 1968, Brundage had gone back to Hodler and demanded that the FIS either do better or the IOC would chop Alpine events from the Grenoble Games—that is to say, eliminate the only events that the host country expected to win. The result: a sullen running argument among the affected parties.

Fiscal purity was a real problem for skiers. Their sport was expensive, requiring extensive gear, travel, and training, especially at the championship level. The best skiers required a subsidy, and everyone knew it. In the effort to make that fact more palatable, Hodler tried to disguise it as a performance issue. The racers claimed, Hodler told the IOC Executive Board, that "the procedure of unmarking would either upset the balance of the skis, or, in the case of the marks on the underside, would interfere with the actual running of the skis." The Executive Board didn't buy it. In a kind of punitive aside, the IOC forced Jean-Claude Killy to renege on a profitable deal with a ski-pole manufacturer.

Eventually, the FIS and the IOC reached a

brief and uneasy truce: The racers would not pose for photographs with their skis in the finish area. Of course, nothing prevented manufacturers from advertising that their boy or girl had ridden to victory on their skis. And nothing kept the skiers from posing for victory photographs in goggles, gloves, headgear, and other togs emblazoned with their sponsors' names.

The shaky compromise would collapse in June, months after Grenoble had passed into Olympic history. Then the FIS would take a brave stand: Alpine racers would be permitted to take openly what they had formerly received on the sly. This left Avery Brundage and the IOC with a handful of poor choices: Stand pat for pure amateurism and effectively purge the Winter Games of their best skiers, adjust their views to accommodate economic realities, eliminate Alpine racing from the Games, or cancel the Winter Games entirely, since fewer than half the countries with national Olympic committees participated. Brundage vowed to resolve the matter before the 1972 Winter Games began at Sapporo, and

Unique in Winter Games history, the Grenoble winners' medals differed for each sport. The front *(above, left)* features a pictogram of one of the nine Olympic events. Wavy lines representing motion are superimposed over the symbol. The obverse *(above, right)* shows the Olympic rings and a snowflake with three roses, a symbol of Grenoble, and an inscription in French: 10th Olympic Winter Games.

The commemorative medals given to all the athletes pay homage to Greece, birthplace of the Games, and to Grenoble, the host city. The front *(below, left)* has a profile of a classical Greek athlete surrounded by snowflakes. The reverse presents a panoramic view of Grenoble with the Alps as a backdrop.

Diplomas were awarded to the top six finishers in each event. The design features the Grenoble snowflakes-and-roses logo.

his voice carried the old Alpine sound of anathema. To some people gathered in the French Alps that winter, Grenoble may have looked like the end. In fact, it was the beginning.

No one understood this better than a battalion of people, most of them Americans, billeted in a tiny Alpine hotel called Les Trois Roses after the three flowers in Grenoble's coat of arms. Located about 12 miles north of the city, the hotel became a command center for one of the great gambles in sports broadcasting history. The American Broadcasting Company had successfully bid $2.5 million for rights to the Grenoble Games—four times their winning bid for Innsbruck 1964. The ABC Sports team was led by 36-year-old wunderkind Roone Arledge and his production director, Charles Howard, 35.

Both men were keenly aware that Grenoble would take them into a terra incognita of television programming—and could very well make or break their network.

In America, "the concept of sports being in prime time was inconceivable," recalls Howard. "There was no *Monday Night Football*, then. It was a totally different world." Plus, ABC was having a tough time keeping up with its competitors, NBC and CBS. "Some of the people we did business with were concerned about the network surviving."

Nor did ABC have much in the way of successful models: Television had been part of the Olympics since Berlin 1936, but it had provided little live or thorough coverage. As recently as Tokyo 1964, television had failed badly. NBC bought the broadcast rights for $1.5 million, a lot of money at the time, and the U.S. and Japanese

Norway's Magnar Solberg *(No. 3)* and Poland's Stanislaw Szczepaniak lie prone during a shooting stage in the 20-kilometer biathlon.

governments had jumped to provide a satellite link to carry the broadcasts to America; still, the network had managed not to bring its audience some of the most exciting sports triumphs in U.S. history: No one saw Billy Mills win the 1,500-meter, or Joe Frazier punch his German foe with a broken hand, until well after the Games had ended. The network had been spooked by the time difference and, of course, by the industry taboo against airing sports in prime time.

Arledge and Howard had done one Winter Olympics together, Innsbruck 1964. "We didn't do much television then," Howard says. "We had a satellite with a one-minute window every two or three days, so we did Tuesday highlights, reduced to 15-minute to half-hour running times. The tapes were driven to Munich to put on the satellite and aired Wednesday evening from New York. They weren't live or even the same day."

Grenoble was going to be different—that, at least, was the gamble. Howard and his crews had tramped the Alpine courses the year before, spotting their cameras. "We thought we could put cameras where there was a sense of danger," he recalls, laughing at the remembered exertions. "We were young then." So, too, was the

contingent of energetic and inventive Grenoble students hired to help out the ABC regulars—natives who, if they didn't know television, did know the terrain.

Along with youth, Arledge and crew had a little international experience. By 1968, ABC had for seven years aired a program called *Wide World of Sports*—a weekend staple that put together as much as two and a half hours of taped events from around the world for broadcast from New York. "That was what gave us confidence," says Howard. That, and new equipment that permitted them to get a camera up the side of a mountain.

At Grenoble, ABC taped all day, from 8 a.m. until 10 p.m. "This was fed for a three-and-a-half-to four-and-a-half-hour program," Howard recounts, "47 minutes of Alpine skiing, 32 minutes of women's figure skating, divided into segments. As things were edited, two or three of us decided what to do. Only McKay"—ABC Sports' amiable anchor, Jim McKay—"was live." They fed their stuff directly from Les Trois Roses to the Early Bird satellite hovering above the equator, for relay to New York, where the network had only to add commercials.

THE WINTER HUNT

The first known image of a skier is a Norwegian rock painting dating back to 3,000 BC. It depicts a man on skis, carrying a weapon. The biathlon, an event that demands both long-distance skiing and marksmanship, is a modern version of that Stone Age canvas of a hunt through the taiga.

February 12, 1968, brought the start at Grenoble of the 20-kilometer biathlon, a race that includes four shooting stops where athletes fire five shots with a rifle at targets nearly 500 feet away. They fire from a prone position once, from an erect stance four times. Each missed shot imposes a 1-minute penalty. The biathlon gold medal went to a 31-year-old Norwegian policeman from Trondheim, Magnar Solberg, whose 1:13:45.9 time was good enough to win, given his flawless marksmanship. The Soviet Union's Aleksandr Tikhonov took the silver medal with a time of 1:14:40.0, reflecting 2 penalty minutes. Tikhonov's score also suffered from two bad shots that missed the target. Another Soviet, Vladimir Goundartsev, took the bronze.

In the biathlon relay—making its Olympic debut at Grenoble—each of four athletes on a team skis 10 kilometers, completing two shooting exercises entailing eight shots at five targets. For each target missed, the racer has to retreat 100 meters. Superior skiing won this event for the Soviets at Grenoble, while perfect shooting was not enough to carry Sweden to more than the bronze. The silver medal went to Norway.

ABC didn't tape everything. Instead, it took primary events covered by French television, then augmented that footage with its own shots. "At Grenoble," Howard says, "we didn't have downhill top to bottom. We took what the French provided, which was the bottom half of the hill." Everything was taped using a French line system, to make it compatible with French footage. But ABC Sports had become proficient in converting the French film to the American line system as they fed the stories to the satellite—another payoff from the *Wide World of Sports* experience.

Once the Games began, television coverage itself became an Olympic event: the marathon. "A good number of people never finished until 5 a.m.—11 p.m. eastern time," Howard remembers. He himself would stay around the broadcast center until 2 or 3, then go to his room in Les Trois Roses to squeeze in some sleep. To make the widely scattered sports sites more accessible, ABC used French helicopters staging out of a pad by the hotel to cover events above Chamrousse and the Alpe d'Huez. People covering events in town could drive it in a few minutes.

But Arledge, Howard, and their army of announcers, reporters, photographers, technicians, editors, grips, and gofers were doing much more than merely covering a collage of athletic events under difficult conditions. They were opening a portal on a universe that only a relatively few people had ever seen.

Europeans had always skied—the Alps drew them irresistibly—but skiing was exotic and remote to most Americans. Snowy slopes were where the rich went to escape the boredom of infinite possibility, and the famous went to be alone. Wealthy men and women in grand, insulating feathers drifted from a sensual languor to vertical runs, skiing with easy, enviable grace, eluding gravity, life's quotidian problems, even age and death. For many, this was a world as inaccessible as Shangri-la—until this fortnight in Grenoble.

The colored images flowing from Les Trois Roses to the rest of the world opened a gateway into that universe and showed that it was exciting and dangerous and intensely attractive—but also human, attainable. The pictures meant that as Jean-Claude Killy sprang into space on the Croix de Chamrousse, he was seen not just by the shivering hundreds pressed against the snow fence bordering the course but by all the world. (And so, Avery Brundage might have grumbled,

America's Jim Barrows follows an unconventional path down the Casserousse course at Grenoble. The crash landed him in the hospital and ended any medal hopes for American men in the downhill.

24-year-old who promised to bring a medal home from Grenoble—his silver at Innsbruck had been the first Alpine medal ever for an American male—had said of Casserousse that it was like "trying to ski on the outside of a basketball." Racing 11th, Kidd made a fine start, hurtling across the Sun Dial, then hairpinning toward the gully. But as he entered another right-hand turn, a hurricane-strength blast of wind dusted him with snow, disorienting him. He thought he saw something flash under him and flinched away, crossing his skis. Then he showed the world how badly things could go wrong on Casserousse.

When Kidd lost his balance, the TV cameras unblinkingly showed viewers—repeatedly and in slow motion—the terrible 60-mile-an-hour crash that tore away his helmet and skis and tossed him through the air like a rag doll. The spectacular spill didn't kill him, but it murdered American hopes for a medal in the downhill.

His teammate Jere Elliott lunged for speed and spun out of control, plowing into a snow fence and roughing up one shoulder. Steamboat Springs' big Jim "Moose" Barrows crashed at the Col de la Balme, where 15 racers had already gone down. "Yeah, I was going too fast," Barrows would concede later from his hospital bed, "but you don't win medals cooling it."

Of course, Jean-Claude Killy had never cooled anything in his life. He was 0.7 of a second ahead of Périllat before he even reached the two rolls at the Col de la Balme and was faster through the two low jumps, skittering dangerously close to the edge on the hairpin, going all out for speed. He cut through the S turns with the risky, abandoned skating and digging that were his trademark. Killy entered the final lap—the narrows of Krieg Passage and the corrugations of the Allais bumps—1.1 seconds ahead of Périllat. Now he was on the warm snow, on skis that had lost virtually all their wax.

was the brand name Dynamic stenciled under the tips of his fast-running fiberglass skis.)

Killy's teammate Guy Périllat had been the first out of the gate at Casserousse and remained the man to beat, with a brisk time of 1:59.93. Of the next 11 racers, Switzerland's John Daniel Dätwyler had managed a 2:00.32 and three others—Heinrich Messner and Karl Schranz of Austria and Italy's Ivo Mahlknecht—had done 2:02 or better. But the unpredictable course had taken its toll.

America, fielding its best Alpine team ever, had tumbled into catastrophe. Billy Kidd, the

Coach Bonnet watched in horror. "He was losing speed," he would recall later, "losing speed with every meter he raced. He was slowing the whole last half of the course. If he had had to go another two meters, he could not have won." On this section, Périllat was a full second faster than Killy and might have taken the gold medal—except that Killy had one last secret weapon: "I knew about the finish line," he would say after the race. "Early in the practice runs, I had realized that if I cut a sharp line just at the pole on the right, I could actually gain a couple of meters." The last-instant swerve brought him in at 1:59.85, a minuscule 0.08 of a second faster than his teammate. His speed over the course: an average 54 miles per hour.

At the finish, Killy duly posed for photographs without his skis. Next to him stood his friend Michel Arpin, with his own skis—Dynamics, of course. Even when claiming a gold medal, it was irresistible to tweak Brundage, who had declined to present medals to Alpine skiers.

Four days later, Killy set the pace for the first run of the giant slalom, which twisted down another tortured slope above Chamrousse, an undulating piece of ground as ideal for its event as Casserousse was marginal. This was the first time in Olympic history that the giant slalom medals would go for the best total time on two runs on different days on different courses; it would also mark Killy's picking up the least familiar tool in his extensive kit: restraint.

The long, 70-gate course was stiff and icy on the first day, but Killy took it in stride: No one in the first seed of 15 came within 1.2 seconds of his time of 1:42.74. Swiss racer Willi Favre swept to second place, 0.8 of a second ahead of Guy Périllat. The rest of the field huddled just over the 1:45 mark. But in that huddle were two skiers bearing hope for an American medal.

Amazingly, Billy Kidd had survived his scenic crash in the downhill with only an ankle injury. Now he raced with the ankle heavily bound and marinated in novocaine, and he managed a solid 8th in his first run, just behind teammate Jim Heuga. America also had some good news in the second seed, where Spider Sabich and Rich Chaffee placed 12th and 13th.

On the second day, however, the giant slalom seemed an altogether different race. An overnight snowstorm had laid a blanket of soft powder over the hard-packed snow, and in the storm's wake came lighter snow and dense fog. Along some sections of the 57-gate second run, visibility dropped to three or four gates. Killy skied gingerly, protecting his perilous lead, and his time was beaten by Kidd, who came in 0.08 of a second faster than the Frenchman. But no one could displace Killy, and he had his second gold medal of the Grenoble Games. Willi Favre held in second place, even though he raced seventh on the second day, and Austria's Heini Messner managed to pick off the bronze, with Périllat a close fourth.

The giant slalom had yielded mixed news. The French monopoly on Alpine events appeared to have cracked: France had the gold, true, but silver had gone to Switzerland, bronze to the old rival, Austria. For America, whose team had suffered terrible crashes, it looked like good news indeed. For the first time in history, all four men on the U.S. team had finished in the first 15: Kidd 5th, Heuga, Sabich, and Chaffee 10th, 14th, and 15th respectively.

What the world was watching, however, was the progress of Jean-Claude Killy, the man with a chance to win three Alpine golds. The only other man to do so had been Austria's Toni Sailer, the "black lightning of Kitzbühel," at Cortina 1956. The Austrians mustered nervously, hoping to keep that mantle from draping the shoulders of this brash Frenchman.

It would be hard to say whether the Austrian cause was helped or hindered by the comedy that now unfolded for the final event, the slalom. The rules had been altered two years earlier by the FIS, which had decided to use a

MONTI'S MOMENT

Italy's Eugenio Monti, a 40-year-old native of the Dolomite valley village of Dobaccio, had problems with Father Time. Monti had come to Grenoble hoping to win a bobsled gold medal before age and infirmity made it impossible for him to continue his sport. He'd been a promising Alpine skier in his youth, but crashes had ruined his knees. Then he'd tried other sports before finding his passion in the extreme velocity and centrifugal madness of bobsledding. At Cortina 1956 he won two silver medals, and he soon had a pocketful of world titles as well—but no Olympic gold.

The Grenoble bob run at Alpe d'Huez was a fast course that dropped 459 feet in less than a mile. Athletes had found it nightmarish at a 1967 tune-up. Monti himself had come off a curve upside down and plowed along on his face for several yards before the sled halted in a trench. On one terrible Wednesday, only an Austrian team made it all the way down.

At the Games the devilish run seemed worse than ever. Races scheduled for daytime had to be deferred so that night could refreeze ice that kept thawing in warm winds. As the competition unfolded on February 11, races were run in the pitch darkness of 5 a.m. with the course lit by searchlights.

Monti's chance for an elusive gold looked shaky after the first three of four runs of the two-man bob contest: He was 0.2 of a second behind Germany's Horst Floth. But a great fourth run moved him into a tie with Floth. Officials decided the gold should go to Monti because his first run had been faster. Racers were only required to make two runs in the four-man contest because a sudden freeze had made the course dangerously fast. Monti's sled ran first in both races, followed by teams from Austria and Switzerland. Monti had made doubly good on his last chance for gold.

complex system of trials to halve the number of racers before the final run. Moreover, the federation had established a classification race to determine the starting order in the slalom final. The idea was advanced in pursuit of fairness: The later one skis in the slalom, the more tracks and chatter marks there are to cross, so that late runners are disadvantaged. Traditionally, skiers were seeded in groups of 15, depending on the points they had earned in competition. At Grenoble, to level the field for skiers who had not competed often enough to earn many points, officials proposed the classification race.

To the Alpine elite, this only meant that dark horses would run very hard—they had nothing to lose, after all—in hopes of displacing the favorites in the early starting places. A group of the top racers—French, Austrians, Americans—signed a petition urging the FIS to drop the race and return to the old point system. In the end, no petition was needed. The infamous Belledonne

Mountain weather decided the matter, spreading the course with such a dense fog that the racers refused to compete.

The fog had done what a more formal protest had not, for now officials discarded the classification slalom and applied the former point system to determine starting order. Unfortunately, they could not reorder the weather. Patchy fog persisted, sometimes offering clear skiing, sometimes cutting visibility to only a few of the 62 gates in the first run. Historians would call it the Ghost Slalom, its skiers gliding like doomed spirits through the mist. Killy had the day's only bit of sun, which lighted his way to a first-place 49.37 first run. But the race was very close: a dozen racers were within one second of his time.

For the second run, Killy started first, keenly aware of the vast pack of racers stalking him. His time down the fog-shrouded course was 50.36 seconds. The first contender was Erik Grahn of Sweden, who fell. Then came Heuga, too slow to win. Then Haakon Mjoen of Norway flashed down the course in 49.67, pushing Killy from first place—a terrible irony, to lose an Alpine event to a Norwegian! (The Scandinavians were traditionally premier Nordic skiers who regarded the Alpine events as somewhat effete.) Two more racers shot out of the gloom, but neither was fast enough to dislodge Mjoen. Then Karl Schranz of Austria started, but even minutes later he hadn't reached the finish line. It seemed that a policeman had crossed the track ahead of him, causing him to miss two gates, and the racer had returned to the start, insisting on a second chance. Officials

Fog obscures Karl Schranz's view of the slalom course at Chamrousse. In spite of the conditions, Schranz turned in the fastest time of the second run.

agreed. The Austrian streaked down the run this time, moving ahead of Killy by half a second; he was second only to the Norwegian.

Such joy as the supposed winner savored was short-lived, however. Word began to percolate down the mountain that Mjoen had omitted one of the gates; he was disqualified. Killy moved up to silver, and Schranz waved his poles in elation—the gold medal seemed to be his. But the entire mountain had begun to buzz with alternative possibilities.

Schranz had told officials that a distracting shadow crossing the snow several gates ahead of him had made him miss the two gates on his original run. But as the matter was probed further, it turned out that the missed gates—18 and 19—were above gate 21, where a policeman had

crossed ahead of Schranz. In the French view, the "shadow" couldn't have been a distraction because Schranz couldn't have seen it at that distance through the thick fog. While Schranz talked to reporters about his victory, officials muttered about the missed gates and the possible impropriety of allowing him a second run in any case. Ultimately, they sided with the French by a 3-2 vote, the only point of disagreement being whether Schranz had really been able to see the policeman. Some thought the matter academic. "He'd run down his grandmother if he thought it would do him any good," observed one of Schranz's compatriots. "I can't see him ducking away from a shadow."

The gold went to Killy, and some said it was more a matter of natural gravitation than of skiing

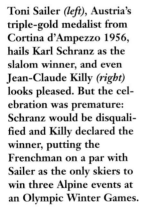

Toni Sailer *(left)*, **Austria's triple-gold medalist from Cortina d'Ampezzo 1956, hails Karl Schranz as the slalom winner, and even Jean-Claude Killy** *(right)* **looks pleased. But the celebration was premature: Schranz would be disqualified and Killy declared the winner, putting the Frenchman on a par with Sailer as the only skiers to win three Alpine events at an Olympic Winter Games.**

prowess. Schranz's cockiness had earned him the sobriquet "the Sonny Liston of skiing." In what came down to a contest of character, how could such a man prevail against the unflappable, telegenic, humorous Casse-cou, now better known as *le Superman?* Killy retired from amateur skiing soon afterward; some said he merely ratified a step taken years before. As for France and Austria, they had experienced worse tensions than this—at Austerlitz, for example, where, thanks to Napoleon, the result had been ominously similar.

Indeed, so brightly did the Frenchman from Val-d'Isère shine at Grenoble that details seemed to vanish in his amiable glare. Killy pervaded the Alpine events in particular, not only as a racer but also as an icon for his female counterparts. Had there been a female Killy in those ranks—in fact, there was not—it might have been Canada's petite 24-year-old Nancy

Greene, who, like Killy, dealt in conflicting nicknames. The press liked to call her a pixie, or Mary Poppins, for her fresh, freckled good looks and wholesome aura. But on the slopes, her comrades called her Tiger for the way she clawed toward victory.

A native of Rossland, British Columbia, Greene had joined Canada's national team at 15; a year later she competed at Squaw Valley 1960, finishing 22nd in the downhill. She came in seventh in that event at Innsbruck 1964. Grenoble was supposed to be the end of her long apprenticeship.

Greene's style would have broadened the famous Killy smile, for it mimicked his wild aggression: She liked to jam her edges into the ice, squirting her skis out ahead of her the way Jean-Claude did. "Killy is my hero," she said. "He's got terrific balance, he's got the quickness of a cat, and he's smart. He has realized that the

Fearless runs in the giant slalom made Canada's Nancy Greene the skier to watch. Greene mimicked Jean-Claude Killy's style in her slalom races with the stiff-armed, lateral positioning of her poles and the way she jammed the edges of her skis into the snow in front of her.

Spectators crowd the final turn of the women's downhill course at Chamrousse. The women started at the same elevation as the men, but their course was 2,390 feet (730 meters) shorter.

fastest way down a mountain is not always the way it says in the book."

The women's downhill course started from the same high point as the men's and dropped a little under half a mile before it ended in the skiing stadium of Recoin on the edge of Chamrousse. It began rather flat, then swept through a quartet of wide turns, skirting fallaways that looked like eternity, an average schuss crossing a few rolls, the relatively flat section of the Cote Belle, then veering to the left from Marmot Schuss for a big finish. Some thought the track too easy for an Olympic contest.

Easy or not, the course preserved the aura of ill luck that the U.S. men had discovered on

Casserousse. Only an hour or two before the race began on February 10, America's Karen Budge, the fastest of her team on the nonstop practice run, had been testing wax in the Belledonne fog when a careless Moroccan skier slammed into her, dislocating her shoulder and removing her from contention. Perhaps after this, the American women decided they had nothing to lose.

The fog dictated the type of wax the downhill racers would use. Most teams had concentrated on waxing for speed on the flats near the end of the course, overlooking the flat portion at its start. But toward midday, just as the races began, the sun burned away the fog and mantled the slopes with brilliant light—and heat. Stopwatches were showing 4-second differences in times during the first 20 seconds of the race, indicating that the wrong wax was gluing the skiers to the snow at the start of their runs. No matter how well the women skied at the bottom, they were losing the race in its first seconds. Thus, in a contest usually decided by hundredths of a second, times were spaced out by several seconds; for example, America's Suzee Chaffee was an amazing 6.8 seconds slower than Olga Pall of Austria on the upper turns of the course and ended in 28th place.

The other problem was that the turns, which had once seemed demanding, proved relatively easy; the racers were entering them with too much caution—and too little speed. Nancy Greene, once favored to win, ended ignominiously in 10th place. France's Marielle Goitschel, the other favorite, finished eighth. Victory went to Olga Pall, who had read the mountain and the

sky correctly. Pall, the 20-year-old racer from the Tyrol, took the gold with a 1:40.87 run, and her Austrian teammate Christl Haas, gold medalist at Innsbruck, took the bronze. But it wasn't like the old days, when the women's downhill was all the red and white flag of Austria. As the French spectators chanted, "Mirabelle, Mirabelle," little Isabelle Mir, a teenager from the French Pyrenees, swept to the finish just 0.46 of a second slower than Pall, wrapping the silver medal in the tricolor of France.

The two runs of the women's slalom were conducted three days later, taking the racers through 56 gates in the first heat, 57 in the second, over a steep hill that dropped more than 500 feet over the 1,400-foot course. The favorites were Nancy Greene, Marielle Goitschel, and France's Annie Famose. Goitschel had taken the silver medal at Innsbruck—just behind her older sister, Christin, who won the gold—and Famose had won at

Carving deep into the snow, France's Marielle Goitschel makes a sharp turn on the slalom course. In two Winter Games, Goitschel won two gold medals and one silver, making her France's most accomplished Olympic woman skier.

Only German speakers won medals in the men's single luge as Austria's Manfred Schmid *(right)* claimed the gold, and Thomas Köhler *(first on left)* and Klaus Bonsack *(third from left)*, both from East Germany, won the silver and bronze respectively.

Klaus Bonsack and East German teammate Thomas Köhler look like a four-legged creature as they keep tightly in line during a run in the doubles luge. Bonsack, the driver, was a luge medalist in three consecutive Winter Games.

FIRE AND ICE

The luge events at Villard-de-Lans came under a two-pronged attack at the Grenoble Games. First there was the overly warm weather that turned the course to slush. Then there was the controversy.

The singles competition was going forward in spite of the iffy ice. East Germans were in first, second, and fourth place in the women's singles, and a sweep seemed probable after the third of four runs. But the team's habit of arriving late for runs and leaving immediately afterward aroused suspicion. A Polish official filed a protest alleging that the East Germans were illegally heating the runners of their sleds, a practice that makes the vehicles slide faster. Judges confirmed the allegation, and all three East Germans were disqualified. Weather made the final run impossible, so Italy's Erica Lechner, who'd stood in third place after the three completed runs, was awarded the gold medal. Christa Schmuck and Angelika Dönhaupt, both of West Germany, became the silver and bronze medalists.

Suspicion then focused on the East German men. Seven of the luge teams threatened a walkout if the German men weren't disqualified as well. Officials decided against it. Nobody walked. Weather cut short the second controversy, as it had the first: The men's event ended after three runs. Austria's Manfred Schmid won, and two East Germans, Thomas Köhler and Klaus Bonsack, finished second and third respectively. The next day Köhler and Bonsack turned the tables on Schmid by winning the two-seater, relegating Schmid and his partner, Ewald Walch, to second.

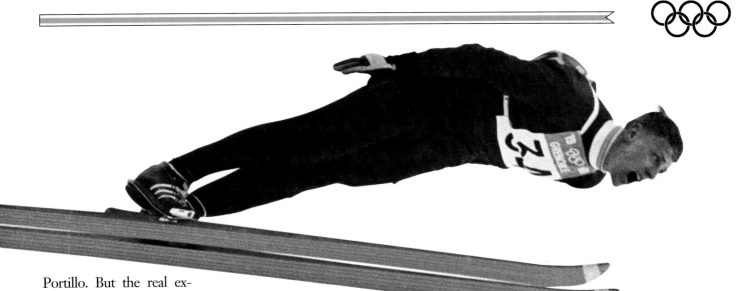

Portillo. But the real excitement was expected to come from the American women, who had found a kind of niche in the slalom. Against all odds, four of them had worked their way into the first-seeded group of 15 to race—only France had as many—and two of the Americans had arrived in Europe only three weeks earlier, with nothing like the FIS points needed for an early starting berth.

Once on the course, the American women went flat out. Kiki Cutter flew down the run in 41.46, a time that would have been almost fast enough to win, had her great speed not taken her past a couple of gates. Judy Nagel, just 16, produced what observers called the best women's slalom in years, whipping gracefully through the gates to finish in 40.19. A third American, Rosie Fortna, hit a stick and missed the next gate but finished at 41.31. The fourth in this breakneck quartet, Wendy Allen, missed some gates but came in with an amazing 39.25. In the stadium, the scoreboard showed the United States in first, second, fourth, and sixth positions after this first run. Then, like fireworks winking out, three of the four women vanished from the board, disqualified. Only little Judy Nagel remained, and she found it lonely beyond telling at the top.

Nagel got off to a bad start on her second run, hesitated at gate three, then drifted off the track as though hypnotized, then returned to ski a few more gates before falling, and, finally, making a good run out of what remained. On the tough lower part of the course, Nagel ran half a second faster than Marielle Goitschel. But what the European press called the Americans' hara-kiri slalom had thrown the event to the favorites. Nagel was disqualified for missing a gate. Goitschel, had the fastest second

run and a winning total time of 1:25.86. Greene took silver with 1:26.15. Bronze went to Famose with 1:27.89.

For Nancy Greene, who had come to the Games as Canada's great hope, a silver medal was nothing like enough. She needed to take home a gold medal—and she had a tigerish appetite for a big win. The giant slalom two days later would be her last chance.

The weather and the Gaboureaux course—a demanding mile of gently undulating ground that dropped about a third of a mile before finishing in the Chamrousse stadium—were perfect for the giant slalom. And here Greene dominated the race as her hero, Killy, might have done. She sprang like a cat from the start, and by the time she had run 50 seconds she had picked up 0.9 of a second on the rest of the field; 80 seconds into the race she was 1.3 seconds ahead. She posted 1:51.97 at the finish, 2.6 seconds ahead of her nearest competitor, Annie Famose, who was followed—one might say dogged—by Switzerland's Fernande Bochatay, 0.07 of a second out of second place.

France had two more women in the first six, Florence Steurer in fourth place by just 0.01 of a second, and Isabelle Mir in sixth. The only Austrian in the group was Olga Pall, in fifth. As for the American women who had brought such dazzling futility to the slalom, there seemed to be nothing left. They skied the giant slalom as though running on empty, sliding poorly and given to such careless errors as an out-of-order run through the gates.

Nancy Greene took more home than the gold and silver medals. She was also named the

Good aerodynamic form floats Czechoslovakia's Jiři Raška out to nearly 300 feet off the 90-meter hill at St. Nizier. The Soviet Union's Vladimir Beloussov won the event, with Raška second. The outcome marked the first time in Winter Games history that a Scandinavian failed to finish in one of the top spots.

outstanding female Alpine skier of the 10th Winter Olympics and earned the FIS's world combined championship. The little tiger had come to the slopes around Grenoble hunting for victory; on Gaboureaux she had made her stunning kill.

Across the valley from the ski runs of Chamrousse, at St. Nizier and Autrans some 20 miles west of Grenoble, skiers were harnessing gravity in a very different way. Two ski jumps had been built for the Grenoble Games, a 70-meter at Autrans and a 90-meter at St. Nizier, both dauntingly vertiginous slopes. As the downhill races are called Alpine, these events, along with the arduous cross-country treks, are called Nordic—because, some would have said, only Scandinavians could win them.

No one expected that to change at Grenoble. Norway's Björn Wirkola was favored to take home two gold medals, one for the 70-meter special jump, another for the 90-meter. If he didn't, his teammate Lars Grini, who had set a 492-foot (150-meter) world record for ski flying, would. Such aspiring leapers as Japan's Takashi Fujisawa, Finland's Veikko Kankkonen, East Germany's Dieter Neuendorf, Czechoslovakia's Jiři Raška, and the Soviet Union's Pjotr Kovalenkov would no doubt have to wait. This would have been true in any year, but it was especially so in 1968, where the rules had been changed. Instead of counting the best two of three jumps, athletes would be given only two chances, and both would count. Without doubt, the new rules would hand victory to the favorites.

Before a middling crowd of spectators at Autrans, Jiři Raška, a 27-year-old from Prague, proved everyone dead wrong with a first jump of almost 260 feet (79 meters), followed by a second of 253 feet (77 meters). His first jump put him third behind another non-Scandinavian, Baldur Preiml of Austria, who had jumped a meter farther, and Soviet jumper Alex Jeglanow of the Soviet Union. But Raška's style—the way he

held his body as he flew, the confidence of his jumps—gave him the points he needed to win. Austria's Reinhold Bachler took the silver medal and Preiml the bronze. Favorite Björn Wirkola finished fourth, Finland's Topi Mattila fifth.

A week later, Raška tried again on the 90-meter platform at St. Nizier and found himself engaged in an aerial duel with a Russian, a Moscow student named Vladimir Beloussov. The Soviet beat Raška on both jumps by a narrow half-meter and took the gold medal with 231.3 points, followed by Raška with 229.4. Norway's Lars Grini took the bronze but ran well back with 214.3 points. Wirkola came in a distant 23rd, some said because he had preferred Grenoble's nightlife, such as it was, to his training.

No matter, the Scandinavians' day would come in the combined, a harrowing contest in which three jumps off the 70-meter platform were followed by a grueling 15-kilometer cross-country race. In the nine previous Olympic Winter Games, 27 medals had been on offer in this event, and Scandinavian athletes had taken 22 of them.

Even so, many observers picked Franz Keller, from Nesselwang in West Germany, to win, with a caveat: His jumping would have to be good enough to make up for his relative slowness on skis. That failing, the contest would almost certainly go to one of the many first-rate long-distance skiers in the field: Switzerland's Alois Kälin or Italy's great cross-country man, Ezio Damolin.

Keller led the field of jumpers with a total of 240.1 points. Poland's Józef Gąsienica was a poor second with 217.7, and Alois Kälin had jumped into the 24th spot with an indifferent 193.2 points. Still, Kälin had only to beat Keller on skis by 3 ½ minutes to take the gold medal. That, as it happened, was exactly the length of Keller's start on the Swiss skier. For 15 kilometers, Kälin trailed the German like a hungry wolf, moving inexorably closer as the race approached the finish. In the final 100 meters Keller led Kälin by 70 meters, and each long, smooth, gliding step brought him closer. When Keller dashed across the finish line, Kälin was only 12 meters behind him—very near, but too far to overcome the poor jumping. Keller won the gold with a total of 449.04 points, Kälin the silver with 447.99: Had he traveled only 2.3 seconds faster, or jumped a meter farther, the gold would have been his. Andreas Kunz of East Germany won the bronze.

And Scandinavia? Sweden had dropped out of the contest altogether, and Finland and Norway finished in the basement between 20th and 40th place. Clearly, the world was changing. Even the long-distance cross-country ski tracks imposed in the mostly open, rolling countryside around Vercors and Autrans had a faint Alpine flavor, with every race opening with a wearing climb

and ending with a breathless downhill finish.

Cross-country ski racing is about strength and stamina, but it is also about wax. On the morning of the 30,000-meter competition, the big, powerful Vikings sniffed the Belledonne weather, thought the day might warm, and picked their ski wax accordingly. The Italians thought differently. They waxed with a homemade cold-snow concoction under the boot portions of their skis, then spread another very-cold-snow wax along the length of their boards. If the day warmed, they were lost. If it stayed cold, however, they would have an edge. On the other hand, what did it matter? Italy had never even placed in an Olympic Nordic-skiing event.

That, too, was about to change.

Racing under perfect conditions, his boards running beautifully with their waxen sheath, 27-

Proud German countrymen carry Franz Keller on their shoulders as they celebrate his victory in the Nordic combined. Keller won one of the closest combined events in Olympic history by beating the second-place finisher, Switzerland's Alois Kälin, by a slim 1.05 points.

Scandinavian hegemony in cross-country skiing comes under attack as Italy's Franco Nones marches over the snow. Nones' conquest in the 30-kilometer race was touted as a harbinger of a new era in men's Nordic events. Still, Scandinavians won 12 of the 21 medals in contention.

year-old Franco Nones, a customs official from the Fieme Valley in the Dolomites, swept to victory in 1:35:39.2. Then, as if to show the world this was no anomaly, his teammate Giulio de Florian placed fifth, about a minute and a half behind Nones. The silver medal went to Odd Martinsen of Norway, who followed Nones by just under one minute, the bronze to Eero Mäntyranta of Finland, who had taken home two gold medals from Innsbruck.

Then, like a machine coming back into adjust-

ment, the Nordic competitions became once again...Nordic. Three days after Nones' victory, the 15-kilometer race took the skiers into a swirl of dense fog, over a course that was uphill for the first half, downhill for the last, on a day of rising temperatures that would change crisp snow to cold mush in the wake of the leaders. Norway's 33-year-old Harald Grönningen, starting fifth, was able to bull his way past the four men ahead of him, then race along an undisturbed track to victory. Eero Mäntyranta of Finland finished just 1.9 seconds slower to win the silver, and Sweden's Gunnar Larsson took the bronze. Scandinavians also triumphed in the 10-kilometer relay on February 14. A Norwegian powerhouse composed of Grönningen, Odd Martinsen, Pål Tyldum, and Ole Ellefsaeter won the race, with Sweden a close second and Finland third.

Finland's Mäntyranta was supposed to make his mark with a victory in the grueling 50-kilometer race—cross-country skiing's equivalent of the marathon—on February 17. But the earlier events appear to have taken their toll on the 30-year-old champion. This heroic skier, one of the finest long-distance racers in sports history, finished a melancholy 15th.

The race was run as two circuits of a 25-kilometer track, and at the end of the first circuit, Norway's Ole Ellefsaeter, who turned 29 the day of the race, held a commanding lead—except that a very capable Russian, Vyacheslav Vedinine, was right behind him and closing. In the end, Ellefsaeter saved the gold medal for Norway, and Vedinine took a silver back to the Soviet Union. Josef Haas, a dark horse from Switzerland, skied to a bronze medal, telling the world that Alpine skiers could do long-distance racing too.

The women made sure the main cross-country medals stayed in Scandinavia and demonstrated that one did not have to look like a Viking to ski like one. Both the 5- and 10-kilometer races were won by Toini Gustafsson, a pretty, blonde 29-

Austria's Franz Vetter *(No. 35)* loses ground to Sweden's Pål Tyldum in the 50-kilometer cross-country. In these endurance events, skiers enter the course at 30-second intervals and race against the clock, not each other.

Focusing carefully on the course ahead, Sweden's Toini Gustafsson maintains perfect form in the middle of the 10-kilometer race. Competition could almost keep up with Gustafsson in the 5-kilometer race—she won by a scant 3.2 seconds—but in the longer event her superior strength carried her away from the field.

year-old mother from Stöllet, Sweden. Born Toini Karvonen in the tiny Finnish village of Haapovaara in 1938, Gustafsson—her first husband's surname—had come to a foster home in Sweden during World War II and had grown up in the province of Värmland. For years she had been a world-class champion skier, and she had raced at Innsbruck 1964. But she had never finished first in an Olympic event. In the 10-kilometer course, Gustafsson outsmarted the Belledonne snows to finish in 36:46.5, more than a minute ahead of Norway's Berit Mördre. Inger Aufles of Norway won the bronze. Four days later, Gustafsson would win the 5-kilometer race with a time of 16:45.2. She would also help Sweden's 3 x 5-kilometer relay team to a silver medal in a race won by fellow Scandinavians, the Norwegians.

Like Scandinavia, the Soviet Union has long, deep winters. Given that fact, it was perhaps inevitable that the Russians would eventually become preeminent in at least one winter sport. Maybe it was also inevitable that

ice hockey would be that sport: There is something exquisitely Russian about the game. While fast and rudely physical, it also contains the strategic elements of chess—a perfect sport for big, fearless skaters who are reflective as well.

Oddly, hockey didn't invade the Soviet Union until after World War II. But once it came, its conquest was total. By the 1950s it was the sport of choice for thousands of young Russians. At the Olympics, from 1956 onward, ice hockey became mainly the province of the American, Canadian, and Soviet sixes, with occasional intrusions by Sweden and Czechoslovakia. And the Russians were becoming progressively harder to beat. At Innsbruck they had taken the gold, followed by Sweden and the Czechs. Now, in the French Alps, the North American teams hoped to gain back some ground.

Ice hockey had also attracted the attention of IOC president Avery Brundage, who took note of the fact that the boundaries between amateur and professional teams in North America were blurred, to put it mildly. A Canada-led move to permit professionals to skate in the Olympics had seemed to arm him with artillery to excommunicate the sport entirely. But at the same time, there was the embarrassment of expertise on the Communist side, where keen interest and heavy subsidies from the government put its "amateur" team into a clearly professional class.

The Soviet team that came to Grenoble showed why its system had come to dominate the sport. About half the players had Olympic experience, and all had come from the rigorous school of two legendary Soviet coaches, Arkadi Chernyshov and Anatoli Tarasov, who developed the national team from talent evolving in local and junior clubs. The Russian players had spent their adolescence on the ice together and could sense one another's moves. Mobile and tough, superbly conditioned and tireless, and as attentive to positioning as any chess grand master, they played an almost perfect game that made the styles of other countries seem clumsy.

Given the Soviet mastery, spectators at the rink in Grenoble were at first not much gripped by suspense. The American team seemed powerless, and Canada, the Russians' only real competition, had suffered a discouraging loss to Finland. Nevertheless, the tournament would become a true nail-biter, with three teams fighting all the way to the wire on the final day of the Games.

The excitement came in the first phase of the contest, when Czechoslovakia—highly rated, but not seen as much of a contender—upset the Russians 5-4. For the Czechs it was a heady whiff of ursine blood; they hadn't beaten the Russians in seven years. The upset also meant that the gold could go to the Soviet Union, Canada, or Czechoslovakia. If the Czechs could whip Sweden, which was no longer in contention, and Canada could beat the Soviets, Czechoslovakia would take home a gold medal.

In the end, Czechoslovakia played first, exhausted from the hard win over the Russians, and tied with Sweden. Some observers thought the Czechs had played timidly, and the tie cost them a vital point and put the Soviets back in winning position. Their speed and clever stickwork demolished Canada 5-0 and gave Moscow the gold medal that had, for an illusory moment, seemed to fall into Czech hands. The dark

A pileup in the Czech goal keeps the Russians from a tying score. The Czechs beat the Soviets 5-4 but failed to capitalize on the upset during a lackluster performance against Sweden the next day.

horses took a silver medal back to Prague, however, and the Canadians consoled themselves with the bronze. The American team, always a forlorn hope in the Games, finished sixth, after Sweden and Finland.

The curious absence of ice hockey in pre-war Russia had an equally odd counter-point in the Netherlands, where centuries of ice-skating on frozen canals had produced a grand Hans Brinker tradition—but not a single Olympic gold medal. Yet at Grenoble, Dutch speed skaters, male and female, were favored to take home at least three golds, and perhaps more; some thought they would win six of the eight on offer.

Christina Kaiser, a 29-year-old secretary at the Delft police station, had taken the world championship away from the Soviets in 1967, winning at 1,000, 1,500, and 3,000 meters. At Grenoble, however, she would face daunting competition. Lydia Skoblikova, who had left Innsbruck with gold medals in those three events, would be there for the Soviet Union; and an American, 16-year-old Dianne Holum, was a favorite to win the 500-meter race. Kaiser also faced a

Finland's Kaija Mustonen ties her laces as she readies herself for the speed-skating competition. Mustonen collected a gold and a silver medal, becoming the outsider in events otherwise dominated by the Netherlands, the Soviet Union, and the United States.

threat from her own teammates, among them Carolina Geijssen.

Among the flying Dutchmen at Grenoble were two more strong contenders. Ard Schenk, 23, had skated second in the world championships of 1966 and 1967 and had a strong chance to win the 1,500 meters, but Kees Verkerk appeared to be Holland's best hope for a gold. Compact but powerful, the 25-year-old from Puttershoek had won the world and European championships in 1967, the first skater to take both in one season.

The women began racing with the 500-meter on February 9, and for a time it looked as if American Mary Meyers' 46.3-second run would be golden. But she was overtaken by Soviet skater Ludmila Titova, who posted 46.1. The silver was shared among three skaters from the United States: Meyers, Dianne Holum, and Jennifer Fish.

In the 1,500 meters, run the next day, second and third place went to two Dutch favorites, Carolina Geijssen and Christina Kaiser, with times of 2:22.7 and 2:24.5, respectively. But Finland's Kaija Mustonen streaked in 0.03 of a second under Geijssen's time for the gold. The Soviet woman picked to win, Lydia Skoblikova, finished a poor 11th.

A day later, in the 1,000-meter, Geijssen scooped up the Netherlands' first skating gold, beating out the 500-meter winner, Ludmila Titova. Dianne Holum took the bronze.

The longest event, the 3,000 meters, was run on February 12 in a light rain. Some observers blamed the weather for depriving Christina Kaiser of the gold medal in her best distance. Not that the Netherlands came up empty: Teammate Johanna Schut won with an Olympic-record time of 4:56.2, with Finland's Mustonen about 4 seconds behind her. Trailing the Finn by a scant 0.3 of a second was Kaiser, taking her second Grenoble bronze.

On the men's side, the 500-meter was a free-

for-all, with a dozen skaters clocking times under 40 seconds. In the end, the spread among the first six would be 0.04 of a second. World-record holder Erhard Keller of West Germany led the pack at 40.3, followed by Magne Thomassen of Norway, who tied at 40.5 with an American, Terry McDermott, an Innsbruck gold medalist.

The 5,000-meter race the next day seemed to belong to Kees Verkerk, who shaved 3 seconds off the world record held by world champion Fred Anton Maier of Norway. Another Dutchman, Petrus Nottet, also bested Maier's world

Holland's Johanna Schut glides through a turn in the 3,000-meter race. Schut turned in one of three Olympic-record times in women's speed skating at the 1968 Winter Games. Despite the new Olympic standards, the Grenoble ice was slow: Only one world record was set during the meet.

A hard-charging finish leads Erhard Keller to the first of two consecutive Winter Games victories in the 500-meter race. Keller was the first German man to win a speed-skating gold medal.

record. Then Maier turned on some mental afterburner and took the gold in 7:22.4, 0.8 of a second better than Verkerk, who had to settle for a silver. Nottet took the bronze. But the tireless Verkerk bounced back in the next event, the 1,500 meters, to win with a time of 2:03.4. His friend and teammate Ard Schenk tied for second place with Norway's Ivar Eriksen at 2:05.0.

The final skating event was the 10,000 meters, skated in a high wind. Gliding easily, Sweden's Johnny Höglin won with a time of 15:23.6, followed by Maier, and, in third place, another Swede, Örjen Sandler. Again, the Scandinavians asserted their primacy in the Winter Games.

But if they skated rapidly, the Scandinavians did not always skate beautifully. The last Nordic female to win an Olympic gold medal in figure skating had been Norway's pert Sonja Henie, who won in

an unprecedented three successive Games from 1928 to 1936; the last Nordic man had been Sweden's Gillis Grafström at St. Moritz 1928. Since then, figure-skating championships had fanned out to Austria and France, Germany and Holland, and—especially—America and the Soviet Union, two countries that would offer Grenoble in figure skating what France had already given in Alpine skiing: champions with the candlepower of M. Killy himself.

This was not quite so clear in the men's figure-skating competition on February 16, where the Austrian world champion, Emmerich Danzer, was expected to win with his incomparable artistry; and if not Danzer, one of his gifted fellow Europeans—Wolfgang Schwarz, also of Austria, or France's Patrick Pera. There was also a long-shot chance for America's Timothy Wood, who seemed to get better and better.

But Wood's performance, dazzling though it was, earned only a silver medal, and Danzer dropped to fourth place after doing poorly in the compulsory figures. The gold went to Wolfgang Schwarz, Danzer's compatriot, the bronze to Pera of France.

But, as some Alpine events had been obscured by Killy's brilliance, so were the men's events lost in the aura of the women's competition several days earlier. Peggy Fleming, a 19-year-old California native, hadn't exactly come out of nowhere when she appeared at Grenoble's new Stade de Glace, a soaring glass and wood structure in Mistral Park. She had followed a long, tough road from her birthplace in San Jose, California, to Cleveland,

Ohio, where she began skating at nine, to Pasadena, California, where she honed her talent. In 1960 she began winning regional championships, then national ones. She had finished sixth at Innsbruck 1964.

Soon afterward, her family had moved to Colorado Springs so that Peggy could train at the renowned Broadmoor Skating Club. There she and her coach, the great Carlo Fassi, crafted the blend of power and grace that, by the time of Grenoble, had become Fleming's trademark. In February 1966 she became the first American woman in almost 10 years to win the world figure-skating championship. She brought a

Kees Verkerk skates a tight oval during the 1,500-meter race. The Dutchman was dominant during the 1966 season, winning three of four races at the world championships. He was the world's best again in 1967, but the improved competition at Grenoble permitted him only two medals, a gold in the 1,500 and silver in the 5,000.

Peggy Fleming completes a spin during her free-skate routine. A 1967 rules change that made compulsory figures count for only 50 percent of a skater's score (previously the number was 60 percent) strengthened her standing as the gold-medal favorite at Grenoble.

without muscularity, emanating a charm and skill that brought the event to her, along with the heart of every spectator. Her gold medal was not won so much as coaxed into her finely poised hand. It was the only gold the United States took home from Grenoble, but it was supremely lustrous. Most critics agreed that no woman skater had shone quite so brilliantly since the days of Sonja Henie.

Other skaters gamely tried to outdo Fleming, of course, and some won medals of their own. Gabriele Seyfert of East Germany skated through a technically difficult routine for the silver medal, and Czechoslovakia's lithe Hana Mašková, in a program filled with difficult jumps, took the bronze. Peggy Fleming proved an impossible act to follow in the amateur ranks—but only briefly. A month after Grenoble, she successfully defended her world crown in Geneva, then announced her retirement from amateur skating. The staggering costs of amateurism had almost ruined her family financially, and it was time for her to pay them back. By April she had a contract with NBC and plans to tour the world as a professional. When she returned to the Olympics, it would be as a commentator. In the coming years she would take the ice from time to time in exhibitions, her serene loveliness intact, her grace unchallenged by skaters years younger. Like Killy, she would always be a star.

decade's and some 20,000 hours' training with her to the French Alps, along with her national and world titles.

She also brought a good deal of residual sorrow. In 1961 an airplane crash in Belgium had decimated the American skating team; she had lost friends and teammates, as well as her first coach, Will Kipp. And only minutes after she won her world title, her beloved father, who had worked two jobs to pay for her training, had died of a heart attack. The radiant beauty who took flight under the lights of the Stade de Glace was not just a pretty face; she had paid dearly for her place on the ice.

Fleming skated flawlessly, building a lead of 77 points in the compulsory figures, then flowing incomparably to the strains of Tchaikovsky, Verdi, Saint-Saëns, and Rossini in the free skating. She was supremely feminine, expressing power

Lyudmila and Oleg Protopopov, of what was then Leningrad, had not come to Grenoble as favorites. They had won the pairs skating world championships in 1963 and 1966 and the gold medal at Innsbruck in 1964, but even then they were close to the edge in terms of age. Now, Lyudmila was 32, Oleg 35—far too old, some believed, for world-class skating.

Appropriately enough, they skated in Grenoble

Austria's Wolfgang Schwarz strikes a regal pose during figure skating at Grenoble. Austria's best chance for a gold medal was thought to be Schwarz's teammate, Emmerich Danzer, the world champion from 1966 to 1968. Danzer had defeated Schwarz eight times in previous championships, but his poor performance in the compulsories pushed him out of Olympic medal contention.

Elegant lifts embelished the routines of Soviet pairs champions Oleg and Lyudmila Protopopov. Passion, however, was the real secret to the couple's success. "Art cannot be measured by points," Oleg said. "We skate from the heart."

The Grenoble logotype pin *(left)*, an ABC pin from 1968, one of the earlier pins issued by a broadcaster *(center)*, and a Czechoslovakian team pin *(right)*.

on February 14—Valentine's Day. Where other pairs opened with a bang, the Protopopovs began in stillness, blooming into action to the lyricism of Beethoven's *Moonlight Sonata*, then accelerating into the opening bars of Beethoven's *Fifth*, always with a technical precision that left the competition foundering in their icy wake.

Some desperate skaters countered with a variety of novel flips and leaps and lifts that, while inadequate to the night, would eventually extend the sport's bag of tricks. The Soviet Union's Tamara Moskvina and Alexei Michine pursued their technically complex program of athletic, high-flying maneuvers with real abandon, only to end in fifth place. Their compatriots, Tatyana Zhukchesternava and Aleksandr Gorelik, skated more sedately to the silver medal, and a West German pair, Margot Glockshuber and Wolfgang Danne, took the bronze.

Nothing could touch the couple from Leningrad. "Some of the loveliest moments," wrote Dennis Bird in London's *Times*, "were the simplest—for instance, the spirals where Lyudmila glided away from her partner, and then returned as though drawn to him by a magnet, with the hint of a kiss. And their forward spiral together, the two united as one, and then the girl going forward alone as her partner stopped in supplication." It was ballet, in the finest tradition of the nation that gave the world the Bolshoi and the Kirov.

There was never the slightest chance that

anyone would take away the Protopopovs' gold, and no one did—at least no one in Grenoble. A year after the Games, however, the pair was dethroned by the explosive performances of Irina Rodnina and Aleksei Ulanov, who dazzled audiences and judges with their speed and gravity-defying bravado. Back in Leningrad after the competition, the Protopopovs were told by their government that they would have to retire. When they declined, they found that they could get ice time only between midnight and 2 or 3 a.m., and that only with the help of a friend. They vanished from Soviet newspapers, their standings dropped year by year. No longer valued by the homeland they had graced, they left it, defecting in 1979 and ending up in Switzerland after a season with America's Ice Capades. Russia may have forgotten them, but aficionados of their sport never would. For decades, the name Protopopov would be invoked as the hallmark of elegance in pairs skating.

In fact, in the years to come a soft and nostalgic glow would seem to envelop the XVIII Olympiad, the valiant underdogs and peerless champions of Tokyo, the glamorous darlings of Grenoble. Of course, new Olympic heights would be scaled in following Games, and new champions would come—athletes stronger, faster, more skilled. But the world was changing, the Happy Games were over, and the newcomers would shine in a far harsher light.

Flagbearers lead national delegations into Grenoble's Ice Stadium at the start of the closing ceremony. The festivities featured a skating exposition, medal presentations, speeches, and songs bidding farewell.

APPENDIX

CALENDAR OF THE XVIII OLYMPIAD........151

TOKYO 1964

    PROGRAM OF EVENTS 152

    MEDAL COUNT 155

    STATISTICS 156

GRENOBLE 1968

    PROGRAM OF EVENTS 166

    MEDAL COUNT 166

    STATISTICS 167

RECORD OF THE XVIII OLYMPIAD 170

    OLYMPIC OFFICERS 170

    IOC MEMBERSHIP 170

    IOC AWARDS..170

    OFFICIAL OLYMPIC PUBLICATIONS.....171

1964

OCTOBER 3	10th IOC Executive Board meeting with NOCs at Tokyo
OCTOBER 4-5, 16	68th IOC Executive Board meeting at Tokyo
OCTOBER 7-8	**63rd Session of the IOC at Tokyo**
OCTOBER 10-24	**TOKYO 1964 15th Olympic Games**
NOVEMBER 6-14	2nd Paralympic Games at Tokyo

1965

APRIL 11, 13	69th IOC Executive Board meeting at Lausanne
APRIL 12	18th IOC Executive Board meeting with IFs at Lausanne
JUNE 20-JULY 3	10th World Games for the Deaf at Washington, D.C.
JULY 9-10	70th IOC Executive Board meeting at Paris
JULY 18-25	1st All-African Games at Brazzaville
AUGUST 20-29	4th University Games at Budapest
OCTOBER 4	11th IOC Executive Board meeting with NOCs at Madrid
OCTOBER 5, 8	71st IOC Executive Board meeting at Madrid
OCTOBER 6-9	**64th Session of the IOC at Madrid**

NOVEMBER 29	12th USOC Quadrennial meeting at the Willard Hotel, Washington, D.C.
DECEMBER 14-21	3rd South East Asian Games at Kuala-Lampur

1966

FEBRUARY 5-13	4th University Winter Games at Sestriere
APRIL 21-24	72nd IOC Executive Board meeting at Rome
APRIL 23	19th IOC Executive Board meeting with IFs at Rome
APRIL 25-28	**65th Session of the IOC at Rome**
JUNE 11-25	10th Central American and Caribbean Games at San Juan
AUGUST 4-13	8th Commonwealth Games at Kingston
OCTOBER 22	73rd IOC Executive Board meeting at Mexico City
DECEMBER 9-20	5th Asian Games at Bangkok

1967

FEBRUARY 11-12	74th IOC Executive Board meeting at Copenhagen
FEBRUARY 20-25	6th World Winter Games for the Deaf at Berchtesgaden
MAY 2-3	75th IOC Executive Board meeting at Teheran
MAY 3	12th IOC Executive Board meeting with NOCs at Teheran

MAY 6-9	66th Session of the IOC at Teheran
JULY 22-AUGUST 7	5th Pan-American Games at Winnipeg
AUGUST 26-SEPTEMBER 9	5th University Games at Tokyo
SEPTEMBER 8-17	5th Mediterranean Games at Tunis
DECEMBER 9-16	4th South East Asian Games at Bangkok
DECEMBER 16-17	76th IOC Executive Board meeting at Lausanne

1968

JANUARY 2-28	77th IOC Executive Board meeting at Lausanne
JANUARY 21-28	5th University Winter Games at Innsbruck
JANUARY 27-28	20th IOC Executive Board meeting with IFs at Lausanne
JANUARY 29-31 & FEBRUARY 5-6	78th IOC Executive Board meeting at Grenoble
FEBRUARY 1-5	**67th Session of the IOC at Grenoble**
FEBRUARY 4-18	**GRENOBLE 1968 10th Olympic Winter Games**
JUNE 27-JULY 3	11th World Games for the Deaf at Washington, D.C.
JULY 19-20	1st International Special Olympics at Chicago

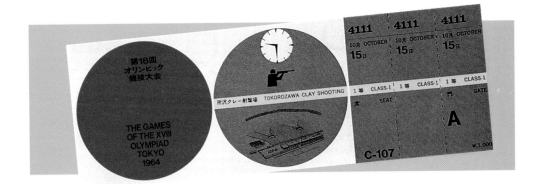

Saturday, OCTOBER 10

PM	EVENT	VENUE
1:30	OPENING CEREMONY	National Stadium

Sunday, OCTOBER 11

AM	EVENT	VENUE
9:00	MODERN PENTATHLON	Asaka Nezu Park
	equestrian	
	BASKETBALL	National Gymnasium Annex
	1st round	
9:30	DIVING	National Gymnasium
	women's springboard, elimination round (1st half)	
10:00	FIELD HOCKEY	Komazawa Hockey Grounds 1, 2, and 3
	preliminaries (6 games)	
	ROWING	Toda Rowing Course
	• four-oared shell with coxswain (3 heats)	
	• four-oared shell without coxswain (3 heats)	
	WATER POLO	Tokyo Metropolitan Indoor Swimming Pool
	eliminations (4 games)	
	WEIGHT LIFTING	Shibuya Public Hall
	bantamweight	
10:30	BASKETBALL	National Gymnasium Annex
	1st round	
11:00	VOLLEYBALL	Komazawa Volleyball Court
	women's (1 game)	
	WRESTLING	Komazawa Gymnasium
	freestyle, all weights	

PM	EVENT	VENUE
12:00	BASKETBALL	National Gymnasium Annex
	1st round	
1:00	VOLLEYBALL	Komazawa Volleyball Court
	women's (1 game)	
1:30	BASKETBALL	National Gymnasium Annex
	1st round	
	SWIMMING	National Gymnasium
	• 100-meter freestyle, heats	
	• women's 200-meter breaststroke, heats	
2:00	BOXING	Korakuen Ice Palace
	eliminations	
	ROWING	Toda Rowing Course
	• single sculls (3 heats)	
	• pair-oared shell with coxswain (3 heats)	
	• four-oared shell without coxswain (3 heats)	
	SOCCER	National Stadium; Komazawa Stadium; Mitsuzawa Football Field; Omiya Football Field
	preliminaries (4 games)	
2:15	FIELD HOCKEY	Komazawa Hockey Grounds 2 and 3
	preliminaries (2 games)	
3:00	VOLLEYBALL	Komazawa Volleyball Court
	(1 game)	
4:00	BASKETBALL	National Gymnasium Annex
	1st round	
	WEIGHT LIFTING	Shibuya Public Hall
	bantamweight	

4:30	DIVING	National Gymnasium
	women's springboard, elimination round (2nd half)	
	WATER POLO	Tokyo Metropolitan Indoor Swimming Pool
	eliminations (4 games)	
5:30	BASKETBALL	National Gymnasium Annex
	1st round	
6:00	WRESTLING	Komazawa Gymnasium
	freestyle, all weights	
7:00	BASKETBALL	National Gymnasium Annex
	1st round	
	BOXING	Korakuen Ice Palace
	eliminations	
8:30	BASKETBALL	National Gymnasium Annex
	1st round	
9:00	SWIMMING	National Gymnasium
	• 100-meter freestyle, semifinals	
	• women's 200-meter breaststroke, semifinals	
	• 200-meter backstroke, heats	

Monday, OCTOBER 12

AM	EVENT	VENUE
8:00	MODERN PENTATHLON	Waseda Memorial Hall
	fencing	
9:00	BASKETBALL	National Gymnasium Annex
	1st round (2 games)	
10:00	FIELD HOCKEY	Komazawa Hockey Grounds 1, 2, and 3
	preliminaries (5 games)	
	ROWING	Toda Rowing Course
	• double sculls (3 heats)	
	• eight-oared shell with coxswain (3 heats)	
	DIVING	National Gymnasium
	women's springboard, final	
	WEIGHT LIFTING	Shibuya Public Hall
	featherweight	
	WATER POLO	Tokyo Metropolitan Indoor Swimming Pool
	eliminations (4 games)	
11:00	WRESTLING	Komazawa Gymnasium
	freestyle, all weights	
	YACHTING	Enoshima Yacht Harbor
	all classes, 1st race	

PM	EVENT	VENUE
12:00	BASKETBALL	National Gymnasium Annex
	1st round (2 games)	
1:00	SWIMMING	National Gymnasium
	• women's 100-meter freestyle, heats	
	• 400-meter medley, heats	
2:00	BOXING	Korakuen Ice Palace
	eliminations	
	ROWING	Toda Rowing Course
	• four-oared shell with coxswain (3 repechages)	
	• pair-oared shell with coxswain	
	• single sculls (3 repechages)	
	SOCCER	Komazawa Stadium; Mitsuzawa Football Field; Omiya Football Field
	preliminaries (3 games)	
2:15	FIELD HOCKEY	Komazawa Hockey Grounds 2 and 3
	preliminaries (2 games)	
4:00	BASKETBALL	National Gymnasium Annex
	1st round (4 games)	

	WEIGHT LIFTING	Shibuya Public Hall
	featherweight	
4:30	WATER POLO	Tokyo Metropolitan Indoor Swimming Pool
	eliminations (4 games)	
5:00	VOLLEYBALL	Komazawa Volleyball Court
	women's (1 game)	
	DIVING	National Gymnasium
	springboard, 1st elimination round	
6:00	WRESTLING	Komazawa Gymnasium
	freestyle, all weights	
7:00	BOXING	Korakuen Ice Palace
	eliminations	
	VOLLEYBALL	Komazawa Volleyball Court
	women's (1 game)	
9:00	SWIMMING	National Gymnasium
	• 200-meter backstroke, semifinals	
	• women's 100-meter freestyle, semifinals	
	• women's 200-meter breaststroke, final	
	• 100-meter freestyle, final	

Tuesday, OCTOBER 13

AM	EVENT	VENUE
8:30	FENCING	Waseda Memorial Hall
	individual foil, preliminaries	
9:00	BASKETBALL	National Gymnasium Annex
	1st round (2 games)	
	MODERN PENTATHLON	Asaka Shooting Range
	shooting	
9:30	DIVING	National Gymnasium
	springboard, 2nd elimination round	
10:00	FIELD HOCKEY	Komazawa Hockey Grounds 2 and 3
	preliminaries (2 games)	
	ROWING	Toda Rowing Course
	pair-oared shell with coxswain (6 repechages)	
	WATER POLO	Tokyo Metropolitan Indoor Swimming Pool
	eliminations (4 games)	
	WEIGHT LIFTING	Shibuya Public Hall
	lightweight	
11:00	VOLLEYBALL	Komazawa Volleyball Court
	(1 game)	
	WRESTLING	Komazawa Gymnasium
	freestyle, all weights	
	YACHTING	Enoshima Yacht Harbor
	all classes, 2nd race	
11:40	FIELD HOCKEY	Komazawa Hockey Ground 1
	preliminaries (1 game)	

PM	EVENT	VENUE
12:00	BASKETBALL	National Gymnasium Annex
	1st round (2 games)	
1:00	VOLLEYBALL	Komazawa Volleyball Court
	(1 game)	
1:30	SWIMMING	National Gymnasium
	• 4 x 100-meter freestyle relay, heats	
	• women's 100-meter backstroke, heats	
2:00	BOXING	Korakuen Ice Palace
	eliminations	

	SOCCER	Prince Chichibu Memorial Football Field; Komazawa Stadium; Mitsuzawa Football Field; Omiya Football Field
	preliminaries (4 games)	
	ROWING	Toda Rowing Course
	• double sculls (3 repechages)	
	• eight-oared shell with coxswain	
3:30	DIVING	National Gymnasium
	springboard, 3rd elimination round	
4:00	BASKETBALL	National Gymnasium Annex
	1st round (4 games)	
	WEIGHT LIFTING	Shibuya Public Hall
	lightweight	
4:30	WATER POLO	Tokyo Metropolitan Indoor Swimming Pool
	eliminations (4 matches)	
5:00	VOLLEYBALL	Komazawa Volleyball Court
	• (1 game)	
	• women's (1 game)	
6:00	WRESTLING	Komazawa Gymnasium
	freestyle, all weights	
7:00	BOXING	Korakuen Ice Palace
	eliminations	
	VOLLEYBALL	Komazawa Volleyball Court
	(2 games)	
9:00	SWIMMING	National Gymnasium
	• 200-meter breaststroke, heats	
	• women's 100-meter backstroke, semifinals	
	• women's 100-meter freestyle, final	
	• 200-meter backstroke, final	

Wednesday, OCTOBER 14

AM	EVENT	VENUE
8:30	FENCING	Waseda Memorial Hall
	women's individual foil, preliminaries	
9:00	BASKETBALL	National Gymnasium Annex
	1st round (2 games)	
10:00	ATHLETICS	National Stadium
	• 100 meters, heats	
	• women's long jump, qualifying	
	• javelin, qualifying	
	CYCLING	Hachioji Cycling Road Race Course
	road team time trial	
	FIELD HOCKEY	Komazawa Hockey Grounds 1, 2, and 3
	preliminaries (4 games)	
	WATER POLO	Tokyo Metropolitan Indoor Swimming Pool
	• (3 games)	
	• semifinals (1 game)	
	WEIGHT LIFTING	Shibuya Public Hall
	middleweight	
11:00	VOLLEYBALL	Komazawa Volleyball Court
	(1 game)	
	WRESTLING	Komazawa Gymnasium
	freestyle, all weights	
	YACHTING	Enoshima Yacht Harbor
	all classes, 3rd race	

PM	EVENT	VENUE
12:00	BASKETBALL	National Gymnasium
	1st round (2 games)	

1:00 VOLLEYBALL . *Komazawa Volleyball Court*
(1 game)
WATER POLO . *Tokyo Metropolitan Indoor Swimming Pool*
semifinals
1:30 SWIMMING . *National Gymnasium*
• 400-meter freestyle, heats
• women's 4 x 100-meter freestyle relay, heats
• 200-meter breaststroke, semifinals
2:00 ATHLETICS . . . . . *National Stadium*
• 400-meter hurdles, heats
• javelin, final
BOXING . . . . *Korakuen Ice Palace*
eliminations
ROWING . . . *Toda Rowing Course*
• four-oared shell with coxswain, semifinal
• pair-oared shell without coxswain, semifinal
• single sculls, semifinal
• pair-oared shell with coxswain, semifinal
• four-oared shell without coxswain, semifinal
• double sculls, semifinal
• eight-oared shell with coxswain, semifinal
SOCCER . . . . *Prince Chichibu Memorial Football Field; Komazawa Stadium; Mitsuzawa Football Field*
preliminaries (5 games)
2:30 MODERN PENTATHLON . . . .*National Gymnasium*
swimming
2:40 ATHLETICS . . . . . *National Stadium*
100 meters, 2nd round
3:00 ATHLETICS . . . . . *National Stadium*
women's long jump, final
3:15 ATHLETICS . . . . . *National Stadium*
800 meters, heats
4:00 ATHLETICS . . . . . *National Stadium*
10,000 meters, final
BASKETBALL . *National Gymnasium Annex*
1st round (4 games)
WEIGHT LIFTING . . . . *Shibuya Public Hall*
middleweight
5:00 VOLLEYBALL . *Komazawa Volleyball Court*
(2 games)
5:30 FENCING . *Waseda Memorial Hall*
individual foil, final
6:00 WRESTLING *Komazawa Gymnasium*
freestyle, all weights
6:30 DIVING . *National Gymnasium*
springboard, final
7:00 BOXING . . . . *Korakuen Ice Palace*
eliminations
VOLLEYBALL . *Komazawa Volleyball Court*
• (1 game)
• women's (1 game)
9:00 SWIMMING . *National Gymnasium*
• 4 x 100-meter freestyle, final
• women's 100-meter backstroke, final
• 400-meter individual medley, final

Thursday, OCTOBER 15

AM	EVENT	VENUE

8:30 FENCING . *Waseda Memorial Hall*
team foil, preliminaries
9:00 SHOOTING . *Asaka Shooting Range*
free rifle, three positions
9:30 SHOOTING . . . . . *Tokorozawa Trap Shooting Range*
trap
DIVING . . . *National Gymnasium*
women's platform, eliminations
10:00 ATHLETICS . . . . . *National Stadium*
• women's 100 meters, heats
• women's high jump, qualifying
• discus, qualifying
FIELD HOCKEY . *Komazawa Hockey Grounds 1, 2, and 3*
preliminaries (5 games)
WATER POLO . *Tokyo Metropolitan Indoor Swimming Pool*
semifinals (3 games)
VOLLEYBALL . *Komazawa Volleyball Court*
(1 game)
YACHTING . *Enoshima Yacht Harbor*
all classes, 4th race
11:00 ATHLETICS . . . . . *National Stadium*
women's 400 meters, heats

PM	EVENT	VENUE

1:00 ATHLETICS . . . . . *National Stadium*
pole vault, qualifying
VOLLEYBALL . *Komazawa Volleyball Court*
(1 game)
1:15 FIELD HOCKEY . *Komazawa Hockey Ground 2*
preliminaries (1 game)
1:30 SWIMMING . *National Gymnasium*
• 400-meter individual medley, heats
• 4 x 100-meter medley relay, heats
2:00 ATHLETICS . . . . . *National Stadium*
• 100 meters, semifinals
• women's high jump, final
BOXING . . . . *Korakuen Ice Palace*
eliminations
SOCCER . . . . *Prince Chichibu Memorial Football Field; Komazawa Stadium; Mitsuzawa Football Field; Omiya Football Field*
preliminaries (4 games)
MODERN PENTATHLON . . . . . *Tokyo University Kemigawa Playing Grounds*
running
2:15 ATHLETICS . . . . . *National Stadium*
400-meter hurdles, heats
FIELD HOCKEY . *Komazawa Hockey Ground 3*
preliminaries (1 game)
2:30 ATHLETICS . . . . . *National Stadium*
• women's 100 meters, 2nd round
• discus, final
3:00 ATHLETICS . . . . . *National Stadium*
800 meters, semifinals
3:20 ATHLETICS . . . . . *National Stadium*
20,000-meter walk, final
3:30 ATHLETICS . . . . . *National Stadium*
100 meters, final
ROWING . . . *Toda Rowing Course*
• four-oared shell with coxswain, final
• pair-oared shell without coxswain, final
• single sculls, final
• pair-oared shell with coxswain, final
• four-oared shell without coxswain, final
• double sculls, final
• eight-oared shell with coxswain, final
3:50 ATHLETICS . . . . . *National Stadium*
3,000-meter steeplechase
5:00 DIVING . . . *National Gymnasium*
women's platform, final
VOLLEYBALL . *Komazawa Volleyball Court*
(2 games)
5:30 FENCING . *Waseda Memorial Hall*
women's individual foil, final
7:00 BOXING . . . . *Korakuen Ice Palace*
eliminations
VOLLEYBALL . *Komazawa Volleyball Court*
(2 games)
7:20 WATER POLO . *Tokyo Metropolitan Indoor Swimming Pool*
semifinal (1 game)
9:00 SWIMMING . *National Gymnasium*
• women's 100-meter butterfly, heats
• 400-meter freestyle, final
• 200-meter breaststroke, final
• women's 4 x 100-meter freestyle relay, final

Friday, OCTOBER 16

AM	EVENT	VENUE

8:30 FENCING . *Waseda Memorial Hall*
• team foil, preliminaries
• women's team foil, preliminaries
9:00 SHOOTING . *Asaka Shooting Range*
small-bore rifle
BASKETBALL . *National Gymnasium Annex*
1st round (2 games)
9:30 EQUESTRIAN . *Karuizawa Equestrian Events Grounds*
three-day event (dressage)
SHOOTING . . . . . *Tokorozawa Trap Shooting Range*
trap
10:00 ATHLETICS . . . . . *National Stadium*
• women's javelin, qualifying
• women's pentathlon (80-meter hurdles, shot put)
CYCLING . . . . *Hachioji Velodrome*
individual pursuit, series
FIELD HOCKEY . *Komazawa Hockey Grounds 2 and 3*
preliminaries (2 games)
DIVING . . . *National Gymnasium*
platform, 1st elimination round
WEIGHT LIFTING . . . . *Shibuya Public Hall*
light heavyweight
10:30 ATHLETICS . . . . . *National Stadium*
• 200 meters, heats
• triple jump, qualifying
11:00 WRESTLING *Komazawa Gymnasium*
Greco-Roman, all weights
11:40 FIELD HOCKEY . *Komazawa Hockey Ground 1*
preliminaries (1 game)

PM	EVENT	VENUE

12:00 BASKETBALL . *National Gymnasium Annex*
1st round (2 games)
1:00 SWIMMING . *National Gymnasium*
• 200-meter butterfly, heats
• women's 4 x 100-meter medley relay, heats
2:00 ATHLETICS . . . . . *National Stadium*
women's 100 meters, semifinals
BOXING . . . . *Korakuen Ice Palace*
eliminations
CYCLING . . . . *Hachioji Velodrome*
• 1,000-meter time trial
• individual team pursuit, quarterfinals
SOCCER . . . . *Prince Chichibu Memorial Football Field; Komazawa Stadium; Omiya Football Field*
preliminaries (3 games)
2:30 ATHLETICS . . . . . *National Stadium*
• 200 meters, 2nd round
• triple jump, final
3:00 ATHLETICS . . . . . *National Stadium*
• 5,000 meters, heats
• women's pentathlon (high jump)
3:40 ATHLETICS . . . . . *National Stadium*
800 meters, final
4:00 ATHLETICS . . . . . *National Stadium*
400-meter hurdles, final
BASKETBALL . . *National Gymnasium Annex*
1st round (4 games)
WEIGHT LIFTING . . . . *Shibuya Public Hall*
light heavyweight
4:20 ATHLETICS . . . . . *National Stadium*
women's 100 meters, final
5:00 FENCING . . *Waseda Memorial Hall*
team foil, final
5:30 SWIMMING . . *National Gymnasium*
1,500-meter freestyle, heats
6:00 WRESTLING *Komazawa Gymnasium*
Greco-Roman, all weights
7:00 BOXING . . . . . *Korakuen Ice Palace*
eliminations
9:00 SWIMMING . *National Gymnasium*
• women's 100-meter butterfly, final
• 4 x 100-meter medley relay, final

Saturday, OCTOBER 17

AM	EVENT	VENUE

8:30 FENCING . . *Waseda Memorial Hall*
women's team foil, preliminaries
9:00 BASKETBALL . . *National Gymnasium Annex*
1st round (2 games)
9:30 EQUESTRIAN . *Karuizawa Equestrian Events Grounds*
three-day event (dressage)
SHOOTING . . . . . *Tokorozawa Trap Shooting Range*
trap
DIVING . . . . *National Gymnasium*
platform, 2nd elimination round
10:00 ATHLETICS . . . . . *National Stadium*
• 400 meters, heats
• hammer throw, qualifying
• shot put, qualifying
CYCLING . . . . *Hachioji Velodrome*
• scratch race series & repechages
• individual pursuit, semifinals
FIELD HOCKEY . *Komazawa Hockey Grounds 1, 2, and 3*
preliminaries (4 games)
WATER POLO . *Tokyo Metropolitan Indoor Swimming Pool*
final round (3 games)
WEIGHT LIFTING . . . . *Shibuya Public Hall*
middle heavyweight

11:00 **ATHLETICS** . . . . . *National Stadium*
1,500 meters, heats
VOLLEYBALL . *Komazawa Volleyball Court*
(1 game)
WRESTLING *Komazawa Gymnasium*
Greco-Roman, all weights

PM	EVENT	VENUE

12:00 **BASKETBALL** . *National Gymnasium Annex*
1st round (2 games)
VOLLEYBALL . *Komazawa Volleyball Court*
women's (1 game)
1:00 **ATHLETICS** . . . . . *National Stadium*
• pole vault, final
• 110-meter hurdles, heats
1:30 **SWIMMING** . . *National Gymnasium*
• women's 400-meter freestyle, heats
• 4 x 200-meter freestyle relay, heats
2:00 **ATHLETICS** . . . . . *National Stadium*
women's pentathlon (long jump)
BOXING . . . . *Korakuen Ice Palace*
eliminations
CYCLING . . . . *Hachioji Velodrome*
• scratch race, round of 16
• individual pursuit, final (2 races, 1-4 places)
• scratch race, repechages round of 16
2:30 **ATHLETICS** . . . . . *National Stadium*
200 meters, semifinals
3:00 **ATHLETICS** . . . . . *National Stadium*
• 400 meters, 2nd round
• shot put, final
VOLLEYBALL . *Komazawa Volleyball Court*
(1 game)
3:40 **ATHLETICS** . . . . . *National Stadium*
women's 400 meters, final
4:00 **ATHLETICS** . . . . . *National Stadium*
200 meters, final
BASKETBALL . . . . *National Gymnasium Annex*
1st round (4 games)
DIVING . . . *National Gymnasium*
platform, 3rd elimination round
WEIGHT LIFTING . . . . *Shibuya Public Hall*
middle heavyweight
4:20 **ATHLETICS** . . . . . *National Stadium*
women's pentathlon (200 meters)
4:50 **ATHLETICS** . . . . . *National Stadium*
3,000-meter steeplechase, final
5:00 **FENCING** . *Waseda Memorial Hall*
women's team foil, finals
VOLLEYBALL . *Komazawa Volleyball Court*
(1 game)
6:00 **WRESTLING** *Komazawa Gymnasium*
Greco-Roman, all weights
7:00 **BOXING** . . . . *Korakuen Ice Palace*
eliminations
VOLLEYBALL . *Komazawa Volleyball Court*
(1 game)
9:00 **SWIMMING** . *National Gymnasium*
• 200-meter butterfly, semifinals
• 1,500-meter freestyle, final
• women's 4 x 100-individual medley, final
WATER POLO . . *Tokyo Metropolitan Indoor Swimming Pool*
final round (1 game)

Sunday, OCTOBER 18

AM	EVENT	VENUE

8:30 **FENCING** . *Waseda Memorial Hall*
individual épée, preliminaries
GYMNASTICS . . *Tokyo Metropolitan Gymnasium*
compulsory exercises
9:00 **SHOOTING** . *Asaka Shooting Range*
free pistol
BASKETBALL . *National Gymnasium Annex*
1st round (2 games)
9:30 **EQUESTRIAN** . *Karuizawa Equestrian Events Grounds*
three-day event (endurance test)
10:00 **ATHLETICS** . . . . . *National Stadium*
• women's 200 meters, heats
CYCLING . . . . *Hachioji Velodrome*
• scratch race, quarterfinals, 1st & 2nd rounds
• team pursuit, series
• scratch race, belle
FIELD HOCKEY . *Komazawa Hockey Grounds 1, 2, and 3*
preliminaries (5 games)
DIVING . . . *National Gymnasium*
platform, final
WEIGHT LIFTING . . . . *Shibuya Public Hall*
heavyweight
WATER POLO . *Tokyo Metropolitan Indoor Swimming Pool*
final round (3 games)
10:30 **ATHLETICS** . . . . . *National Stadium*
• women's 800 meters, heats
• long jump, qualifying
11:00 **VOLLEYBALL** . *Komazawa Volleyball Court*
(1 game)
WRESTLING *Komazawa Gymnasium*
Greco-Roman, all weights

PM	EVENT	VENUE

12:00 **BASKETBALL** . *National Gymnasium Annex*
1st round (2 games)
SWIMMING . *National Gymnasium*
• women's 400-meter freestyle, final
• 200-meter butterfly, final
12:20 **ATHLETICS** . . . . . *National Stadium*
• 50,000-meter walk, final
1:00 **ATHLETICS** . . . . . *National Stadium*
hammer throw, final
VOLLEYBALL . *Komazawa Volleyball Court*
• (1 game)
• women's (1 game)
2:00 **ATHLETICS** . . . . . *National Stadium*
110-meter hurdles, semifinals
BOXING . . . . *Korakuen Ice Palace*
eliminations
CYCLING . . . . *Hachioji Velodrome*
• scratch race, semifinals (1st and 2nd rounds)
• scratch race, belle
• team pursuit, quarterfinals
• scratch race, final
SOCCER . . . . *Prince Chichibu Memorial Football Field; Komazawa Stadium; Mitsuzawa Football Field; Omiya Football Field*
quarterfinals (4 games)
2:15 **FIELD HOCKEY** . *Komazawa Hockey Grounds 2 and 3*
preliminaries (2 games)
2:25 **ATHLETICS** . . . . . *National Stadium*
women's 200 meters, semifinals

2:50 **ATHLETICS** . . . . . *National Stadium*
women's 80-meter hurdles, heats
3:00 **ATHLETICS** . . . . . *National Stadium*
long jump, final
VOLLEYBALL . *Komazawa Volleyball Court*
(1 game)
3:20 **ATHLETICS** . . . . . *National Stadium*
400 meters, semifinals
3:50 **ATHLETICS** . . . . . *National Stadium*
110-meter hurdles, final
4:00 **BASKETBALL** . . . . *National Gymnasium Annex*
1st round (4 games)
WATER POLO . *Tokyo Metropolitan Indoor Swimming Pool*
final round (1 game)
WEIGHT LIFTING . . . . *Shibuya Public Hall*
heavyweight
4:05 **ATHLETICS** . . . . . *National Stadium*
5,000 meters, final
5:00 **GYMNASTICS** . . *Tokyo Metropolitan Gymnasium*
compulsory exercises
VOLLEYBALL . *Komazawa Volleyball Court*
(1 game)
6:00 **WRESTLING** *Komazawa Gymnasium*
Greco-Roman, all weights
SWIMMING . *National Gymnasium*
• women's 4 x 100-meter medley relay, final
• 4 x 200-meter freestyle relay, final
7:00 **BOXING** . . . . *Korakuen Ice Palace*
eliminations
VOLLEYBALL . *Komazawa Volleyball Court*
(1 game)

Monday, OCTOBER 19

AM	EVENT	VENUE

8:30 **FENCING** . . *Waseda Memorial Hall*
individual saber, preliminaries
GYMNASTICS . . *Tokyo Metropolitan Gymnasium*
women's compulsory exercises
9:00 **SHOOTING** . *Asaka Shooting Range*
rapid-fire pistol (1st course)
10:00 **ATHLETICS** . . . . . *National Stadium*
• decathlon (100 meters, long jump)
• women's discus, qualifying
CYCLING . . . . *Hachioji Velodrome*
• tandem series, repechages
• team pursuit, semifinals
• tandem race, quarterfinals (1st and 2nd rounds)
FIELD HOCKEY . *Komazawa Hockey Grounds 1, 2, and 3*
preliminaries (6 games)
11:00 **ATHLETICS** . . . . . *National Stadium*
1,500 meters, semifinals
VOLLEYBALL . *Komazawa Volleyball Court*
(1 game)
WRESTLING *Komazawa Gymnasium*
Greco-Roman, all weights
YACHTING . *Enoshima Yacht Harbor*
all classes, 5th race

PM	EVENT	VENUE

1:00 **SHOOTING** . *Asaka Shooting Range*
rapid-fire pistol (2nd course)

EQUESTRIAN . *Karuizawa Equestrian Events Grounds*
three-day event (jumping test)
VOLLEYBALL . *Komazawa Volleyball Court*
(1 game)
1:15 **FIELD HOCKEY** . *Komazawa Hockey Ground 2*
preliminaries (1 game)
2:00 **ATHLETICS** . . . . . *National Stadium*
• women's 80-meter hurdles, semifinals
• decathlon (shot put)
BOXING . . . . . *Korakuen Ice Palace*
all weights, quarterfinals
2:20 **ATHLETICS** . . . . . *National Stadium*
women's 800 meters, semifinals
2:30 **ATHLETICS** . . . . . *National Stadium*
women's discus, final
2:40 **ATHLETICS** . . . . . *National Stadium*
women's 200 meters, final
3:00 **ATHLETICS** . . . . . *National Stadium*
400 meters, final
3:20 **ATHLETICS** . . . . . *National Stadium*
women's 80-meter hurdles, final
3:30 **ATHLETICS** . . . . . *National Stadium*
decathlon (high jump)
5:00 **ATHLETICS** . . . . . *National Stadium*
decathlon (400 meters)
GYMNASTICS . . *Tokyo Metropolitan Gymnasium*
women's compulsory exercises
VOLLEYBALL . *Komazawa Volleyball Court*
• (1 game)
• women's (1 game)
5:30 **FENCING** . *Waseda Memorial Hall*
individual épée, final
6:00 **WRESTLING** *Komazawa Gymnasium*
Greco-Roman, all weights
7:00 **BOXING** . . . . *Korakuen Ice Palace*
all weights, quarterfinals
VOLLEYBALL . *Komazawa Volleyball Court*
(2 games)

Tuesday, OCTOBER 20

AM	EVENT	VENUE

8:30 **FENCING** . *Waseda Memorial Hall*
team épée, preliminaries
GYMNASTICS . . *Tokyo Metropolitan Gymnasium*
optional exercises
9:00 **ATHLETICS** . . . . . *National Stadium*
decathlon (110-meter hurdles)
SHOOTING . *Asaka Shooting Range*
small-bore rifle
9:40 **ATHLETICS** . . . . . *National Stadium*
decathlon (discus)
10:00 **ATHLETICS** . . . . . *National Stadium*
• high jump, qualifying
• women's shot put
CANOEING . . . . *Lake Sagami*
all classes, heats
10:10 **ATHLETICS** . . . . . *National Stadium*
women's 4 x 100-meter relay, heats
11:00 **YACHTING** . *Enoshima Yacht Harbor*
all classes, 6th race

PM	EVENT	VENUE

1:00 **ATHLETICS** . . . . . *National Stadium*
• decathlon (pole vault)
• women's shot put, final
JUDO . . . . *Nippon Budokan Hall*
lightweights

2:00	**ATHLETICS** . . . . *National Stadium* 4 x 100-meter relay, heats
	BOXING . . . . *Korakuen Ice Palace* quarterfinals
	CYCLING . . . . *Hachioji Velodrome* • tandem race, semifinals and finals • team pursuit, finals
	SOCCER . . . . *Prince Chichibu Memorial Football Field; Komazawa Stadium* semifinals (2 games)
	BASKETBALL . *National Gymnasium Annex* semifinals (2 games)
3:00	**ATHLETICS** . . . . *National Stadium* • decathlon (javelin) • 4 x 400-meter relay, heats
	CANOEING . . . . *Lake Sagami* all classes, heats
3:30	**ATHLETICS** . . . . *National Stadium* women's 800 meters, final
4:00	**ATHLETICS** . . . . *National Stadium* 4 x 100-meter relay, semifinals
5:00	**ATHLETICS** . . . . *National Stadium* decathlon (1,500 meters)
	GYMNASTICS . . *Tokyo Metropolitan Gymnasium* optional exercises
5:30	**FENCING** . *Waseda Memorial Hall* individual saber, final
6:30	**BASKETBALL** . *National Gymnasium Annex* semifinals (2 games)
7:00	**BOXING** . . . . *Korakuen Ice Palace* all weights, quarterfinals

Wednesday, OCTOBER 21

AM	EVENT	VENUE
8:30	**FENCING** . . *Waseda Memorial Hall* team épée , preliminaries	
	GYMNASTICS . . *Tokyo Metropolitan Gymnasium* women's optional exercises	
10:00	**CANOEING** . . . . *Lake Sagami* all classes, semifinals	
11:00	**VOLLEYBALL** . *Komazawa Volleyball Court* women's (1 game)	
	YACHTING . *Enoshima Yacht Harbor* all classes, 7th race	

PM	EVENT	VENUE
12:15	**FIELD HOCKEY** . *Komazawa Hockey Grounds 1 and 2* semifinals (4 games)	
1:00	**ATHLETICS** . . . . *National Stadium* marathon	
	JUDO . . . . . *Nippon Budokan Hall* middleweights	
	VOLLEYBALL . *Komazawa Volleyball Court* (1 game)	
1:20	**ATHLETICS** . . . . *National Stadium* 1,500 meters, final	
1:50	**ATHLETICS** . . . . *National Stadium* 4 x 100-meter relay, final	
2:00	**ATHLETICS** . . . . *National Stadium* high jump, final	
	BOXING . . . . *Korakuen Ice Palace* semifinals	
	BASKETBALL . . *National Gymnasium Annex* semifinals (2 games)	
2:20	**ATHLETICS** . . . . *National Stadium* women's 4 x 100-meter relay, final	
2:50	**ATHLETICS** . . . . *National Stadium* 4 x 400-meter relay, final	
3:00	**CANOEING** . . . . *Lake Sagami* all classes, semifinals	
5:00	**FENCING** . . *Waseda Memorial Hall* team épée, final	
	GYMNASTICS . . *Tokyo Metropolitan Gymnasium* women's optional exercises	
	VOLLEYBALL . *Komazawa Volleyball Court* (2 games)	
6:30	**BASKETBALL** . . *National Gymnasium Annex* semifinals (2 games)	
7:00	**BOXING** . . . . *Korakuen Ice Palace* semifinals	
	VOLLEYBALL . *Komazawa Volleyball Court* (2 games)	

Thursday, OCTOBER 22

AM	EVENT	VENUE
8:30	**EQUESTRIAN** . . . . . . *Equestrian Park* dressage	

	FENCING . . *Waseda Memorial Hall* team saber, preliminaries
10:00	**CYCLING** . . . . . . *Hachioji Cycling Road Race Course* individual road race
11:00	**VOLLEYBALL** . *Komazawa Volleyball Court* (1 game)

PM	EVENT	VENUE
1:00	**JUDO** . . . . . *Nippon Budokan Hall* heavyweights	
	VOLLEYBALL . *Komazawa Volleyball Court* (1 game)	
1:55	**FIELD HOCKEY** . *Komazawa Hockey Ground 1* 5th place	
2:00	**CANOEING** . . . . *Lake Sagami* all events, finals	
	BASKETBALL . *National Gymnasium Annex* finals (2 games)	
5:00	**GYMNASTICS** . . *Tokyo Metropolitan Gymnasium* • team and individual • women's team and individual	
	VOLLEYBALL . *Komazawa Volleyball Court* (2 games)	
6:00	**GYMNASTICS** . . *Tokyo Metropolitan Gymnasium* individual final (floor, horse, rings)	
6:30	**BASKETBALL** . *National Gymnasium Annex* finals (2 games)	
7:00	**VOLLEYBALL** . *Komazawa Volleyball Court* • (1 game) • women's (1 game)	
8:00	**GYMNASTICS** . . *Tokyo Metropolitan Gymnasium* women's individual finals (horse, vault, uneven bars)	

Friday, OCTOBER 23

AM	EVENT	VENUE
8:30	**FENCING** . *Waseda Memorial Hall* team saber, preliminaries	
10:00	**EQUESTRIAN** . . . . . . *Equestrian Park* dressage	

| 11:00 | **VOLLEYBALL** . *Komazawa Volleyball Court*
(2 games) |

PM	EVENT	VENUE
12:00	**SOCCER** . . . . . *National Stadium* consolation	
12:15	**FIELD HOCKEY** . *Komazawa Hockey Ground 1* consolation and final	
1:00	**EQUESTRIAN** . . . . . . *Equestrian Park* dressage	
	JUDO . . . . . *Nippon Budokan Hall* all weights, finals	
	VOLLEYBALL . *Komazawa Volleyball Court* (2 games)	
2:00	**BASKETBALL** . *National Gymnasium Annex* finals (2 games)	
2:30	**SOCCER** . . . . . . *National Stadium* final	
5:00	**FENCING** . . *Waseda Memorial Hall* team saber, final	
	VOLLEYBALL . *Komazawa Volleyball Court* (1 game)	
6:00	**GYMNASTICS** . . *Tokyo Metropolitan Gymnasium* women's individual finals	
6:30	**BASKETBALL** . . *National Gymnasium Annex* finals (2 games, 1-4 places)	
7:00	**BOXING** . . . . *Korakuen Ice Palace* all weights, finals	
	VOLLEYBALL . *Komazawa Volleyball Court* women's (1 game)	
7:30	**GYMNASTICS** . . *Tokyo Metropolitan Gymnasium* individual finals	

Saturday, OCTOBER 24

AM	EVENT	VENUE
7:30	**EQUESTRIAN** . . . . *National Stadium* jumping, 1st round	

PM	EVENT	VENUE
1:00	**EQUESTRIAN** . . . . *National Stadium* jumping, 2nd round	
3:30	**CLOSING CEREMONY** . . . . *National Stadium*	

NATIONAL MEDAL COUNT

COMPETITORS   COUNTRIES: 94   ATHLETES: 5,140   MEN: 4,457   WOMEN: 683

	GOLD	SILVER	BRONZE	TOTAL		GOLD	SILVER	BRONZE	TOTAL		GOLD	SILVER	BRONZE	TOTAL		GOLD	SILVER	BRONZE	TOTAL
URS	30	31	35	96	RUM	2	4	6	12	BEL	2		1	3	ARG	1			1
USA	36	26	28	90	BUL	3	5	2	10	KOR		2	1	3	IRL		1		1
GER	10	22	18	50	NLD	2	4	4	10	TRT		1	2	3	BRA			1	1
JPN	16	5	8	29	SWE	2	2	4	8	TUN		1	1	2	NGA			1	1
ITA	10	10	7	27	TUR	2	3	1	6	IRN			2	2	KEN			1	1
POL	7	6	10	23	DEN	2	1	3	6	IND	1			1	URU			1	1
HUN	10	7	5	22	FIN	3		2	5	BAH	1			1	MEX			1	1
AUS	6	2	10	18	NZL	3		2	5	ETH	1			1	GHA			1	1
GBR	4	12	2	18	YUS	2	1	2	5	PHI		1		1					
FRA	1	8	6	15	SWI	1	2	1	4	PAK		1		1					
CZS	5	6	3	14	CAN	1	2	1	4	CUB		1		1					

TOKYO 1964
15TH OLYMPIC GAMES

ATHLETICS (TRACK & FIELD)

Event	Gold	Silver	Bronze	4	5	6
100 METERS	USA 10.0 ROBERT HAYES	CUB 10.2 E. FIGUEROLA CAMUE	CAN 10.2 HARRY JEROME	4. POL Wieslaw Maniak 10.4	5. GER Heinz Schumann 10.4	6. two-way tie 10.4
200 METERS	USA 20.3 HENRY CARR	USA 20.5 O. PAUL DRAYTON	TRT 20.6 EDWIN ROBERTS	4. CAN Harry Jerome 20.7	5. ITA Livio Berruti 20.8	6. POL Marian Foik 20.8
400 METERS	USA 45.1 MICHAEL LARRABEE	TRT 45.2 WENDELL MOTTLEY	POL 45.6 ANDRZEJ BADEŃSKI	4. GBR Robbie Brightwell 45.7	5. USA Ulis Williams 46.0	6. GBR Timothy Graham 46.0
800 METERS	NZL 1:45.1 PETER SNELL	CAN 1:45.6 WILLIAM CROTHERS	KEN 1:45.9 W. KIPRUGUT CHUMA	4. JAM George Kerr 1:45.9	5. USA Thomas Farrell 1:46.6	6. USA Jerome Siebert 1:47.0
1,500 METERS	NZL 3:38.1 PETER SNELL	CZS 3:39.6 JOSEF ODLOŽIL	NZL 3:39.6 JOHN DAVIES	4. GBR Alan Simpson 3:39.7	5. USA Dyrol Burleson 3:40.0	6. POL Witold Baran 3:40.3
5,000 METERS	USA 13:48.8 ROBERT SCHUL	GER 13:49.6 HARALD NORPOTH	USA 13:49.8 WILLIAM DELLINGER	4. FRA Michel Jazy 13:49.8	5. KEN Kipchoge Keino 13:50.4	6. NZL William Baillie 13:51.0
10,000 METERS	USA 28:24.4 WILLIAM MILLS	TUN 28:24.8 MOHAMED GAMMOUDI	AUS 28:25.8 RONALD CLARKE	4. ETH Mamo Wolde 28:31.8	5. URS Leonid Ivanov 28:53.2	6. JPN Kokichi Tsuburaya 28:59.4
MARATHON	ETH 2:12:11.2 ABEBE BIKILA	GBR 2:16:19.2 BASIL HEATLEY	JPN 2:16:22.8 KOKICHI TSUBURAYA	4. GBR Brian Kilby 2:17:02.4	5. HUN József Sütő 2:17:55.8	6. USA Leonard Edelen 2:18:12.4
110-METER HURDLES	USA 13.6 HAYES JONES	USA 13.7 H. BLAINE LINDGREN	URS 13.7 ANATOLY MIKHAILOV	4. ITA Eddy Ottoz 13.8	5. IND G. Randhawa Singh 14.0	6. FRA Marcel Duriez 14.0
400-METER HURDLES	USA 49.6 WARREN CAWLEY	GBR 50.1 JOHN COOPER	ITA 50.1 SALVATORE MORALE	4. AUS Gary Knoke 50.4	5. USA James Luck 50.5	6. ITA Roberto Frinolli 50.7
3,000-METER STEEPLECHASE	BEL 8:30.8 GASTON ROELANTS	GBR 8:32.4 MAURICE HERRIOTT	URS 8:33.8 YVAN BELYAYEV	4. POR Manuel de Oliveira 8:36.2	5. USA George Young 8:38.2	6. FRA Guy Texereau 8:38.6
4 X 100-METER RELAY	USA 39.0 O. PAUL DRAYTON GERRY ASHWORTH RICHARD STEBBINS ROBERT HAYES	POL 39.3 ANDRZEJ ZIELIŃSKI WIESLAW MANIAK MARIAN FOIK MARIAN DUDZIAK	FRA 39.3 PAUL GENEVAY BERNARD LAIDEBEUR CLAUDE PIQUEMAL JOCELYN DELECOUR	4. JAM McNeill/Robinson/ Headley/Johnson 39.4	5. URS Ozolin/Zubov/ Kosanov/Savchuk 39.4	6. VEN Herrera/Murad/ Romero/Herrera Fucil 39.5
4 X 400-METER RELAY	USA 3:00.7 OLLAN CASSELL MICHAEL LARRABEE ULIS WILLIAMS HENRY CARR	GBR 3:01.6 TIMOTHY GRAHAM ADRIAN METCALFE JOHN COOPER ROBBIE BRIGHTWEL	TRT 3:01.7 EDWIN SKINNER KENT BERNARD EDWIN ROBERTS WENDELL MOTTLEY	4. JAM Kahn/Spence/ Spence/Kerr 3:02.3	5. GER Jüttner/Schulz/ Schmitt/Kinder 3:04.3	6. POL Filipiuk/Kluczek/ Swatowski/Badeński 3:05.3
20,000-METER WALK	GBR 1:29:34.0 KENNETH MATTHEWS	GER 1:31:13.2 DIETER LINDNER	URS 1:31:59.4 VLADIMIR GOLUBNICHY	4. AUS Noel Freeman 1:32:06.8	5. URS Gennady Solodov 1:32:33.0	6. USA Ronald Zinn 1:32:43.0
50,000-METER WALK	ITA 4:11:12.4 ABDON PAMICH	GBR 4:11:31.2 PAUL NIHILL	SWE 4:14:17.4 INGVAR PETTERSSON	4. GER Burkhard Leuschke 4:15:26.8	5. AUS Robert Gardiner 4:17:06.8	6. GER Christoph Höhne 4:17:41.6
HIGH JUMP	URS 2.18 VALERY BRUMEL	USA 2.18 JOHN THOMAS	USA 2.16 JOHN RAMBO	4. SWE Stig Pettersson 2.14	5. URS Robert Shavlakadze 2.14	6. two-way tie 2.09
POLE VAULT	USA 5.10 FREDERICK HANSEN	GER 5.05 WOLFGANG REINHARDT	GER 5.00 KLAUS LEHNERTZ	4. GER Manfred Preussger 5.00	5. URS Gennady Bliznyetsov 4.95	6. CZS Rudolf Tomášek 4.90

Event	Gold	Silver	Bronze	4th	5th	6th
LONG JUMP	GBR 8.07 Lynn Davies	USA 8.03 Ralph Boston	URS 7.99 Igor Ter-Ovanesyan	NGA Wariboko West 7.60	FRA Jean Cochard 7.44	SPA Luis Felipe Areta 7.34
TRIPLE JUMP	POL 16.85 Józef Szmidt	URS 16.58 Oleg Fyedoseyev	URS 16.57 Viktor Kravchenko	GBR Frederick Alsop 16.46	RUM Şerban Ciochină 16.23	GER Manfred Hinze 16.15
SHOT PUT	USA 20.33 Dallas Long	USA 20.20 James Randy Matson	HUN 19.39 Vilmos Varju	USA W. Parry O'Brien 19.20	HUN Zsigmond Nagy 18.88	URS Nikolai Karasyov 18.86
DISCUS THROW	USA 61.00 Alfred Oerter	CZS 60.52 Ludvík Daněk	USA 59.49 David Weill	USA L. Jay Silvester 59.09	HUN József Szécsényi 57.23	POL Zenon Begier 57.06
JAVELIN THROW	FIN 82.66 Pauli Nevala	HUN 82.32 Gergely Kulcsár	URS 80.57 Jānis Lūsis	POL Janusz Sidlo 80.17	SWI Urs von Wartburg 78.72	FIN Jorma Kinnunen 76.94
HAMMER THROW	URS 69.74 Romuald Klim	HUN 69.09 Gyula Zsivótzky	GER 68.09 Uwe Beyer	URS Yury Nikulin 67.69	URS Yury Bakarinov 66.72	USA Harold Connolly 66.65
DECATHLON	GER 7,887 Willi Holdorf	URS 7,842 Rein Aun	GER 7,809 Hans-Joachim Walde	USA Paul Herman 7,787	TWN Yang Chuan-Kwang 7,650	GER Horst Beyer 7,647
100 METERS	USA 11.4 Wyomia Tyus	USA 11.6 Edith McGuire	POL 11.6 Ewa Klobukowska	USA Marilyn White 11.6	CUB Miguelina Cobián 11.7	AUS Marilyn Black 11.7
200 METERS	USA 23.0 Edith McGuire	POL 23.1 Irena Kirszenstein	AUS 23.1 Marilyn Black	JAM Una Morris 23.5	URS Lyudmila Samotyosova 23.5	POL B. Sobotta-Janiszewska 23.9
400 METERS	AUS 52.0 Betty Cuthbert	GBR 52.2 Ann Packer	AUS 53.4 Judith Amoore	HUN Antonia Munkácsi 54.4	URS Mariya Itkina 54.6	NLD Mathilda van der Zwaard 55.2
800 METERS	GBR 2:01.1 Ann Packer	FRA 2:01.9 Maryvonne Dupureur	NZL 2:02.8 M. A. Chamberlain	HUN Zsuzsa Szabó 2:03.5	GER Antje Gleichfeld 2:03.9	URS Laine Erik 2:05.1
80-METER HURDLES	GER 10.5 Karin Balzer	POL 10.5 T. Ciepla-Wieczorek	AUS 10.5 Pamela Kilborn	URS Irina Press 10.6	JPN Ikuko Yoda 10.7	POL Maria Piatkowska 10.7
4 X 100-METER RELAY	POL 43.6 T. Ciepla-Wieczorek, Irena Kirszenstein, Halina Górecka-Richter, Ewa Klobukowska	USA 43.9 Willy White, Wyomia Tyus, Marilyn White, Edith McGuire	GBR 44.0 Janet Simpson, Mary Rand, Daphne Arden, Dorothy Hyman	URS Gaide/Latse/Samotyosova/Popova 44.4	GER Frisch/Pollmann/Pensberger-Langbein/Heine 44.7	AUS Bowering/Black/Burvill/Bennett 45.0
HIGH JUMP	RUM 1.90 Iolanda Balaş	AUS 1.80 M. Mason-Brown	URS 1.78 Taisiya Chenchik	BRA Aida Dos Santos 1.74	CAN Dianne Gerace 1.71	GBR Frances Slaap 1.71
LONG JUMP	GBR 6.76 Mary Rand	POL 6.60 Irena Kirszenstein	URS 6.42 Tatyana Schelkanova	GER Ingrid Becker 6.40	RUM Viorica Viscopoleanu 6.35	BUL Diana Yorgova 6.24
SHOT PUT	URS 18.14 Tamara Press	GER 17.61 R. Garisch-Culmberger	URS 17.45 Galina Zybina	NZL Valerie Sloper-Young 17.26	GER Margitta Helmboldt 16.91	URS Irina Press 16.71
DISCUS THROW	URS 57.27 Tamara Press	GER 57.21 Ingrid Lotz	RUM 56.97 Lia Manoliu	BUL Virzhinia Mikhailova 56.70	URS Yevgeniya Kuznetsova 55.17	HUN Jolán Kleiber 54.87
JAVELIN THROW	RUM 60.54 Mihaela Peneş	HUN 58.27 Márta Rudas	URS 57.06 Yelena Gorchakova	URS Birute Kalediene 56.31	URS Elvira Ozolina 54.81	RUM Maria Diaconescu 53.71
PENTATHLON	URS 5,246 Irina Press	GBR 5,035 Mary Rand	URS 4,956 Galina Bystrova	GBR Mary Peters 4,797	YUS Draga Stamejčič 4,790	GER Helga Hoffman 4,737

BASKETBALL

Event	Gold	Silver	Bronze	4th	5th	6th
FINAL STANDINGS	USA	URS	BRA	PUR	ITA	POL

BOXING

FLYWEIGHT 112.5 lbs. (51 kg)	ITA FERNANDO ATZORI	POL ARTUR OLECH	USA ROBERT CARMODY / URS STANISLAV SOROKIN	5. four-way tie
BANTAMWEIGHT 119.5 lbs. (54 kg)	JPN TAKAO SAKURAI	KOR CHUNG SHIN-CHO	MEX JUAN FABILA MENDOZA / URU WASHINGTON RODRIGUEZ	5. four-way tie
FEATHERWEIGHT 126 lbs. (57 kg)	URS STANISLAV STEPASHKIN	PHI ANTHONY VILLANUEVA	USA CHARLES BROWN / GER HEINZ SCHULZ	5. four-way tie
LIGHTWEIGHT 132 lbs. (60 kg)	POL JÓZEF GRUDZIEŃ	URS VELIKTON BARANNIKOV	USA RONALD ALLAN HARRIS / IRL JAMES MCCOURT	5. four-way tie
LIGHT WELTERWEIGHT 140 lbs. (63.5 kg)	POL JERZY KULEJ	URS YEVGENY FROLOV	GHA EDDIE BLAY / TUN HABIB GALHIA	5. four-way tie
WELTERWEIGHT 148 lbs. (67 kg)	POL MARIAN KASPRZYK	URS RIČARDAS TAMULIS	ITA SILVANO BERTINI / FIN PERTTI PURHONEN	5. four-way tie
LIGHT MIDDLEWEIGHT 156 lbs. (71 kg)	URS BORIS LAGUTIN	FRA JOSEPH GONZALES	POL JÓZEF GRZESIAK / NGA NOJIM MAIYEGUN	5. four-way tie
MIDDLEWEIGHT 165.5 lbs. (75 kg)	URS VALERY POPENCHENKO	GER EMIL SCHULZ	ITA FRANCO VALLE / POL TADEUSZ WALASEK	5. four-way tie
LIGHT HEAVYWEIGHT 179 lbs. (81 kg)	ITA COSIMO PINTO	URS ALEKSEI KISSELYOV	BUL ALEXANDER NIKOLOV / POL ZBIGNIEW PIETRZYKOWSKI	5. four-way tie
HEAVYWEIGHT 200.5 lbs. (91 kg)	USA JOSEPH FRAZIER	GER HANS HUBER	ITA GIUSEPPE ROS / URS VADIM YEMELYANOV	5. four-way tie

CANOEING

KAYAK SINGLES 1,000 METERS	SWE 3:57.13 ROLF PETERSON	HUN 3:57.28 MIHÁLY HESZ	RUM 4:00.77 AUREL VERNESCU	4. GER Erich Suhrbier 4:01.62 5. AUT Günther Pfaff 4:03.56 6. NLD Antonius Geurts 4:04.48
KAYAK PAIRS 1,000 METERS	SWE 3:38.54 SVEN-OLOV SJÖDELIUS NILS GUNNAR UTTERBERG	NLD 3:39.30 ANTONIUS GEURTS PAUL HOEKSTRA	GER 3:40.69 HEINZ BÜKER HOLGER ZANDER	4. RUM Ivanov/Nicoară 3:41.12 5. HUN Mészáros/Szöllösi 3:41.39 6. ITA Beltrami/Zilioli 3:43.55
KAYAK FOURS 1,000 METERS	URS 3:14.67 MYKOLA CHUZHYKOV ANATOLY GRISHIN VYACHESLAV IONOV VOLODYMYR MOROZOV	GER 3:15.39 GÜNTHER PERLEBERG BERNHARD SCHULZE FRIEDHELM WENTZKE HOLGER ZANDER	RUM 3:15.51 SIMION CUCIUC ATANASE SCIOTNIC MIHAI TURCAŞ AUREL VERNESCU	4. HUN Kemecsey/Mészáros/ 3:16.24 Szente/Szöllösi 5. SWE Peterson/Sjödelius/ 3:17.47 Utterberg/von Gerber 6. ITA Agnisetta/Beltrami/ 3:19.32 Pedroni/Zilioli

Event	Gold	Silver	Bronze	4th–6th
CANADIAN SINGLES 1,000 METERS	GER 4:35.14 JÜRGEN ESCHERT	RUM 4:37.89 ANDREI IGOROV	URS 4:38.31 YEVGENY PENYAYEV	4. HUN András Törö 4:39.95 5. SWE Ove Emanuelsson 4:42.70 6. BUL Bogdan Ivanov 4:44.76
CANADIAN PAIRS 1,000 METERS	URS 4:04.64 ANDREY KHIMICH STEPAN OSCHEPKOV	FRA 4:06.52 JEAN BOUDEHEN MICHEL CHAPUIS	DEN 4:07.48 PEER NORRBOHM NIELSEN JOHN SÖRENSEN	4. HUN Hajba/Soltesz 4:08.97 5. RUM Lipalit/Sidorov 4:09.88 6. GER Böhle/Lewe 4:13.18
KAYAK SINGLES 500 METERS	URS 2:12.87 LYUDMILA KHVEDOSYUK	RUM 2:15.35 HILDE LAUER	USA 2:15.68 MARCIA JONES	4. GER Elke Felten 2:15.94 5. SWE Else Marie Ljungdahl 2:16.00 6. AUT Hanneliese Spitz 2:16.11
KAYAK PAIRS 500 METERS	GER 1:56.95 ROSWITHA ESSER ANNEMARIE ZIMMERMANN	USA 1:59.16 FRANCINE FOX GLORIANE PERRIER	RUM 2:00.25 HILDE LAUER CORNELIA SIDERI	4. URS Gruzintseva/Seredina 2:00.69 5. DEN Hansen/Werner-Hansen 2:00.88 6. SWE Ljungdahl/Sisth 2:02.24

CYCLING

Event	Gold	Silver	Bronze	4th–6th
1,000-METER SPRINT	ITA 2-0 GIOVANNI PETTENELLA	ITA SERGIO BIANCHETTO	FRA DANIEL MORELON	4. FRA Pierre Trentin 5. four-way tie
2,000-METER TANDEM	ITA 10.85 10.75 ANGELO DAMIANO SERGIO BIANCHETTO	URS 10.80 IMANT BODNIEKS VIKTOR LOGUNOV	GER WILLI FUGGERER KLAUS KOBUSCH	4. NLD de Graaf/van der Touw 5. four-way tie
1,000-METER TIME TRIAL	BEL 1:09.59 PATRICK SERCU	ITA 1:10.09 GIOVANNI PETTENELLA	FRA 1:10.42 PIERRE TRENTIN	4. NLD Pieter van der Touw 1:10.68 5. CZS Jiří Pecka 1:10.70 6. GER Lothar Claesges 1:10.86
TEAM TIME TRIAL	NLD 2:26:31.19 EVERT DOLMAN GERBEN KARSTENS JOHANNES PIETERSE HUBERTUS ZOET	ITA 2:26:55.39 SEVERINO ANDREOLI LUCIANO DALLA BONA PIETRO GUERRA FERRUCIO MANZA	SWE 2:27:11.52 SVEN HAMRIN ERIK PETTERSSON GÖSTA PETTERSSON STURE PETTERSSON	4. ARG Acosta/Breppe/Delmastro/Placanica 2:27:58.55 5. URS Melikhov/Petrov/Olizarenko/Saidkhuschin 2:28:26.48 6. FRA Bidault/Chappe/Desvages/Wuillemin 2:28:52.74
4,000-METER INDIVIDUAL PURSUIT	CZS 5:04.75 JIŘI DALER	ITA 5:05.96 GIORGIO URSI	DEN 5:01.90 PREBEN ISAKSSON	4. NLD Tiemen Groen 5:04.21 5. four-way tie
4,000-METER TEAM PURSUIT	GER 4:35.67 LOTHAR CLAESGES KARLHEINZ HENRICHS KARL LINK ERNST STRENG	ITA 4:35.74 LUIGI RONCAGLIA VINCENZO MANTOVANI CARLO RANCATI FRANCO TESTA	NLD 4:38.99 GERARD KOEL HENDRIK CORNELISSEN JACOB OUDKERK CORNELIS SCHUURING	4. AUS Brislin/Baird/Browne/Vogels 4:39.42 5. four-way tie
ROAD RACE 144.83 KILOMETERS	ITA 4:39:51.63 MARIO ZANIN	DEN 4:39:51.65 K. ÅKERSTRÖM RODIAN	BEL 4:39:51.74 WALTER GODEFROOT	4. AUS Raymond Bilney 4:39:51.74 5. SPA J. Lopez Rodriguez 4:39:51.74 6. GER Wilfried Peffgen 4:39:51.74

DIVING

Event	Gold	Silver	Bronze	4th–6th
PLATFORM	USA 148.58 ROBERT WEBSTER	ITA 147.54 KLAUS DIBIASI	USA 146.57 THOMAS GOMPF	4. MEX R. Madrigal Garcia 144.27 5. URS Viktor Palagin 143.77 6. GBR Brian Phelps 143.18
SPRINGBOARD	USA 159.90 KENNETH SITZBERGER	USA 157.63 FRANCIS GORMAN	USA 143.77 LARRY ANDREASEN	4. GER Hans-Dieter Pophal 142.58 5. SWE Göran Lundqvist 138.65 6. URS Boris Polulyakh 138.64
PLATFORM	USA 99.80 LESLEY BUSH	GER 98.45 INGRID ENGEL-KRÄMER	URS 97.60 GALINA ALEKSEYEVA	4. USA Linda Cooper 96.30 5. GER Christine Lanzke 92.92 6. AUT Ingeborg Pertmayr 92.70
SPRINGBOARD	GER 145.00 INGRID ENGEL-KRÄMER	USA 138.36 JEANNE COLLIER	USA 138.18 MARY WILLARD	4. USA Sue Gossick 129.70 5. URS Tamara Fyedosova 126.33 6. URS Yelena Anokhina 125.60

EQUESTRIAN

Event	Gold	Silver	Bronze	4th–6th
THREE-DAY EVENT INDIVIDUAL	ITA +64.40 MAURO CHECCOLI	ARG +56.40 CARLOS MORATORIO	GER +49.20 FRITZ LIGGES	4. USA Michael Page +47.40 5. IRL Anthony Cameron +46.53 6. GER Horst Karsten +36.60

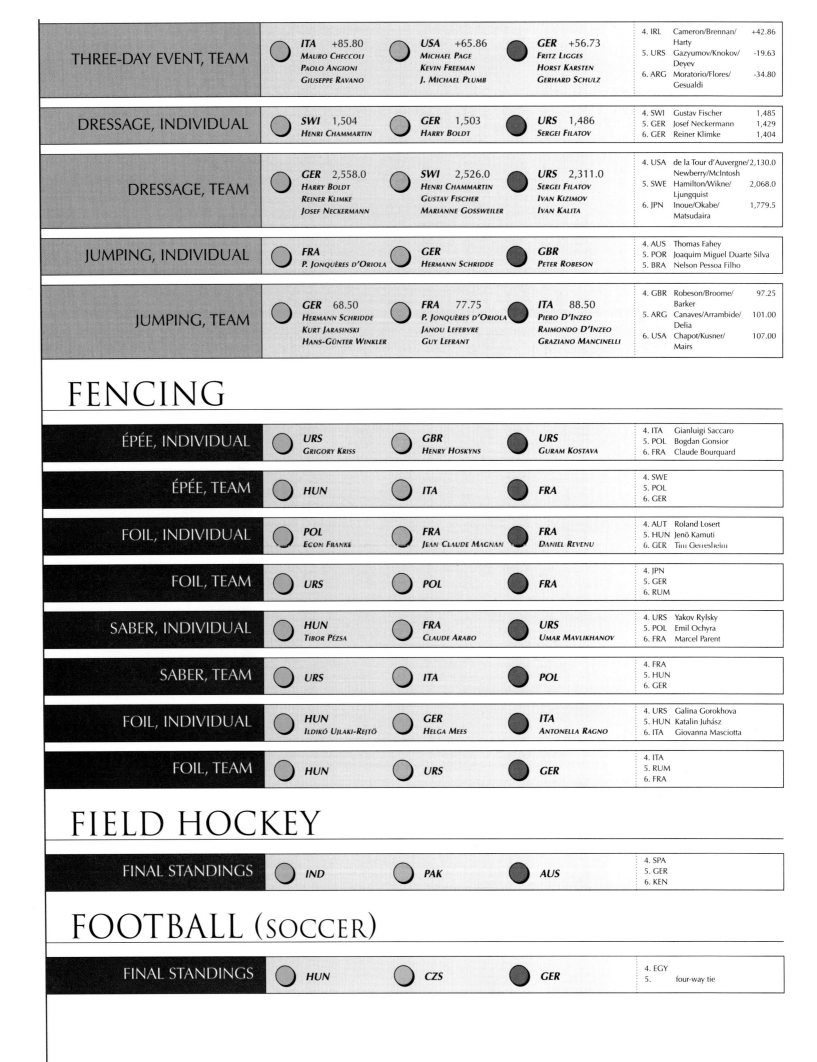

THREE-DAY EVENT, TEAM
- 🥇 ITA +85.80 — Mauro Checcoli, Paolo Angioni, Giuseppe Ravano
- 🥈 USA +65.86 — Michael Page, Kevin Freeman, J. Michael Plumb
- 🥉 GER +56.73 — Fritz Ligges, Horst Karsten, Gerhard Schulz
- 4. IRL Cameron/Brennan/Harty +42.86
- 5. URS Gazyumov/Knokov/Deyev -19.63
- 6. ARG Moratorio/Flores/Gesualdi -34.80

DRESSAGE, INDIVIDUAL
- 🥇 SWI 1,504 — Henri Chammartin
- 🥈 GER 1,503 — Harry Boldt
- 🥉 URS 1,486 — Sergei Filatov
- 4. SWI Gustav Fischer 1,485
- 5. GER Josef Neckermann 1,429
- 6. GER Reiner Klimke 1,404

DRESSAGE, TEAM
- 🥇 GER 2,558.0 — Harry Boldt, Reiner Klimke, Josef Neckermann
- 🥈 SWI 2,526.0 — Henri Chammartin, Gustav Fischer, Marianne Gossweiler
- 🥉 URS 2,311.0 — Sergei Filatov, Ivan Kizimov, Ivan Kalita
- 4. USA de la Tour d'Auvergne/Newberry/McIntosh 2,130.0
- 5. SWE Hamilton/Wikne/Ljungquist 2,068.0
- 6. JPN Inoue/Okabe/Matsudaira 1,779.5

JUMPING, INDIVIDUAL
- 🥇 FRA — P. Jonquères d'Oriola
- 🥈 GER — Hermann Schridde
- 🥉 GBR — Peter Robeson
- 4. AUS Thomas Fahey
- 5. POR Joaquim Miguel Duarte Silva
- 5. BRA Nelson Pessoa Filho

JUMPING, TEAM
- 🥇 GER 68.50 — Hermann Schridde, Kurt Jarasinski, Hans-Günter Winkler
- 🥈 FRA 77.75 — P. Jonquères d'Oriola, Janou Lefebvre, Guy Lefrant
- 🥉 ITA 88.50 — Piero D'Inzeo, Raimondo D'Inzeo, Graziano Mancinelli
- 4. GBR Robeson/Broome/Barker 97.25
- 5. ARG Canaves/Arrambide/Delia 101.00
- 6. USA Chapot/Kusner/Mairs 107.00

FENCING

ÉPÉE, INDIVIDUAL
- 🥇 URS — Grigory Kriss
- 🥈 GBR — Henry Hoskyns
- 🥉 URS — Guram Kostava
- 4. ITA Gianluigi Saccaro
- 5. POL Bogdan Gonsior
- 6. FRA Claude Bourquard

ÉPÉE, TEAM
- 🥇 HUN
- 🥈 ITA
- 🥉 FRA
- 4. SWE
- 5. POL
- 6. GER

FOIL, INDIVIDUAL
- 🥇 POL — Egon Franke
- 🥈 FRA — Jean Claude Magnan
- 🥉 FRA — Daniel Revenu
- 4. AUT Roland Losert
- 5. HUN Jenö Kamuti
- 6. GER Tim Gerresheim

FOIL, TEAM
- 🥇 URS
- 🥈 POL
- 🥉 FRA
- 4. JPN
- 5. GER
- 6. RUM

SABER, INDIVIDUAL
- 🥇 HUN — Tibor Pézsa
- 🥈 FRA — Claude Arabo
- 🥉 URS — Umar Mavlikhanov
- 4. URS Yakov Rylsky
- 5. POL Emil Ochyra
- 6. FRA Marcel Parent

SABER, TEAM
- 🥇 URS
- 🥈 ITA
- 🥉 POL
- 4. FRA
- 5. HUN
- 6. GER

FOIL, INDIVIDUAL
- 🥇 HUN — Ildikó Ujlaki-Rejtö
- 🥈 GER — Helga Mees
- 🥉 ITA — Antonella Ragno
- 4. URS Galina Gorokhova
- 5. HUN Katalin Juhász
- 6. ITA Giovanna Masciotta

FOIL, TEAM
- 🥇 HUN
- 🥈 URS
- 🥉 GER
- 4. ITA
- 5. RUM
- 6. FRA

FIELD HOCKEY

FINAL STANDINGS
- 🥇 IND
- 🥈 PAK
- 🥉 AUS
- 4. SPA
- 5. GER
- 6. KEN

FOOTBALL (SOCCER)

FINAL STANDINGS
- 🥇 HUN
- 🥈 CZS
- 🥉 GER
- 4. EGY
- 5. four-way tie

GYMNASTICS

ALL-AROUND, INDIVIDUAL
- JPN 115.95 — Yukio Endo
- JPN 115.40 — Shuji Tsurumi
- URS 115.40 — Boris Shakhlin
- URS 115.40 — Viktor Lisitsky
- 5. ITA Franco Menichelli 115.15
- 6. JPN Haruhiro Yamashita 115.10

ALL-AROUND, TEAM
- JPN 577.95
- URS 575.45
- GER 565.10
- 4. ITA 560.90
- 5. POL 559.50
- 6. CZS 558.15

FLOOR EXERCISES
- ITA 19.450 — Franco Menichelli
- URS 19.350 — Viktor Lisitsky
- JPN 19.350 — Yukio Endo
- 4. URS Viktor Leontyev 19.200
- 5. JPN Takashi Mitsukuri 19.100
- 6. URS Yuri Tsapenko 18.850

HORIZONTAL BAR
- URS 19.625 — Boris Shakhlin
- URS 19.550 — Yury Titov
- YUS 19.500 — Miroslav Cerar
- 4. URS Viktor Lisitsky 19.325
- 5. JPN Yukio Endo 19.050
- 6. JPN Takashi Ono 19.000

HORSE VAULT
- JPN 19.600 — Haruhiro Yamashita
- URS 19.325 — Viktor Lisitsky
- FIN 19.300 — Hannu Rantakari
- 4. JPN Shuji Tsurumi 19.225
- 5. URS Boris Shakhlin 19.200
- 6. JPN Yukio Endo 19.075

PARALLEL BARS
- JPN 19.675 — Yukio Endo
- JPN 19.450 — Shuji Tsurumi
- ITA 19.350 — Franco Menichelli
- 4. URS Sergei Diomidov 19.225
- 5. URS Viktor Lisitsky 19.200
- 6. YUS Miroslav Cerar 18.450

POMMELED HORSE
- YUS 19.525 — Miroslav Cerar
- JPN 19.325 — Shuji Tsurumi
- URS 19.200 — Yury Tsapenko
- 4. JPN Haruhiro Yamashita 19.075
- 5. NOR Harald Wigaard 18.925
- 6. JPN Takashi Mitsukuri 18.650

RINGS
- JPN 19.475 — Takuji Haytta
- ITA 19.425 — Franco Menichelli
- URS 19.400 — Boris Shakhlin
- 4. URS Viktor Leontyev 19.350
- 5. JPN Shuji Tsurumi 19.275
- 6. JPN Yukio Endo 19.250

ALL-AROUND, INDIVIDUAL
- CZS 77.564 — Vera Čáslavská
- URS 76.998 — Larissa Latynina
- URS 76.965 — Polina Astakhova
- 4. GER Birgit Radochla 76.431
- 5. CZS Hana Ružičková 76.097
- 6. JPN Keiko Ikeda (Tanaka) 76.031

ALL-AROUND, TEAM
- URS 380.890
- CZS 379.989
- JPN 377.889
- 4. GER 376.038
- 5. HUN 375.455
- 6. RUM 371.984

BALANCE BEAM
- CZS 19.449 — Vera Čáslavská
- URS 19.399 — Tamara Manina
- URS 19.382 — Larissa Latynina
- 4. URS Polina Astakhova 19.366
- 5. CZS Hana Ružičková 19.349
- 6. JPN Keiko Ikeda 19.216

FLOOR EXERCISES
- URS 19.599 — Larissa Latynina
- URS 19.500 — Polina Astakhova
- HUN 19.300 — Anikó Jánosi-Ducza
- 4. GER Birgit Radochla 19.299
- 5. GER Ingrid Föst 19.266
- 6. CZS Vera Čáslavská 19.099

HORSE VAULT
- CZS 19.483 — Vera Čáslavská
- URS 19.283 — Larisa Latynina
- GER 19.283 — Birgit Radochla
- 4. JPN Toshiko Aihara 19.282
- 5. URS Yelena Volchetskaya 19.149
- 6. GER Ute Starke 19.116

UNEVEN BARS
- URS 19.332 — Polina Astakhova
- HUN 19.216 — Katalin Makray
- URS 19.199 — Larissa Latynina
- 4. JPN Toshiko Aihara 18.782
- 5. CZS Vera Čáslavská 18.416
- 6. URS Tamara Azamotailova 17.833

JUDO

LIGHTWEIGHT
156.5 lbs. (71 kg)
- JPN — Takehide Nakatani
- SWI — Eric Hänni
- URS — Oleg Stepanov
- URS — Aron Bogoljubov
- 5. four-way tie

MIDDLEWEIGHT
189.5 lbs. (86 kg)
- JPN — Isao Okano
- GER — Wolfgang Hofmann
- USA — James Bregman
- KOR — Kim Eui-Tae
- 5. four-way tie

HEAVYWEIGHT
> 209 lbs. (95 kg)
- JPN — Isao Inokuma
- CAN — A. Douglas Rogers
- URS — Anzor Kiknadze
- URS — Parnaoz Chikviladze
- 5. four-way tie

	Gold	Silver	Bronze	4–6	
OPEN	 **NLD** ANTONIUS GEESINK	**JPN** AKIO KAMINAGA	**GER** KLAUS GLAHN **AUS** THEODORE BORONOVSKIS		

MODERN PENTATHLON

	Gold	Silver	Bronze	4–6	
INDIVIDUAL	**HUN** 5,116 FERENC TÖRÖK	**URS** 5,067 IGOR NOVIKOV	**URS** 5,039 ALBERT MOKEYEV	4. AUS Peter Macken 5. URS Viktor Mineyev 6. USA James Moore	4,897 4,894 4,891
TEAM	**URS** 14,961 IGOR NOVIKOV ALBERT MOKEYEV VIKTOR MINEYEV	**USA** 14,189 JAMES MOORE DAVID KIRKWOOD PAUL PESTHY	**HUN** 14,173 FERENC TÖRÖK IMRE NAGY OTTO TÖRÖK	4. SWE Jansson/Junefelt/ Liljenwall 5. AUS Macken/McMiken/ Page 6. GER Gödicke/Adler/ Frings	14,056 13,703 13,599

ROWING

	Gold	Silver	Bronze	4–6	
SINGLE SCULLS	**URS** 8:22.51 VYACHESLAV IVANOV	**GER** 8:26.24 ACHIM HILL	**SWI** 8:29.68 GOTTFRIED KOTTMANN	4. ARG Alberto Demiddi 5. NZL Murray Watkinson 6. USA Donald Spero	8:31.51 8:35.57 8:37.53
DOUBLE SCULLS	**URS** 7:10.66 OLEG TYURIN BORIS DUBROVSKY	**USA** 7:13.16 SEYMOUR CROMWELL JAMES STORM	**CZS** 7:14.23 VLADIMÍR ANDRS PAVEL HOFMANN	4. SWI Bürgin/Studach 5. GER Lebert/Steffes-Mies 6. FRA Duhamel/Monnereau	7:24.97 7:30.03 7:41.80
PAIR-OARED SHELL WITHOUT COXSWAIN	**CAN** 7:32.94 GEORGE HUNGERFORD ROGER JACKSON	**NLD** 7:33.40 STEVEN BLAISSE ERNST VEENEMANS	**GER** 7:38.63 MICHAEL SCHWAN WOLFGANG HOTTENROTT	4. GBR Nicholson/Farquharson 5. DEN Christiansen/Boye 6. FIN Pitkänen/Lehtelä	7:42.00 7:48.13 8:05.74
PAIR-OARED SHELL WITH COXSWAIN	**USA** 8:21.23 EDWARD FERRY CONN FINDLAY HENRY MITCHELL	**FRA** 8:23.15 JACQUES MOREL GEORGES MOREL JEAN-CLAUDE DAROUY	**NLD** 8:23.42 HERMAN ROUWÉ FREDERIK HARTSUIKER JAN JUSTUS BOS	4. URS Safronov/Rakovschik/ Rudakov 5. CZS Chalupa/Palko/ Mejstrĭk 6. POL Maskrecki/Siejkowski/ Kozera	8:24.85 8:36.21 8:40.00
FOUR-OARED SHELL WITHOUT COXSWAIN	**DEN** 6:59.30 JOHN HANSEN ERIK PETERSEN KURT HELMUDT BJÖRN HASLÖV	**GBR** 7:00.47 JOHN MICHAEL RUSSELL H. A. WARDELL-YERBURGH WILLIAM BARRY JOHN JAMES	**USA** 7:01.37 GEOFFREY PICARD RICHARD LYON THEODORE NASH THEODORE MITTET	4. NLD Wartena/Enters/ Boelen/Castelein 5. ITA Sgheiz/Balatti/ Zucchi/Sgheiz 6. GER Schrörs/Efferta/ Müller/Misselhorn	7:09.98 7:10.05 7:10.33
FOUR-OARED SHELL WITH COXSWAIN	**GER** 7:00.44	**ITA** 7:02.84	**NLD** 7:06.46	4. FRA 5. URS 6. POL	7:13.92 7:16.05 7:28.15
EIGHT-OARED SHELL WITH COXSWAIN	**USA** 6:18.23	**GER** 6:23.29	**CZS** 6:25.11	4. YUS 5. URS 6. ITA	6:27.15 6:30.69 6:42.78

SHOOTING

	Gold	Silver	Bronze	4–6	
RAPID-FIRE PISTOL	 **FIN** 592 PENTTI LINNOSVUO	**RUM** 591 ION TRIPŞA	**CZS** 590 LUBOMIR NACOVSKY	4. SWI Hans Albrecht 5. HUN Szilárd Kun 6. RUM Marcel Roşca	590 589 588
FREE PISTOL	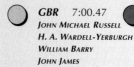 **FIN** 560 VÄINÖ MARKKANEN	**USA** 557 FRANKLIN GREEN	**JPN** 554/26 YOSHIHISA YOSHIKAWA	4. GER Johann Garreis 5. GBR Anthony Chivers 6. PER Antonio Vita Segura	554/24 552 550
SMALL-BORE RIFLE PRONE	**HUN** 597 (Gold) LÁSZLÓ HAMMERL	**USA** 597 (Silver) LONES WIGGER	**USA** 596 TOMMY POOL	4. CAN Gilmour Boa 5. RUM Nicolae Rotaru 6. JPN Akihiro Rinzaki	595 595 594
SMALL-BORE RIFLE THREE POSITIONS	**USA** 1,164 LONES WIGGER	**BUL** 1,152 VELICHKO KHRISTOV	**HUN** 1,151 LÁSZLÓ HAMMERL	4. GER Harry Köcher 5. POL Jerzy Nowicki 6. USA Tommy Pool	1,148 1,147 1,147
FREE RIFLE THREE POSITIONS	**USA** 1,153 GARY ANDERSON	**URS** 1,144 SHOTA KVELIASHVILI	**USA** 1,136 MARTIN GUNNARSSON	4. URS Aleksandr Gerasimenok 5. SWI August Hollenstein 6. FIN Esa Kervinen	1,135 1,135 1,133

162

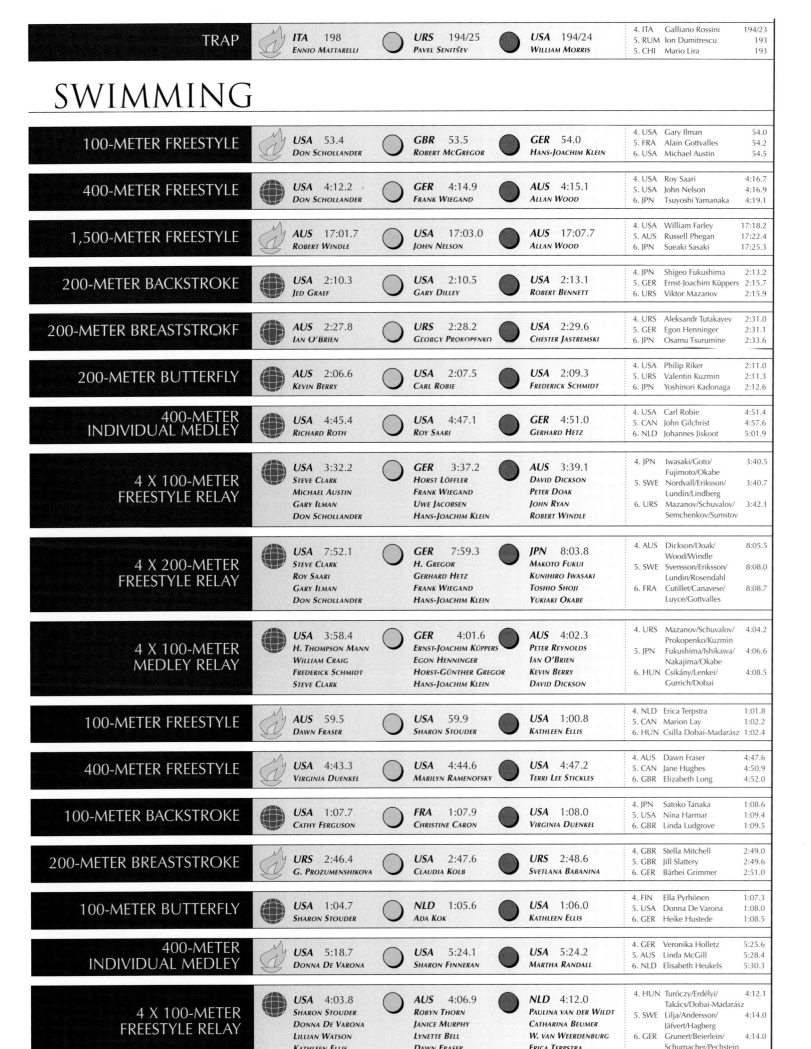

TRAP	ITA 198 ENNIO MATTARELLI	URS 194/25 PAVEL SENITŠEV	USA 194/24 WILLIAM MORRIS	4. ITA Galliano Rossini 194/23
				5. RUM Ion Dumitrescu 193
				5. CHI Mario Lira 193

SWIMMING

100-METER FREESTYLE	USA 53.4 DON SCHOLLANDER	GBR 53.5 ROBERT McGREGOR	GER 54.0 HANS-JOACHIM KLEIN	4. USA Gary Ilman 54.0
				5. FRA Alain Gottvalles 54.2
				6. USA Michael Austin 54.5

400-METER FREESTYLE	USA 4:12.2 DON SCHOLLANDER	GER 4:14.9 FRANK WIEGAND	AUS 4:15.1 ALLAN WOOD	4. USA Roy Saari 4:16.7
				5. USA John Nelson 4:16.9
				6. JPN Tsuyoshi Yamanaka 4:19.1

1,500-METER FREESTYLE	AUS 17:01.7 ROBERT WINDLE	USA 17:03.0 JOHN NELSON	AUS 17:07.7 ALLAN WOOD	4. USA William Farley 17:18.2
				5. AUS Russell Phegan 17:22.4
				6. JPN Sueaki Sasaki 17:25.3

200-METER BACKSTROKE	USA 2:10.3 JED GRAEF	USA 2:10.5 GARY DILLEY	USA 2:13.1 ROBERT BENNETT	4. JPN Shigeo Fukushima 2:13.2
				5. GER Ernst-Joachim Küppers 2:15.7
				6. URS Viktor Mazanov 2:15.9

200-METER BREASTSTROKE	AUS 2:27.8 IAN O'BRIEN	URS 2:28.2 GEORGY PROKOPENKO	USA 2:29.6 CHESTER JASTREMSKI	4. URS Aleksandr Tutakayev 2:31.0
				5. GER Egon Henninger 2:31.1
				6. JPN Osamu Tsurumine 2:33.6

200-METER BUTTERFLY	AUS 2:06.6 KEVIN BERRY	USA 2:07.5 CARL ROBIE	USA 2:09.3 FREDERICK SCHMIDT	4. USA Philip Riker 2:11.0
				5. URS Valentin Kuzmin 2:11.3
				6. JPN Yoshinori Kadonaga 2:12.6

400-METER INDIVIDUAL MEDLEY	USA 4:45.4 RICHARD ROTH	USA 4:47.1 ROY SAARI	GER 4:51.0 GERHARD HETZ	4. USA Carl Robie 4:51.4
				5. CAN John Gilchrist 4:57.6
				6. NLD Johannes Jiskoot 5:01.9

4 X 100-METER FREESTYLE RELAY	USA 3:32.2 STEVE CLARK MICHAEL AUSTIN GARY ILMAN DON SCHOLLANDER	GER 3:37.2 HORST LÖFFLER FRANK WIEGAND UWE JACOBSEN HANS-JOACHIM KLEIN	AUS 3:39.1 DAVID DICKSON PETER DOAK JOHN RYAN ROBERT WINDLE	4. JPN Iwasaki/Goto/ Fujimoto/Okabe 3:40.5
				5. SWE Nordvall/Eriksson/ Lundin/Lindberg 3:40.7
				6. URS Mazanov/Schuvalov/ Semchenkov/Sumstov 3:42.1

4 X 200-METER FREESTYLE RELAY	USA 7:52.1 STEVE CLARK ROY SAARI GARY ILMAN DON SCHOLLANDER	GER 7:59.3 H. GREGOR GERHARD HETZ FRANK WIEGAND HANS-JOACHIM KLEIN	JPN 8:03.8 MAKOTO FUKUI KUNIHIRO IWASAKI TOSHIO SHOJI YUKIAKI OKABE	4. AUS Dickson/Doak/ Wood/Windle 8:05.5
				5. SWE Svensson/Eriksson/ Lundin/Rosendahl 8:08.0
				6. FRA Cutillet/Canavese/ Luyce/Gottvalles 8:08.7

4 X 100-METER MEDLEY RELAY	USA 3:58.4 H. THOMPSON MANN WILLIAM CRAIG FREDERICK SCHMIDT STEVE CLARK	GER 4:01.6 ERNST-JOACHIM KÜPPERS EGON HENNINGER HORST-GÜNTHER GREGOR HANS-JOACHIM KLEIN	AUS 4:02.3 PETER REYNOLDS IAN O'BRIEN KEVIN BERRY DAVID DICKSON	4. URS Mazanov/Schuvalov/ Prokopenko/Kuzmin 4:04.2
				5. JPN Fukushima/Ishikawa/ Nakajima/Okabe 4:06.6
				6. HUN Csikány/Lenkei/ Gurrich/Dobai 4:08.5

100-METER FREESTYLE	AUS 59.5 DAWN FRASER	USA 59.9 SHARON STOUDER	USA 1:00.8 KATHLEEN ELLIS	4. NLD Erica Terpstra 1:01.8
				5. CAN Marion Lay 1:02.2
				6. HUN Csilla Dobai-Madarász 1:02.4

400-METER FREESTYLE	USA 4:43.3 VIRGINIA DUENKEL	USA 4:44.6 MARILYN RAMENOFSKY	USA 4:47.2 TERRI LEE STICKLES	4. AUS Dawn Fraser 4:47.6
				5. CAN Jane Hughes 4:50.9
				6. GBR Elizabeth Long 4:52.0

100-METER BACKSTROKE	USA 1:07.7 CATHY FERGUSON	FRA 1:07.9 CHRISTINE CARON	USA 1:08.0 VIRGINIA DUENKEL	4. JPN Satoko Tanaka 1:08.6
				5. USA Nina Harmar 1:09.4
				6. GBR Linda Ludgrove 1:09.5

200-METER BREASTSTROKE	URS 2:46.4 G. PROZUMENSHIKOVA	USA 2:47.6 CLAUDIA KOLB	URS 2:48.6 SVETLANA BABANINA	4. GBR Stella Mitchell 2:49.0
				5. GBR Jill Slattery 2:49.6
				6. GER Bärbei Grimmer 2:51.0

100-METER BUTTERFLY	USA 1:04.7 SHARON STOUDER	NLD 1:05.6 ADA KOK	USA 1:06.0 KATHLEEN ELLIS	4. FIN Ella Pyrhönen 1:07.3
				5. USA Donna De Varona 1:08.0
				6. GER Heike Hustede 1:08.5

400-METER INDIVIDUAL MEDLEY	USA 5:18.7 DONNA DE VARONA	USA 5:24.1 SHARON FINNERAN	USA 5:24.2 MARTHA RANDALL	4. GER Veronika Holletz 5:25.6
				5. AUS Linda McGill 5:28.4
				6. NLD Elisabeth Heukels 5:30.3

4 X 100-METER FREESTYLE RELAY	USA 4:03.8 SHARON STOUDER DONNA DE VARONA LILLIAN WATSON KATHLEEN ELLIS	AUS 4:06.9 ROBYN THORN JANICE MURPHY LYNETTE BELL DAWN FRASER	NLD 4:12.0 PAULINA VAN DER WILDT CATHARINA BEUMER W. VAN WEERDENBURG ERICA TERPSTRA	4. HUN Turóczy/Erdélyi/ Takács/Dobai-Madarász 4:12.1
				5. SWE Lilja/Andersson/ Jäfvert/Hagberg 4:14.0
				6. GER Grunert/Beierlein/ Schumacher/Pechstein 4:14.0

4 X 100-METER MEDLEY RELAY	USA 4:33.9 CATHY FERGUSON CYNTHIA GOYETTE SHARON STOUDER KATHLEEN ELLIS	NLD 4:37.0 KORNELIA WINKEL KLENA BIMOLT ADA KOK ERICA TERPSTRA	URS 4:39.2 TATYANA SAVELYEVA SVETLANA BABANINA TATYANA DEVYATOVA NATALYA USTINOVA	4. JPN Tanaka/Yamamoto/ Takahashi/Kihara 4:42.0 5. GBR Norfolk/Mitchell/ Cotterill/Long 4:45.8 6. CAN Weir/Lay/ Stewart/Kennedy 4:49.9

VOLLEYBALL

FINAL STANDINGS	URS	CZS	JPN	4. RUM 5. BUL 6. HUN

FINAL STANDINGS	JPN	URS	POL	4. RUM 5. USA 6. KOR

WATER POLO

FINAL STANDINGS	HUN	YUS	URS	4. ITA 5. RUM 6. GER

WEIGHT LIFTING

BANTAMWEIGHT 123 lbs. (56 kg)	URS 357.5 ALEKSEI VAKHONIN	HUN 355.0 IMRE FÖLDI	JPN 347.5 SHIRO ICHINOSEKI	4. POL Henryk Trębicki 342.5 5. KOR Yang Mu-shin 340.0 6. JPN Yukio Furuyama 335.0
FEATHERWEIGHT 132 lbs. (60 kg)	JPN 397.5 YOSHINOBU MIYAKE	USA 382.5 ISAAC BERGER	POL 377.5 MIECZYSLAW NOWAK	4. JPN Hiroshi Fukuda 375.0 5. ITA Sebastiano Mannironi 370.0 6. KOR Kim Hae-nam 367.5
LIGHTWEIGHT 148.75 lbs. (67.5 kg)	POL 432.5 (Gold) W. BASZANOWSKI	URS 432.5 (Silver) VLADIMIR KAPLUNOV	POL 420.0 MARIAN ZIELIŃSKI	4. USA Anthony Garcy 412.5 5. CZS Zdenek Otáhal 400.0 6. JPN Hiroshi Yamazaki 397.5
MIDDLEWEIGHT 165 lbs. (75 kg)	CZS 445.0 HANS ZDRAŽILA	URS 440.0 VIKTOR KURENTSOV	JPN 437.5 MASASHI OUCHI	4. KOR Lee Jong-sup 432.5 5. JPN Sadahiro Miwa 422.5 6. HUN Mihály Huszka 420.0
LIGHT HEAVYWEIGHT 181.5 lbs. (82.5 kg)	URS 475.0 RUDOLF PLUKFELDER	HUN 467.5 GÉZA TÓTH	HUN 467.5 GYÖZÖ VERES	4. POL Jerzy Kaczkowski 455.0 5. USA Gary Cleveland 455.0 6. KOR Hyung-woo Lee 452.5
MIDDLE HEAVYWEIGHT 198.25 lbs. (90 kg)	URS 487.5 VLADIMIR GOLOVANOV	GBR 475.0 LOUIS MARTIN	POL 467.5 IRENEUSZ PALIŃSKI	4. USA William March 467.5 5. RUM Lazăr Baroga 460.0 6. HUN Árpád Nemessányi 460.0
HEAVYWEIGHT 242.5 lbs. (110 kg)	URS 572.5 LEONID ZHABOTINSKY	URS 570.0 YURY VLASOV	USA 537.5 NORBERT SCHEMANSKY	4. USA Gary Gubner 512.5 5. HUN Károly Ecser 507.5 6. UAR M. Mahmoud Ibrahim 495.0

WRESTLING, FREESTYLE

FLYWEIGHT 114.5 lbs. (52 kg)	JPN YOSHIKATSU YOSHIDA	KOR CHANG CHANG-SUN	IRN ALI AKBAR HEIDARI	4. URS Ali Aliyev 5. TUR Cemal Yanilmaz 6. FRA André Zoete
BANTAMWEIGHT 125.5 lbs. (57 kg)	JPN YOJIRO UETAKE	TUR HÜSEYIN AKBAŞ	URS AYDYN IBRAGIMOV	4. USA David Auble 5. KOR Choi Young-kil 6. IND Bishamber Singh
FEATHERWEIGHT 136.5 lbs. (62 kg)	JPN OSAMU WATANABE	BUL STANCHO KOLEV	URS NODAR KHOKHASHVILI	4. USA Robert Douglas 5. AFG Mohammed Ebrahimi 6. IRN Mohammed Ebrahimi Seifpour
LIGHTWEIGHT 149.5 lbs. (68 kg)	BUL ENYU VULCHEV (DIMOV)	GER KLAUS-JÜRGEN ROST	JPN IWAO HORIUCHI	4. TUR Mahmut Atalay 5. IRN Abdollah Movahhed 6. three-way tie
WELTERWEIGHT 163 lbs. (74 kg)	TUR ISMAIL OGAN	URS GULIKO SAGARADZE	IRN M. ALI SANATKARAN	4. BUL Petko Dermendzhiev 5. JPN Yasuo Watanabe 6. CAN Philip Oberlander
MIDDLEWEIGHT 181 lbs. (82 kg)	BUL PRODAN GARDZHEV	TUR HASAN GÜNGÖR	USA DANIEL BRAND	4. IRN Mansour Mehdizadeh 5. HUN Géza Holiósi 5. JPN Tatsuo Sasaki

LIGHT HEAVYWEIGHT 198.5 lbs. (90 kg)	URS ALEKSANDR MEDVED	TUR AHMET AYIK	BUL SAID MUSTAFOV	4. IRN Gholam Reza Takhti 5. SWI Peter Jutzeler 6. USA Gerald Conine
HEAVYWEIGHT 220 lbs. (100 kg)	URS ALEKSANDR IVANITSKY	BUL LYUTVI AHMEDOV	TUR HAMIT KAPLAN	4. CZS Bohumil Kubat 5. GBR Denis McNamara 6. RUM Ştefan Ştîngu

WRESTLING, GRECO-ROMAN

FLYWEIGHT 114.5 lbs. (52 kg)	JPN TSUTOMU HANAHARA	BUL ANGEL KEREZOV	RUM DUMITRU PIRVULESCU	4. four-way tie
BANTAMWEIGHT 125.5 lbs. (57 kg)	JPN MASAMITSU ICHIGUCHI	URS VLADLEN TROSTYANSKY	RUM ION CERNEA	4. CZS Jiří Švec 5. three-way tie
FEATHERWEIGHT 136.5 lbs. (62 kg)	HUN IMRE POLYÁK	URS ROMAN RURUA	YUS BRANISLAV MARTINOVIČ	4. USA Ronald Finley 4. UAR Mostafa Mansour 6. three-way tie
LIGHTWEIGHT 149.5 lbs. (68 kg)	TUR KAZIM AYVAZ	RUM VALERIU BULARCĂ	URS DAVID GVANTSELADZE	4. JPN Tokuaki Fujita 5. YUS Stevan Horvat 6 FIN Eero Tapio
WELTERWEIGHT 163 lbs. (74 kg)	URS ANATOLY KOLESOV	BUL KIRIL PETKOV	SWE BERTIL NYSTRÖM	4. POL Boleslaw Dubicki 5. HUN Antal Rizmayer 5. RUM Ion Tăranu
MIDDLEWEIGHT 181 lbs. (82 kg)	YUS BRANISLAV SIMIČ	CZS JIŘÍ KORMANIK	GER LOTHAR METZ	4. HUN Géza Holiósi 4. URS Valentin Olenik 6. BUL Kraliu Bimbalov
LIGHT HEAVYWEIGHT 198.5 lbs. (90 kg)	BUL BOYAN RADEV	SWE PER SVENSSON	GER HEINZ KIEHL	4. RUM Nicolae Martinescu 5. three-way tie
HEAVYWEIGHT 220 lbs. (100 kg)	HUN ISTVÁN KOZMA	URS ANATOLY ROSHIN	GER WILFRIED DIETRICH	4. CZS Petr Kment 5. SWE Sten Ragnar Svensson 6. USA Robert Pickens

YACHTING

FINN MONOTYPE	GER 7,638 WILHELM KUHWEIDE	USA 6,373 PETER BARRETT	DEN 6,190 HENNING WIND	4. NZL Peter Mander 5,684 5. AUT Hubert Raudaschi 5,405 6. AUS Colin Ryrie 5,273
DRAGON CLASS	DEN 5,854 OLE BERNTSEN CHRISITAN VON BÜLOW OLE POULSEN	GER 5,826 PETER AHRENDT ULRICH MENSE WILFRIED LORENZ	USA 5,523 LOWELL NORTH CHARLES ROGERS RICHARD DEAVE	4. GBR Parry/Harris/ Reade 5,090 5. BER Cooper/Simmons/ Soares 5,055 6. ITA Sorrentino/Furlan/ Pelaschiar 4,636
FLYING DUTCHMAN	NZL 6,255 HELMER PEDERSEN EARLE WELLS	GBR 5,556 FRANKLYN MUSTO ARTHUR MORGAN	USA 5,158 HARRY MELGES WILLIAM BENTSEN	4. DEN Petersen/Fogh 4,500 5. URS Shelkovnikov/Pilchin 4,375 6. NLD Verhagen/de Jong 4,214
5.5-METER CLASS	AUS 5,981 WILLIAM NORTHRAM JAMES SARGEANT PETER O'DONNELL	SWE 5,284 LARS THÖRN STURE STORK ERNST ARNE KARLSSON	USA 5,106 JOHN MCNAMARA FRANCIS SCULLY JOSEPH BATCHELDER	4. ITA Straulino/Petronio/ Minervini 4,738 5. GER Kopperschmidt/Reich/ Wagner/Mares 3,057 6. FIN Gullichsen/Frazer/ Salovaara 3,039
STAR CLASS	BAH 5,664 DURWARD KNOWLES C. CECIL COOKE	USA 5,585 RICHARD STEARNS LYNN WILLIAMS	SWE 5,527 PELLE PETTERSSON HOLGER SUNDSTRÖM	4. FIN Tallberg/Tallberg 5,402 5. URS Pinegin/Shutkov 4,305 6. GER Splieth/Meyer 4,175

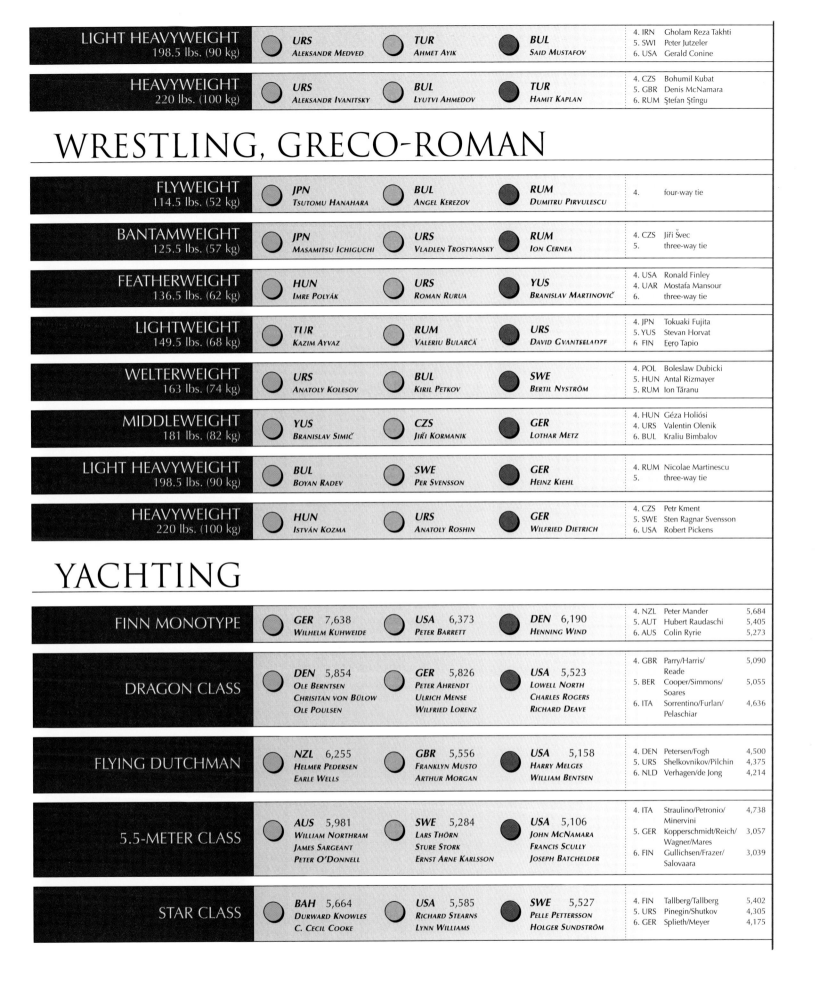

Tuesday, FEBRUARY 6

PM	EVENT	VENUE
3:00	OPENING CEREMONY	Stade d'Inauguration
5:50	HOCKEY	Ice Stadium
9:00	HOCKEY	Ice Stadium

Wednesday, FEBRUARY 7

AM	EVENT	VENUE
7:00	FIGURE SKATING	Ice Stadium
	women's singles, compulsories	
8:30	SKIING, NORDIC	Autrans
	30 kilometers	

PM	EVENT	VENUE
12:00	SKIING, ALPINE	Casserousse
	downhill, practice run	
4:45	HOCKEY	Municipal Ice Rink
	(2 games)	
5:00	HOCKEY	Hockey Ice Stadium
	(2 games)	
6:30	BOBSLED	Alpe d'Huez Bobsled Course
	2-man, 1st and 2nd runs	

Thursday, FEBRUARY 8

AM	EVENT	VENUE
7:30	FIGURE SKATING	Ice Stadium
	women's singles, compulsories	

PM	EVENT	VENUE
5:00	HOCKEY	Ice Stadium
8:30	HOCKEY	Ice Stadium
	(2 games)	

Friday, FEBRUARY 9

AM	EVENT	VENUE
9:00	SKIING, NORDIC	Autrans
	women's 10 kilometers	
10:00	SPEED SKATING	Speed-Skating Oval
	women's 500 meters	
11:00	SKIING, ALPINE	Chamrousse
	women's downhill, practice run	

PM	EVENT	VENUE
12:00	SKIING, ALPINE	Chamrousse
	downhill	
1:00	HOCKEY	Ice Stadium
4:30	HOCKEY	Ice Stadium
	(2 games)	
4:45	HOCKEY	Municipal Ice Rink
	(2 games)	

Saturday, FEBRUARY 10

AM	EVENT	VENUE
8:30	SKIING, NORDIC	Autrans
	15 kilometers	
9:00	SPEED SKATING	Speed-Skating Oval
	women's 1,500 meters	

PM	EVENT	VENUE
12:00	SKIING, ALPINE	Chamrousse
	women's downhill, final	
	HOCKEY	Ice Stadium
1:00	SKIING, NORDIC	Autrans Ski Jump
	combined, 70-meter jump	
3:30	HOCKEY	Ice Stadium
7:00	FIGURE SKATING	Ice Stadium
	women's free skate	
8:00	BOBSLED	Alpe d'Huez Bobsled Course
	2-man, 3rd & 4th runs	
	LUGE	Villard-de-Lans Luge Course
	• singles, 1st & 2nd runs	
	• women's singles, 1st & 2nd runs	
8:30	HOCKEY	Ice Stadium

Sunday, FEBRUARY 11

AM	EVENT	VENUE
9:30	SKIING, NORDIC	Autrans
	combined, 15 kilometers	
10:00	SPEED SKATING	Speed-Skating Oval
	women's 1,000 meters	

PM	EVENT	VENUE
12:00	SKIING, ALPINE	Chamrousse
	giant slalom, 1st run	
1:00	FIGURE SKATING	Ice Stadium
	pairs, compulsories	
1:00	SKI JUMPING	Autrans
	70-meter hill	
4:30	HOCKEY	Ice Stadium
9:00	HOCKEY	Ice Stadium

Monday, FEBRUARY 12

AM	EVENT	VENUE
8:15	BIATHLON	Autrans
	individual event	
9:30	SPEED SKATING	Speed-Skating Oval
	women's 3,000 meters	
	SKIING, NORDIC	Autrans
	combined (15-kilometer cross-country)	

PM	EVENT	VENUE
12:00	SKIING, ALPINE	Chamrousse
	giant slalom, 2nd run	

1:00	HOCKEY	Ice Stadium
4:30	HOCKEY	Municipal Ice Rink
	(2 games)	
4:45	HOCKEY	Ice Stadium
	(2 games)	

Tuesday, February 13

AM	EVENT	VENUE
7:00	FIGURE SKATING	Ice Stadium
	compulsories	
8:00	LUGE	Villard-de-Lans Luge Course
	• singles, 3rd runs	
	• women's singles, 3rd runs	
9:00	SKIING, NORDIC	Autrans
	women's 5 kilometers	
12:00	SKIING, ALPINE	Chamrousse
	women's slalom	

PM	EVENT	VENUE
5:00	HOCKEY	Ice Stadium
8:30	HOCKEY	Ice Stadium
	(2 games)	

Wednesday, February 14

AM	EVENT	VENUE
7:00	FIGURE SKATING	Ice Stadium
	compulsories	
9:00	SKIING, NORDIC	Autrans
	4 x 10-kilometer relay	
10:00	SPEED SKATING	Speed-Skating Oval
	500 meters	

PM	EVENT	VENUE
12:00	SKIING, ALPINE	Chamrousse
	slalom, seeding run	
4:00	HOCKEY	Ice Stadium
	(2 games)	
7:30	FIGURE SKATING	Ice Stadium
	pairs, free skate	

Thursday, FEBRUARY 15

AM	EVENT	VENUE
8:30	BIATHLON	Autrans
	relay	
9:00	SPEED SKATING	Speed-Skating Oval
	5,000 meters	

PM	EVENT	VENUE
12:00	SKIING, ALPINE	Chamrousse
	women's giant slalom, 1st & 2nd runs	
1:00	HOCKEY	Ice Stadium
4:30	HOCKEY	Ice Stadium
8:30	HOCKEY	Ice Stadium

9:00	HOCKEY	Ice Stadium

Friday, FEBRUARY 16

AM	EVENT	VENUE
5:00	BOBSLED	Alpe d'Huez Bobsled Course
	4-man, 1st & 2nd runs	
9:00	SPEED SKATING	Speed-Skating Oval
	1,500 meters	
9:30	SKIING, NORDIC	Autrans
	women's 3 x 5-kilometer relay	

PM	EVENT	VENUE
12:00	SKIING, ALPINE	Chamrousse
	slalom, 1st run	
4:30	HOCKEY	Ice Stadium
8:00	FIGURE SKATING	Ice Stadium
	free skate	
8:30	HOCKEY	Municipal Ice Rink
9:00	HOCKEY	Ice Stadium

Saturday, FEBRUARY 17

AM	EVENT	VENUE
8:00	SPEED SKATING	Speed-Skating Oval
	10,000 meters	
8:00	SKIING, NORDIC	Autrans
	50 kilometers	

PM	EVENT	VENUE
12:00	SKIING, ALPINE	Chamrousse
	slalom, final	
2:00	HOCKEY	Ice Stadium
4:45	HOCKEY	Municipal Ice Rink
5:30	HOCKEY	Ice Stadium
8:30	HOCKEY	Municipal Ice Rink
9:00	HOCKEY	Ice Stadium

Sunday, FEBRUARY 18

AM	EVENT	VENUE
8:00	LUGE	Villard-de-Lans Luge Course
	2-man, 2 runs only	

PM	EVENT	VENUE
1:00	SKI JUMPING	Saint Nizier Ski Jump
	90-meter hill	
Evening	CLOSING CEREMONY	Stade d'Inauguration

NATIONAL MEDAL COUNT

COMPETITORS

COUNTRIES: 35   ATHLETES: 1,006   MEN: 800   WOMEN: 206

	GOLD	SILVER	BRONZE	TOTAL		GOLD	SILVER	BRONZE	TOTAL		GOLD	SILVER	BRONZE	TOTAL		GOLD	SILVER	BRONZE	TOTAL
SOV	8	5	3	16	USA	3	2	3	8	SWE	1	1	2	4	SPA	1			1
GDR	4	3	7	14	FRG	3	1	1	5	JPN	1	1	1	3	CAN	1			1
NOR	2	5	5	12	ITA	2	2	1	5	TCH	1		2	3	HUN		1		1
SUI	4	3	3	10	AUT	1	2	2	5	FRA		1	2	3					
NLD	4	3	2	9	FIN		4	1	5	POL	1			1					

GRENOBLE 1968
10TH OLYMPIC WINTER GAMES

BIATHLON

20 KILOMETERS

NOR 1:13:45.9 **MAGNAR SOLBERG**	SOV 1:14:40.4 **ALEKSANDR TIKHONOV**	SOV 1:18:27.4 **VLADIMIR GOUNDARTSEV**

4. POL S. Szczepaniak 1:18:56.8
5. FIN Arve Kinnari 1:19:47.9
6. SOV Nikolai Pousanov 1:20:14.5

4 X 7.5-KILOMETER RELAY

SOV 2:13:02.4 **ALEKSANDR TIKHONOV** **NIKOLAI POUSANOV** **VICTOR MAMATOV** **VLADIMIR GOUNDARISEV**	NOR 2:14:50.2 **OLA WAEHAVG** **OLAV JORDET** **MAGNAR SOLBERG** **JON ISTAD**	SWE 2:17:26.3 **LARS-GÖRAN ARWIDSON** **TORE ERIKSSON** **OLLE PETRUSSON** **HOLMFRID OLSSON**

4. POL Rózak/Fiedor/ Lukaszczyk/Szczepaniak 2:20:19.6
5. FIN Suutarinen/Floejt/ Vähäkylä/Kinnari 2:20:41.8
6. GDR Kluge/Jahn/ Koschka/Speer 2:21:54.5

BOBSLED

TWO-MAN

ITA 4:41.54 **EUGENIO MONTI** **LUCIANO DE PAOLIS**	FRG 4:41.54 **HORST FLOTH** **PEPI BADER**	RUM 4:44.46 **ION PANȚURU** **NICOLAE NEAGOE**

4. AUT Thaler/Durnthaler 4:45.13
5. GBR Nash/Dixon 4:45.16
6. USA Lamey/Huscher 4:46.03

FOUR-MAN

ITA 2:17.39 **EUGENIO MONTI** **LUCIANO DE PAOLIS** **ROBERTO ZANDONELLA** **MARIO ARMANO**	AUT 2:17.48 **ERWIN THALER** **REINHOLD DURNTHALER** **HERBERT GRUBER** **JOSEF EDER**	SUI 2:18.04 **JEAN WICKI** **HANS CANDRIAN** **WILLI HOFMANN** **WALTER GRAF**

4. RUM Panțuru/Neagoe/ Hristovici/Maftei 2:18.14
5. FRG Floth/Bader/ Schäfer/Lange 2:18.33
6. ITA Gaspari/Cavallini/ Rescigno/Clemente 2:18.36

FIGURE SKATING

SINGLES

AUT 13 **WOLFGANG SCHWARZ**	USA 17 **TIMOTHY WOOD**	FRA 31 **PATRICK PERA**

4. AUT Emmerich Danzer 29
5. USA Gary Visconti 52
6. USA John Petkevich 56

SINGLES

USA 9 **PEGGY FLEMING**	GDR 18 **GABRIELE SEYFERT**	TCH 31 **HANA MASKOVÁ**

4. USA Albertina Noyes 40
5. AUT Beatrix Schuba 51
6. HUN Zsuzsa Almássy 57

PAIRS

SOV 10 **LYUDMILA BELOUSOVA** **OLEG PROTOPOPOV**	SOV 17 **TATYANA ZHUK** **ALEKSANDR GORELIK**	FRG 30 **MARGOT GLOCKSHUBER** **WOLFGANG DANNE**

4. GDR Steiner/Walther 37
5. SOV Moskvina/Michine 44
6. USA Kauffman/Kauffman 58

HOCKEY

FINAL STANDINGS

SOV	TCH	CAN

4. SWE
5. FIN
6. USA

LUGE

SINGLE

AUT 2:52.48 **MANFRED SCHMID**	GDR 2:52.66 **THOMAS KÖHLER**	GDR 2:53.33 **KLAUS-MICHAEL BONSACK**

4. POL Zbigniew Gawior 2:53.51
5. AUT Josef Feistmantl 2:53.57
6. GDR Hans Plenk 2:53.67

TWO-SEATER

GDR 1:35.85 **KLAUS-MICHAEL BONSACK** **THOMAS KÖHLER**	AUT 1:36.34 **MANFRED SCHMID** **EWALD WALCH**	FRG 1:37.29 **WOLFGANG WINKLER** **FRITZ NACHMANN**

4. FRG Plenk/Aschauer 1:37.61
5. GDR Hörnlein/Bredow 1:37.81
6. POL Gawior/Gawior 1:37.85

SINGLE	● ITA 2:28.66 Erika Lechner	● FRG 2:29.37 Christa Schmuck	● FRG 2:29.56 Angelika Dünhaupt	4. POL	Helena Macher	2:30.05
				5. POL	Jadwiga Damse	2:30.15
				6. TCH	Dana Beldová	2:30.35

SKIING, ALPINE

DOWNHILL	● FRA 1:59.85 Jean-Claude Killy	● FRA 1:59.93 Guy Périllat	● SUI 2:00.32 John-Daniel Dätwyler	4. AUT	Heinrich Messner	2:01.03
				5. AUT	Karl Schranz	2:01.89
				6. ITA	Ivo Mahiknecht	2:02.00
SLALOM	● FRA 1:39.73 Jean-Claude Killy	● AUT 1:39.82 Herbert Huber	● AUT 1:40.09 Alfred Matt	4. SWE	Dumeng Giovanoli	1:40.22
				5. USA	Vladimir Sabich	1:40.49
				6. POL	Andrzej Bachleda	1:40.61
GIANT SLALOM	● FRA 3:29.28 Jean-Claude Killy	● SUI 3:31.50 Willy Favre	● AUT 3:31.83 Heinrich Messner	4. FRA	Guy Périllat	3:32.06
				5. USA	William Kidd	3:32.37
				6. AUT	Karl Schranz	3:33.08
DOWNHILL	● AUT 1:40.87 Olga Pall	● FRA 1:41.33 Isabelle Mir	● AUT 1:41.41 Christl Haas	4. AUT	Brigitte Seiwald	1:41.82
				5. FRA	Annie Famose	1:42.15
				6. GBR	Felicity Field	1:42.79
SLALOM	● FRA 1:25.86 Marielle Goitschel	● CAN 1:26.15 Nancy Greene	● FRA 1:27.89 Annie Famose	4. GBR	Gina Hathorn	1:27.92
				5. FRA	Isabelle Mir	1:28.22
				6. FRG	Burgl Färbinger	1:28.90
GIANT SLALOM	● CAN 1:51.97 Nancy Greene	● FRA 1:54.61 Annie Famose	● SUI 1:54.74 Fernande Bochatay	4. FRA	Florence Steurer	1:54.75
				5. AUT	Olga Pall	1:55.61
				6. FRA	Isabelle Mir	1:56.07

SKIING, NORDIC

15 KILOMETERS	● NOR 47:54.2 Harald Grönningen	● FIN 47:56.1 Eero Mäntyranta	● SWE 48:33.7 Gunnar Larsson	4. FIN	Kalevi Laurila	48:37.6
				5. SWE	Jan Halvarsson	48:39.1
				6. SWE	Bjarne Andersson	48:41.1
30 KILOMETERS	● ITA 1:35:39.2 Franco Nones	● NOR 1:36:28.9 Odd Martinsen	● FIN 1:36:55.3 Eero Mäntyranta	4. SOV	Vladimir Voronkov	1:37:10.8
				5. ITA	Giulio De Florian	1:37:12.9
				6. FIN	Kalevi Laurila	1:37:29.8
50 KILOMETERS	● NOR 2:28:45.8 Ole Ellefsæter	● SOV 2:29:02.5 Vyacheslav Vedenin	● SUI 2:29:14.8 Josef Haas	4. NOR	Pål Tyldum	2:29:26.7
				5. SWE	Melcher Risberg	2:29:37.0
				6. SWE	Gunnar Larsson	2:29:37.2
4 X 10-KILOMETER RELAY	● NOR 2:08:33.5 Odd Martinsen Pål Tyldum Harald Grönningen Ole Ellefsaeter	● SWE 2:10:13.2 Jan Halvarsson Bjarne Andersson Gunnar Larsson Assar Rönnlund	● FIN 2:10:56.7 Kalevi Oikarainen Hannu Taipale Kalevi Laurila Eero Mäntyranta	4. SOV	Voronkov/Akentiev/ Tarakanov/Vedenine	2:10:57.2
				5. SUI	Hischier/Haas/ Koch/Kälin	2:15:32.4
				6. ITA	De Florian/Nones/ Serafini/Stella	2:16:32.2
COMBINED	● FRG 449.04 Franz Keller	● SUI 447.99 Alois Kälin	● GDR 444.10 Andreas Kunz	4. TCH	Tomás Kučera	434.14
				5. ITA	Ezio Damolin	429.54
				6. POL	Jósef Gąsienica	428.78
5 KILOMETERS	● SWE 16:45.2 Toini Gustafsson	● SOV 16:48.4 Galina Kulakova	● SOV 16:51.6 Alevtina Kolchina	4. SWE	Barbro Martinsson	16:52.9
				5. FIN	Marjatta Kajosmaa	16:54.6
				6. SOV	Rita Achkina	16:55.1
10 KILOMETERS	● SWE 36:46.5 Toini Gustafsson	● NOR 37:54.6 Berit Mördre	● NOR 37:59.9 Inger Aufles	4. SWE	Barbro Martinsson	38:07.1
				5. FIN	Marjatta Kajosmaa	38:09.0
				6. SOV	Galina Kulakova	38:26.7
3 X 5-KILOMETER RELAY	● NOR 57:30.0 Inger Aufles Babben Damon-Enger Berit Mördre	● SWE 57:51.0 Britt Strandberg Toini Gustafsson Barbro Martinsson	● SOV 58:13.6 Alevtina Kolchina Rita Achkina Galina Kulakova	4. FIN	Pusula/Oikkonen/ Kajosmaa	58:45.1
				5. POL	Budny/Biegun/ Pęksa-Czerniawska	59:04.7
				6. GDR	Köhler/Schmidt/ Nestler	59:33.9

SKI JUMPING

SMALL HILL	● TCH 216.5 Jiři Raška	● AUT 214.2 Reinhold Bachler	● AUT 212.6 Baldur Preiml	4. NOR	Björn Wirkola	212.0
				5. FIN	Topi Mattila	211.9
				6. SOV	Anatoly Zheglanov	211.5
LARGE HILL	● SOV 231.3 Vladimir Beloussov	● TCH 229.4 Jiři Raška	● NOR 214.3 Lars Grini	4. GDR	Manfred Queck	212.8
				5. NOR	Bent Tomtum	212.2
				6. AUT	Reinhold Bachler	210.7

SPEED SKATING

500 METERS		FRG 40.3 ERHARD KELLER		NOR 40.5 MAGNE THOMASSEN		USA 40.5 RICHARD McDERMOTT	4. SOV Yevgeny Grishin 40.6 5. three-way tie

1,500 METERS		NLD 2:03.4 CORNELIS VERKERK		NLD 2:05.0 ADRIANUS SCHENK		NOR 2:05.0 IVAR ERIKSEN	4. NOR Magne Thomassen 2:05.1 5. SWE Johnny Höglin 2:05.2 5. NOR Björn Tveter 2:05.2

5,000 METERS		NOR 7:22.4 FRED ANTON MAIER		NLD 7:23.2 CORNELIS VERKERK		NLD 7:25.5 PETRUS NOTTET	4. NOR Per-Willy Guttormsen 7:27.8 5. SWE Johnny Höglin 7:32.7 6. SWE Örjan Sandler 7:32.8

10,000 METERS		SWE 15:23.6 JOHNNY HÖGLIN		NOR 15:23.9 FRED ANTON MAIER		SWE 15:31.8 ÖRJAN SANDLER	4. NOR Per-Willy Guttormsen 15:32.6 5. NLD Cornelis Verkerk 15:33.9 6. SWE Jonny Nilsson 15:39.6

500 METERS		SOV 46.1 LYUDMILA TITOVA		USA 46.3 MARY MEYERS USA 46.3 JENNIFER FISH		USA 46.3 DIANNE HOLUM	5. NLD Elisabeth van den Brom 46.6 6. FIN Kaija Mustonen 46.7 6. NOR Sigrid Sundby 46.7

1,000 METERS		NLD 1:32.6 CAROLINA GEIJSSEN		SOV 1:32.9 LYUDMILA TITOVA		USA 1:33.4 DIANNE HOLUM	4. FIN Kaija Mustonen 1:33.6 5. SOV Irina Yegorova 1:34.4 6. NOR Sigrid Sundby 1:34.5

1,500 METERS		FIN 2:22.4 KAIJA MUSTONEN		NLD 2:22.7 CAROLINA GEIJSSEN		NLD 2:24.5 CHRISTINA KAISER	4. NOR Sigrid Sundby 2:25.2 5. SOV Lasma Kaouniste 2:25.4 6. FIN Kaija-Lisa Keskivitikka 2:25.8

3,000 METERS		NLD 4:56.2 JOHANNA SCHUT		FIN 5:01.0 KAIJA MUSTONEN		NLD 5:01.3 CHRISTINA KAISER	4. FIN Kaija-Lisa Keskivitikka 5:03.9 5. NLD Wilhelmina Burgmeijer 5:05.1 6. SOV Lydia Skoblikova 5:08.0

RECORD OF THE XVIII OLYMPIAD

OCTOBER 10, 1964 — OCTOBER 11, 1968

OFFICERS OF THE INTERNATIONAL OLYMPIC COMMITTEE

Avery Brundage — President
Armand Emile Massard — Vice President
Marquess of Exeter — Vice President

Other Executive Members:
Guru Dutt Sondhi
Constantin Andrianov
José de J. Clark
Ivar Emil Vind
Giorgio de Stefani
Marc Hodler

INTERNATIONAL OLYMPIC COMMITTEE MEMBERSHIP DURING THE XVIII OLYMPIAD

ARRIVALS: 19

—— 1964 ——

October 7	Alexander de Merode	Belgium
	Sylvio Magalhaes de Padilha	Brazil
	Guilio Onesti	Italy
	Herman van Karnebeek	The Netherlands
	Sang Beck Lee	South Korea

—— 1965 ——

October 7	Amadou Barry	Senegal
	Gunnar Ericsson	Sweden
	Frantisek Kroutil	Czechoslovakia
	Pyrros Lappas	Greece
	Mohammed Mzali	Tunisia

—— 1966 ——

April 25	Georg von Opel	Germany
	Juan-Antonio Samaranch	Spain
	Heinz Schöbel	Germany
	Georg Wilhelm	
	Hanover International Olympic Academy	
	Jan Staubo	Norway

—— 1967 ——

May 6	Key Young Chang	South Korea
	Paavo Honkajuuri	Finland
	Tsunyeoshi Takeda	Japan
	James Worrall	Canada

DEPARTURES: 16

—— 1964 ——

| November 10 | Prince Pierre* | Monaco |

—— 1965 ——

April 6	Ioannis Ketseas*	Greece
October 6	Bo Ekelund	Sweden
October 7	Josef Gruss	Czechoslovakia

—— 1966 ——

January 8	Benedikt Waage*	Iceland
April 25	Olaf Ditlev-Simonsen Jr.	Norway
August 18	Francois Pietri*	France
November 14	Sang Beck Lee*	South Korea
November 19	Guru Dutt Sondhi*	India

—— 1967 ——

February 25	Shingoro Takaishi*	Japan
May 6	Arthur Porritt	New Zealand
	Mohamed Taher Pasha	Egypt
	Johan Ragnell	Finland
	Sidney Dawes	Canada
	Agustin Sosa	Panama

—— 1968 ——

| June 20 | Julio Bustamante* | Venezuela |

* Died in office; all others resigned

Net increase in the IOC membership: 3

Total IOC membership by the end of the XVIII Olympiad: 73

OFFICERS OF THE UNITED STATES OLYMPIC COMMITTEE

11th USOC Quadrennial, December 4, 1961, to November 29, 1965

Kenneth L. Wilson
Wilson, who had previously served two terms as president, was elected president of the USOC on December 4, 1961. His term spanned the XVII and XVIII Olympiads.

Other elected officers were:

Douglas F. Roby	Vice President
Asa S. Bushnell	Secretary
R. Max Ritter	Treasurer
Patrick H. Sullivan	Counselor
J. Lyman Bingham	Executive Director

12th USOC Quadrennial, November 29, 1965, to April 19, 1969

Douglas F. Roby
Roby was elected USOC president November 29, 1965. His term spanned the XVIII and XIX Olympiads.

Other elected officers were:

Franklin L. Orth	First Vice President
Dr. Merritt H. Stiles	Second Vice President
Robert J. Kane	Secretary
Julian K. Roosevelt	Treasurer
Patrick H. Sullivan	Counselor
Arthur G. Lentz	Executive Director *
Everett D. Barnes	Executive Director

* Served as acting director, June 1-December 1, 1968

HONORARY PRESIDENTS OF THE UNITED STATES OLYMPIC COMMITTEE

Starting with President Grover Cleveland, who accepted the honorary presidency of what was then the American Olympic Association in 1895, every United States president has agreed to serve in this capacity. During the XVIII Olympiad, President Lyndon Baines Johnson was the honorary president of the United States Olympic Committee.

OLYMPIC AWARDS

THE OLYMPIC CUP

Beginning in 1906, the Olympic Cup was awarded annually to a person, institution, or association that had contributed significantly to sport or to the development of the Olympic movement. The Olympic Cup was kept at the IOC; honorees received a reproduction. The award was originally conceived by Baron Pierre de Coubertin.

RECIPIENTS

1964	Southern California Committee for the Olympic Games in Los Angeles
1965	Not attributed
1966	International Association for Deaf Sports
1967	Bolivar Games

OLYMPIC DIPLOMA OF MERIT

The Olympic Diploma of Merit, created in 1905 during the third Olympic Congress in Brussels, was awarded to an individual who had been active in the service of sport and/or had contributed substantially to the Olympic movement.

RECIPIENTS

1964	Rudolf Hagelstange	Germany
	Prince Axel	Denmark
1965	Burhan Felek	Turkey
1966	Joseph Barthel	Luxembourg
	Dr. Joseph A. Gruss	Czechoslovakia
1967	Kon Ichikawa	Japan
	Sir Herbert MacDonald	Jamaica
	Antonio Elola Olaso	Spain

SIR THOMAS FEARNLEY CUP

The Fearnley Cup, donated in 1950 by Sir Thomas Fearnley, former member of the International Olympic Committee in Norway from 1927 to 1950, was awarded to a sports club or a local sports association practicing meritorious achievement in the service of the Olympic movement.

RECIPIENTS

1964	Not attributed	
1965	Not attributed	
1966	Not attributed	
1967	Athletic Club of South America	Argentina

THE MOHAMMED TAHER TROPHY

The Mohammed Taher Trophy was donated in 1950 by His Excellency Mohammed Taher Pasha, member of the International Olympic Committee in Egypt from 1934 to 1968. The award went to an amateur athlete, Olympian or otherwise, whose excellence merited special recognition.

RECIPIENTS

1964	Not attributed	
1965	Sixten Jernberg	Sweden
1966	Rodrigo de Castro Pereira	Portugal
1967	Eugenio Monte	Italy

THE COUNT ALBERTO BONACOSSA TROPHY

The Count Alberto Bonacossa Trophy presented in 1954 by the Italian National Olympic Committee in honor of Count Alberto Bonacossa, member of the International Olympic Committee in Italy from 1925 to 1953, was awarded to the national Olympic committee which had done outstanding work in furthering the Olympic movement during the preceding year.

RECIPIENTS

1964	Japanese Olympic Committee
1965	Spanish Olympic Committee
1966	Kenya Olympic and Commonwealth Games Association
1967	Ecuadorian Olympic Committee

THE TOKYO TROPHY

The Tokyo Trophy, presented in 1964 by the city of Tokyo, was awarded to an athlete or group of athletes whose conduct during the Olympic Games exemplified outstanding sportsmanship.

RECIPIENTS

1964	Not attributed
1965	Not attributed
1966	Not attributed
1967	Lars Gunnar Kall and Stig Lennart Kall

OFFICIAL PUBLICATIONS OF THE INTERNATIONAL OLYMPIC COMMITTEE

THE OLYMPIC CHARTER

The Olympic Charter provides the official rules, procedures, and protocols of the IOC, which are periodically updated by vote of the membership at an IOC Session. Nine editions were issued during the XVIII Olympiad.

Edition 13	Issued April 1966 (In French and English)
Edition 14	Issued May 1967 (In French and English)
Edition 14.1	Issued May 1967 (In French and English)
Edition 14.2	Issued May 1967 (In French and English)
Edition 14.3	Issued May 1967 (In French and English)
Edition 14.4	Issued May 1967 (In French and English)
Edition 14.5	Issued May 1967 (In French and English)
Edition 15	Issued September 1967 (In French and English)
Edition 15.1	Issued February 1968 (In French and English)

THE OLYMPIC BULLETIN

International Olympic Committee Bulletin (Bulletin du Comité International Olympique) - Published at IOC headquarters in Lausanne, Switzerland, the *International Olympic Committee Bulletin* was written in French and English with the occasional submission in German, Spanish, or other languages. The first edition came out in October 1946.

#88	November 1964
#89	February 1965
#90	May 1965
#91	August 1965
#92	November 1965
#93	February 1966
#94	May 1966
#95	August 1966
#96	November 1966
#97	February 1967
#98-#99	August 1967

INFORMATION LETTER

Information Letter (Lettre d'Information) - The IOC membership felt the quarterly editions of the *International Olympic Committee Bulletin* did not provide information on IOC matters in a timely fashion. Beginning in October 1967, the IOC began producing a monthly edition entitled the *Information Letter*. Published in Lausanne, the *Information Letter* became the 10th version of the *Olympic Review*, which constituted yet another sequential numbering system.

#1	October 1967
#2	November 1967
#3	December 1967
#4	January 1968
#5	February 1968
#6-#7	March-April 1968
#8	May 1968
#9	June 1968
#10	July 1968
#11	August 1968
#12	September 1968

ACKNOWLEDGMENTS

The publisher would like to thank the following for their invaluable assistance to 1st Century Project and World Sport Research & Publications: Gov. Francisco G. Almeda (Philippine Olympic Committee, Manila); Sheik Fahad Al-Ahmad Al-Sabah (Olympic Committee of Kuwait); Don Anthony; Maj. Gen. Charouck Arirachakaran (Olympic Committee of Thailand, Bangkok); Bibliothèque National de France (Paris); Marie-Charlotte Bolot (University of the Sorbonne Cultural Library and Archives, Paris); Boston Public Library; British Museum and Library (London); Gail Britton; Richard L. Coe; Anita DeFrantz (IOC Member in the United States); Margi Denton; Carl and Lieselott Diem - Archives/Olympic Research Institute of the German Sport University Cologne; Edward L. Doheny, Jr. Library (University of Southern California, Los Angeles); Robert G. Engel; Miguel Fuentes (Olympic Committee of Chile, Santiago); National Library of Greece (Athens); Hollee Hazwell (Columbiana Collection, Columbia University, New York); Rebecca S. Jabbour and Bill Roberts (Bancroft Library, University of California at Berkeley); Diane Kaplan (Manuscripts and Archives, Sterling Library, Yale University, New Haven); David Kelly (Sport Specialist, Library of Congress, Washington, D.C.); Fékrou Kidane (International Olympic Committee, Lausanne); Peter Knight; Dr. John A. Lucas; Los Angeles Public Library; Blaine Marshall; Joachaim Mester, President of the German Sport University Cologne; Ed Mosk; Geoffroy de Navacelle; New York Public Library; Olympic Committee of India (New Delhi); Richard Palmer (British Olympic Association, London); C. Robert Paul; University of Rome Library and Archives; Margaret M. Sherry (Rare Books and Special Collections, Firestone Library, Princeton University); Dr. Ruth Sparhawk; Gisela Terrell (Special Collections, Irwin Library, Butler University, Indianapolis); Walter Teutenberg; The Officers, Directors and Staff (United States Olympic Committee, Colorado Springs); University Research Library, (University of California at Los Angeles); John Vernon (National Archives, Washington, DC); Emily C. Walhout (Houghton Library; Harvard University); Herb Weinberg; Dr. Wayne Wilson, Michael Salmon, Shirley Ito (Paul Ziffren Sports Resource Center Library, Amateur Athletic Foundation of Los Angeles); Patricia Henry Yeomans; Nanci A. Young (Seeley G. Mudd Manuscript Library, Princeton University Archives); Dr. Karel Wendl, Michéle Veillard, Patricia Eckert, Simon Mandl, Ruth Perrenoud, Nikolay Guerguiev, Fani Kakridi-Enz, Laura Leslie Pearman, and Christine Sklentzas (International Olympic Committee Olympic Studies and Research Center, Lausanne); and Pat White (Special Collections, Stanford University Library, Palo Alto).

The publishers recognize with gratitude the special contributions made for Volume 16 by Pat and Billy Mills; Chuck Howard; Daniel Waeger (Koblenz); Val Ching, Neil Loft (Allsport, Pacific Palisades); Michael Shulman (Archive Photos, New York City); Dr. Maurice Vrillac, Veronique Peresset (CNOSF, Paris); Ellen Hansmann, Jurgen Zinke (dpa, Frankfurt); Jean-Pierre Lafarge (Laboratoire National de Dépistage du Dopage (Chatenay-Malabry); Yoshiko Solomon (Little Tokyo Branch of the Los Angeles Public Library, Los Angeles); Ron Morris, Charlie DiMarco (On Track, Burbank); Ken Kishimoto, Shigeaki Matsubara (Photo Kishimoto, Tokyo); Ian Blackwell, Andrew Wrighting (Popperfoto, Overstone); Phillipe Renard (Presse Sports, Issy-Les-Moulineau); Meredith Brosnan (Sovfoto/Eastfoto, New York City); Prem Kalliat (Sports Illustrated Picture Sales, New York City); Deborah Goodsite (The Corbis-Bettmann Archive, New York City); Alexandra Leclef Mandl (The International Olympic Committee, Lausanne); John Fritz (U.S. Equestrian Team, Inc., Gladstone); and Patricia Olkiewicz (United States Olympic Committee, Colorado Springs).

The Publishers would also like to thank the following individuals, institutions and foundations for providing initial funding for the project: The Amelior Foundation (Morristown, New Jersey); Roy and Mary Cullen (Houston); The English, Bonter, Mitchell Foundation (Ft. Wayne, Indiana); Adrian French (Los Angeles); The Knight Foundation (Miami); The Levy Foundation (Philadelphia); and, Jonah Shacknai (New York). And for completion funding: Michael McKie, Optimax Securities, Inc. (Toronto); Graham Turner, Fraser & Beatty (Toronto); and Century of Sport Partnership (Toronto).

And a special thanks to Barron Pittenger (Assistant Executive Director, United States Olympic Committee, September 1981 to August 1987 and Executive Director, August 1987 to December 1989).

BIBLIOGRAPHY

Aaseng, Nathan. *World-Class Marathoners.* Minneapolis, MN: Lerner Publications Company, 1982.

Anonymous. "Big Spending, Mad Building—Japan Prepares for Olympics." *U.S. News & World Report,* December 2, 1963.

Anonymous. "End of an Era—Tokyo Reborn." *Newsweek,* September 7, 1964.

Anonymous. "Kokichi's Last Marathon." *World Sports,* March 1968.

Anonymous. "Tokyo's Olympian Remodeling." *Newsweek,* April 29, 1963.

Anonymous. "Tokyo's Case of Olympic Fever." *Newsweek,* October 19, 1964.

Allen, Neil. "The Involvement of Oerter." *World Sports,* August 1964.

Allen, Neil. "Runners Whom Renown Outran." *World Sports,* November 1968.

Auran, John H. "Canada Loves Nancy Greene." *Skiing,* November 1967.

Auran, John H. "Last Rites at Grenoble." *Skiing,* October 1968.

Bingham, Walter. "Valeri's High, High Jump." *Sports Illustrated,* February 27, 1961.

Brady, Michael. "That Wretched Sex Mess." *Ski,* February 1968.

Brokhin, Yuri. *The Big Red Machine: The Rise and Fall of Soviet Olympic Champions.* New York: Random House, 1977.

Buchanan, Ian. *British Olympians: 100 Years of Gold Medalists.* Enfield, UK: Guiness, 1991.

Cahn, Susan K. *Coming On Strong: Gender and Sexuality in Twentieth-Century Women's Sport.* New York: The Free Press, 1994.

Carlson, Lewis H. and John J. Fogarty. *Tales of Gold.* Chicago: Contemporary Books, 1987.

Connery, Donald S. "Tokyo Changes Face for Asia's First Olympics." *Sports Illustrated,* May 8, 1961.

Cuthbert, Betty. *Golden Girl.* London: Pelham Books, 1966.

Crossman, Jim. *Olympic Shooting.* Washington, DC: National Rifle Association, 1978.

Duncanson, Neil. *The Fastest Men on Earth: The 100m Olympic Champions.* London: Willow Books, 1988.

Duncanson, Neil and Patrick Collins. *Tales of Gold.* London: Queen Anne Press, 1992.

Espy, Richard. *The Politics of the Olympic Games.* Berkeley: University of California Press, 1979.

Flagler, J.M. "Letter From Sendagaya." *The New Yorker,* August 15, 1964.

Fraser, Dawn and Harry Gordon. *Below the Surface: Confessions of an Olympic Champion.* New York: William Morrow & Co., 1965.

Frazier, Joe with Phil Berger. *Smokin' Joe*. New York: Macmillan, 1996.

Gafner, Raymond. *The International Olympic Committee-One Hundred Years: The Ideas-The Presidents-The Achievements, Volume II*. Lausanne: International Olympic Committee, 1995.

Geesink, Anton. *My Championship Judo*. New York: Arco, 1966.

Gibson, Colin. "A New Bikila...or Another?" *World Sports*, August 1964.

Gordon, Barclay. *Olympic Architecture: Building for the Summer Games*. New York: John Wiley & Sons, 1983.

Gordon, Harry. *Australia and the Olympic Games*. St. Lucia, Queensland: University of Queensland Press, 1994.

Graves, William. "Tokyo: The Peaceful Explosion." *National Geographic*, October 1964.

Greene, Nancy. *Nancy Greene: An Autobiography*. Don Mills, OT: Pagurian Press Ltd, 1968.

Guttman, Allen. *The Games Must Go On: Avery Brundage and the Olympic Movement*. New York: Columbia University Press, 1984.

Guttman, Allen. *The Olympics: A History of the Modern Games*. Chicago and Urbana: University of Illinois Press, 1992.

Hayes, Bob with Robert Pack. *Run, Bullet, Run*. New York: Harper & Row Publishers, 1990.

Hemery, David. *The Pursuit of Sporting Excellence*. Champaign, IL: Human Kinetic Books, 1986.

Hendershott, Jon. *Track's Greatest Women*. Los Altos, CA: Tafnews Press, 1987.

Hollobaugh, Jeff. "Top Winning Streaks." *Track and Field News*, December 1991.

Hopkins, John. *The Marathon*. London: Stanley Paul, 1966.

Huberty, Ernest. *The Olympic Games: Mexico, Grenoble, 1968*. Koeln: Lingen Verlag, 1968.

McDonald, David. *For the Recrod: Canada's Greatest Women Athletes*, Toronto: J. Wiley & Sons, 1981.

Jenkins, Dan. "Killy and Bonnet Girl Power Will Save the Day for France." *Sports Illustrated*, February 5, 1968.

Kieran, John and Arthur Daley. *The Story of the Olympic Games*, New York: J.B. Lippincott Co., 1973.

The Lord Killanin and John Rodda. *The Olympic Games: 80 Years of People, Events and Records*. New York: Collier Books, 1976.

Killy, Jean-Claude. *Comeback*. New York: Macmillan Publishing Company, 1974.

Kuznetsov, Victor and Mikhail Lukashev. *USSR-USA Sports Encounters*, Moscow: Progress Publishers, 1977.

Lapchick, Richard E. *The Politics of Race and International Sport: The Case of South Africa*. Westport, CT: Greenwood Press, 1974.

Lester, Gary. *Australians at the Olympics*. Sydney: Lester Townsend Books, 1984.

Lucas, John. *The Modern Olympic Games*. New York: A.S. Barnes and Company, 1980.

Macleod, Ian. "From Hickory to Fibre-Glass." *Athletics Weekly*, April 12, 1986.

Nelson, Cordner and Roberto Quercetani. *Runner and Races: 1,500 m/mile*. Los Altos, CA: Tafnews Press, 1973.

Newman, Bruce. "Striking the Lode." *Sports Illustrated*, January 27, 1988.

Oliver, Guy. *The Guiness Record of World Soccer*. Enfield, UK: Guiness Publishing, 1992.

Olsen, Jack. "The Doves and Gongs of Tokyo." *Sports Illustrated*, October 19, 1964.

Pennacchia, Mario. *Giulio Onesti: Rinascita e indipendenza dello sport in Italia*. Rome: Lucarini, 1986.

Porter, Philip. "Open Weight Olympic Competition." *Black Belt Magazine*, February 1965.

Rand, Mary. *Mary Mary: An Autobiography*. London: Hodder and Stoughton, 1969.

Rogin, Gilbert. "The Fastest is Faster." *Sports Illustrated*, October 5, 1964.

Schollander, Don. *Deep Water*. New York: Crown Publishers, 1971.

Snell, Peter. *No Bugles, No Drums*. Auckland: Minerva, 1966.

Steinback, Valeri. *638 Olympic Champions*. Moscow: Raduga Publishers, 1984.

Suster, Gerald. *Champions of the Ring*. London: Robson, 1992.

Underwood, John. "An Exhuberant Finish in Tokyo." *Sports Illustrated*, November 2, 1964.

Underwood, John. "We Win the Five and Ten." *Sports Illustrated*, October 26, 1964.

Underwood, John. "The Tokyo Games." *Sports Illustrated*, October 5, 1964.

Van Steenwyk, Elizabeth. *Peggy Fleming: Cameo of a Champion*. New York: McGraw-Hill Book Company, 1978.

Various. *How They Reached the Top: Stories of Soviet Sports Champions*. Moscow: Progress Publishers, 1966.

Wallechinsky, David. *The Complete Book of the Olympics*. Boston: Little, Brown and Company, 1992.

Whitehouse, Jo. "First Lady Olympian of Three-Day Eventing." *USCTA Eventing News*, September/October 1994.
Wise, S.F. and Douglas Fisher. *Canada's Sporting Heroes*. Don Mills, OT: General Publishing Company Ltd, 1974.

Wright, Benjamin T. *Skating Around the World, 1892-1992*. Davos, Switzerland: International Skating Union, 1992.

Zarnowski, Frank. *The Decathlon*. Champaign, IL: Leisure Press, 1989.

Ski, Spring Issue, 1968

Skiing, February 1968

Track and Field News, October/November 1964

The Japan Times: XVIII Olympic Games in Tokyo October, 1964, Special Bound Volume

Excerpts from:

The New York Times

Philadelphia Enquirer

PHOTO CREDITS

INDEX

Note: Figures in italics indicate photos or illustrations.

A

ABC (American Broadcasting Company) television network, *109*, 121-3, *147*
African nations, protests against apartheid by, 96, 97
Ali, Muhammad. *See* Clay, Cassius
Allen, Wendy, 133
Alpe d'Huez bobsled course, *115*, 126 (sidebar)
Amateurism, 94, *118*, 119-21, 123-4, 125, 138, 144
Amoore, Judy, 32, 33
Amphetamines, 98-9, 102-3
Antwerp 1920 Olympic Games, 57
Apartheid, 94-7
Argentina, 11 (sidebar), 18
Arledge, Roone, 121-3
Arpin, Michel, 125
Ashworth, Gerald, 68
Association Nationale d'Education Physique, 100, 102
Association of National Olympic Committees. *See* Permanent General Assembly
Athens 1896 Olympic Games, 77 (sidebar)
Aufles, Inger, 138
Augert, Jean-Paul, 120
Australia, 10, 23-6, 27, 29-34, 38, 39, 48, 57; judo and, 85; marathon and, 48; swimming and, 27, 29-30; track events and, 30-4, 38, 39; yachting and, 53 (sidebar)
Austria: alpine skiing and, 116, 126, 131; bobsled and, 126 (sidebar); figure skating and, 142-3, *145*; luge and, *132*; ski jump and, 134
Autrans ski jump, 134

B

Bachler, Reinhold, 134
Badge, *18*
Bahamas, 67
Balaş, Iolanda, 76, 105 (sidebar), *105*
Balzer, Karin, 74
Bannister, Dr. Roger, 51
Barcelona 1992 Summer Games, 40, 97
Barrows, Jim, *124*, 124
Belgium, *38*
Bello, Billy, death of, 99
Beloussov, Vladimir, *133*, 134
Ben Boubaker, Hedhili, 48
Berlin 1936 Summer Olympics, 43, 51, 91; television and, 121
Bernard, Michel, 57
Biathlon, *122*, 123 (sidebar)
Bikila, Abebe, 23, 47, 48-9, *49*, 63, 95; death of, 49
Bobsled, *126*, 126 (sidebar)
Bochatay, Fernande, 133
Bolotnikov, Pyotr, 23

Bonavena, Oscar, 18
Bonnet, Honoré, 116, 125
Bonsack, Klaus, *132*, 132
Boronovskis, Theodore, 85
Boston, Ralph, 41, 43
Boxing, *6*, 7-11, *9*, *10*, 18-9, 21; flyweight, *9*; middleweight, 10
Brazil, 11 (sidebar), 88
Breckenridge, Alex, 22
Brightwell, Robbie, 34, 35, 36
Brumel, Valery, 58-9, *59*, 62-5, *64*, 83; motorcycle accident involving, 64 5
Brundage, Avery, (IOC president), 105, 106 (sidebar), 107-8; amateurism and, *118*-20, 125, 138; Winter Games and, 118, 138
Budge, Karen, 130
Burleson, Dyrol, 57
Bush, Lesley, *81*

C

Calmat, Alain, 110, *116*
Campbell, Ben, 85
Canada, 18, 55, 55, 67, 138, 139
Carr, Henry, *68*
Čáslavská, Vera, 60
Casserousse ski run, 113, 114
CBS television network, 109, 121
Cerutty, Percy, *32*
Chaffee, Rich, 125
Chaffee, Suzee, 131
Chamberlain, Ann, 35
Chernyshov, Arkadi, 138
Choh, Dong-kih, *9*
Chromosomal testing, 104
Chuvalo, George, 18
Clarke, Ron, 23, *24*, 25-6, 38, 39, 48, 54
Clay, Cassius, (Muhammad Ali), *9*, 18, 26, 67
Cold War, 54, 75, 93
Comite Olimpico Nazionale d'Italia (CONI), 105, 107
Commercialism, 94, 97
CONI. *See* Comite Olimpico Nazionale d'Italia
Connolly, Harold, 100, *102*
Coulon, Roger, 107
Cross-Country skiing. *See* Skiing, Nordic
Crothers, William, 55
Cuba, 67
Cuthbert, Betty, 30-4, *32*, *35*
Cutter, Kiki, 133
Cycling, drug use and, 98, 99
Czechoslovakia, 11 (sidebar), 57, 60 (sidebar), *76*, 138-9, *139*

D

Daimatsu, Hirofumi, 88, *88*, 91

Damolin, Ezio, 134
Dan, Shin-geum, 32, 34, 35, *97*
Daněk, Ludvik, 70, *71*, 72
Danne, Wolfgang, 147
Danzer, Emmerich, 142-3
Dätwyler, John Daniel, 124
Davenport, Willie, 38
Davies, John, 57
Davies, Lynn, 40-1, *42*, 43
de Coubertin, Baron Pierre, 104
de Florian, Giulio, 136
de Gaulle, Charles, 110, 118
de Klerk, Jan, 96
de Mérode, Prince Alexandre, 102
Decathlon, 22 (sidebar), *28*
Dellinger, Bill, 39-40
Discus: men's, 69-72; women's, 75
Diving, *81*
Dobai, Gyula, 82
Dönhaupt, Angelika, 132 (sidebar)
Doping. *See* Drug use, Drug testing
Drayton, Paul, 68
Drug testing: methods of, 103; thwarting of, 103
Drug use by athletes: cycling and, 98, 99; dangers of, 98, 99; historically, 97-8
Dugent, Duke, 8
duPont, Lana, 62 (sidebar), *62*
Dupureur, Maryvonne, 35, 36

E

Ellefsaeter, Ole, 136
Elliott, Herb, 57
Elliott, Jere, 124
Ellis, Jimmy, 18
Endo, Yukio, 60 (sidebar), *60*
Engel-Krämer, Ingrid, *81*, *95*
Enoshima yachting center, 14, *53*
Equestrian events, 62 (sidebar), *62*, *63*
Eriksen, Ivar, 142
Ethiopia, 23, 47, *48*, *49*

F

Famose, Annie, 131, 133
Farrell, Thomas, 55
Favre, Willi, 125
Fédération Internationale de Lutte Amateur (FILA), 77 (sidebar), *107*
Fédération Internationale de Natation Amateur, 107
Fédération Internationale de Ski (FIS), 119-20, 125-7
Fencing, *65*
Figuerola, Enrique, 67
Figure skating, 142-7; women's, 143-4, *144*; pairs, 144, *146*, 147; men's, 142-3, *145*

FILA. *See* Fédération Internationale de Lutte Amateur
Finland, 43-5, *45*, 139, *140*, 141
Finlay, Harry, *94*
FIS. *See* Fédération Internationale de Ski
Fish, Jennifer, 141
Fleming, Peggy, 143-4, *144*
Floth, Horst, 126 *(sidebar)*
Football. *See* Soccer
Fortna, Rosie, 133
France, 33, 35, 36, 57, 82, 83, 126; figure skating and, 142-3; men's 5,000 m run and, 39-40; men's skiing and, 124-9
Fraser, Dawn, 27, *27*, 29-31, *30*, 36; arrest of, 29; banning of, 30
Frazier, Joe, *6*, 7-11, 18-9, 21, 122; childhood of, 7-8; early career of, 9; injury to, 11, 18, *19*; later career of, 18-9; training of, 8
Fujisawa, Takashi, 134

G

GAIF. *See* General Assembly of the International Federations
Galen, 97-8, *98*
Games schedules: Grenoble, 119, 166; Tokyo, 8, 152-5
Gammoudi, Mohamed, 23, 25-6, *26*
Gąsienica, Jósef, 134
Geesink, Anton, 84-6, *86*
Geijssen, Carolina, 141
Gender testing, 75, 76-7, 104, 105 *(sidebar)*; Eastern bloc athletes and, 104; methods of, 104
General Assembly of the International Federations (GAIF), 107-8
Germany, *6*, 7, 18, 22 *(sidebar)*, 39-40, 67, 74, *81*, 82, 85; competing as unified team, *95*
Germany, East, 33, 75; figure skating and, 144; luge and, 132 *(sidebar)*, *132*; Nordic combined and, 135; ski jumping and, 134
Germany, West: figure skating and, 147; women's luge and, 132 *(sidebar)*; Nordic combined and, 134; speed skating and, 141
"Ghost Slalom," 127
Glahn, Klaus, 85
Glockshuber, Margot, 147
Goitschel, Marielle, *131*, 131, 133
Gorchakova, Yelena, 46
Gorelik, Aleksandr, 147
Gottvalles, Alain, 82, 83
Goundartsev, Vladimir, 123 *(sidebar)*
Grafström, Gillis, 142
Grahn, Erik, 127
Great Britain, 23, 33, 49, 57, 85; women's 400 m and 800 m run and, 34-6; men's 100 m freestyle swim and, 82-3; women's long jump and, 72-4
Greene, Nancy, 129-30, *129*, 131, 133-4
Grenoble 1968 Winter Olympics, closing ceremonies, *148-9*; drug testing at, 103, *103*, 104; Games schedule, 119, 166; national medal count, 166; opening ceremonies, *110-1*, 118; sites, 113-14, *114*, *115*; torch, *116*; television and *109*
Grini, Lars, 134
Grönningen, Harald, 136
Gustafsson, Toini (Karvonen), 136, 138, *138*
Gymnastics, 60 *(sidebar)*, 60-1

H

Haas, Christl, 131
Haas, Josef, 136
Hachicha, Ali, 85
Haines, George, 80
Halberg, Murray, 23, 54
Hammer throw, *102*
Hammerl, László, *72*
Handa, Yuriko, 88
Hansen, Fred, 28 *(sidebar)*, *28*
"Happy Games," 17, 54, 83, 94, 147
Hary, Armin, 67
Hayes, Bob, 65-9, *66*; childhood of, 66-7; post-Olympic career, 69
Heatley, Basil, 49
Helsinki 1952 Summer Olympics, 9, 28 *(sidebar)*, 62 *(sidebar)*
Henie, Sonja, 142
Heuga, Jim, 125, 127
High jump, men's, 58-9, 62-5
Hill, Albert, 57
Hill, Ralph, 36
Hill, Ron, 23
Hirohito, Emperor, 4, 17
Hiroshima, 4, 17

Hockey. *See* Ice hockey
Hodler, Marc, 119-20
Hogan, Jim, 48
Höglin, Johnny, 142
Holdorf, Willi, 22 *(sidebar)*, *22*
Holum, Dianne, 140-1
Howard, Dick, death of, 99
Huber, Hans, *6*, 7, 18
Hungary, 11 *(sidebar)*, 33, 45, 46, 49, 72, 82
Hungerford, George, *55*

I

Ice hockey, 138-40, *139*; move to admit professionals to, 138
Ichiguchi, Masamitsu, 76
IFs. *See* International Federations
Igloi, Mihaly, 38
Ilman, Gary, 82-3
Innsbruck 1964 Winter Olympics: advertising and, 119; television and, 122
International Federations (IFs), 105, 107-8
International Olympic Committee (IOC): budget of, 108; bureaucratic growth in, 104, 107-8; commercialism and, 94; drug testing and, 102-4; gender testing and, 104; headquarters of, 93; Medical Commission, 102-4; push for democratization in, 105, 107-8; racism and, 94-7; television broadcast rights and, 108-9; Third World and, 107
IOC. *See* International Olympic Committee
Ireland, 48, 85
Isobe, Sata, 88
Italy, 11 *(sidebar)*, *65*, 68, 132 *(sidebar)*, 135-6
Itkina, Maria, 32, 33
Ivory Coast, 67

J

Jackson, Roger, *55*
Jacobsen, Uwe, 82
Jamaica, 55, *56*, 68
Japan (nation), and World War II, 11
Japan (team), 46, 47, 49, 76, 83-4; boxing and, 84; gymnastics and, 60-1, 84; judo and, 84-7; track and field events and, 47, 49; women's volleyball and, 87-8, *88*, *89*, 91; wrestling and, 84
Javelin: men's, 43-5, *45*; women's, 45-7
Jazy, Michel, 39-40
Jeglanow, Alex, 134
Jensen, Knut, 99
Jerome, Harry, 67
Jones, Hayes, *44*
Judo, 14, 84-7

K

Kaiser, Christina, 140, 141
"Kaizuka Amazons" *(Nichibo Kaizuka)*, 88, *89*, 91
Kälin, Alois, 134-5
Kaminaga, Akio, 84-6, *86*
Kankkonen, Veikko, 134
Karuizawa Equestrian Track, 14, *62*
Kasai, Masae, 88
Keino, Kip, 39
Keller, Erhard, 141, *142*
Keller, Franz, 134-5, *135*
Kenya, 39, 55
Kerr, George, 55, *56*
Kidd, Billy, 124
Killy, Jean-Claude, *112*, *113*, 114, 116-8, *117*, 124-5, 127-9, *128*; amateurism and, 120; childhood of, 114, 116
Kinnunen, Jorma, 44
Kiprugut, Wilson, 55
Kirszenstein, Irena, 73
Klein, Hans-Joachim, 82
Klobukowska, Ewa, 76-7
Köhler, Thomas, *132*, 132 *(sidebar)*
Komazawa Olympic Park, 14, *15*, 17
Kone, Gaoussou, 67
Korakuen Ice Palace, 7, *9*, 11, 18
Korea, North, 11 *(sidebar)*, 32, *96*, 97
Korea, South, *9*
Kovalenkov, Pjotr, 134
Kriss, Grigory, *65*
Kulcsár, Gergely, 45
Kunz, Andreas, 135

L

Lakota Sioux nation, 21
Larsson, Gunnar, 136

Latynina, Larissa, 60 *(sidebar)*, 61
Lebret, Evelyne, 33
Lechner, Erica, 132 *(sidebar)*
Lindgren, Blaine, *44*
Lindgren, Gerry, 23, 38
Lisitsky, Viktor, 60 *(sidebar)*
Liston, Sonny, 9, 26, 67
London 1908 Olympics, 77 *(sidebar)*
Long jump: men's, 40-3, *42*; women's, 72-3, *73*
Loren, Valentin, *10*
Lotz, Ingrid, 75
Luge, 132 *(sidebar)*, *132*
Lūsis, Jānis, 45
Lydiard, Arthur, 52-3

M

Machen, Eddie, 18
Maehata, Hideko, 91
Mahlknecht, Ivo, 124
Maier, Fred Anton, 141-2
Mali, *28*
Maniak, Wieslaw, 67
Mäntyranta, Eero, 136
Marathon, 22-3, 47-9, *48*, *49*; route of, 47
Martinsen, Odd, 136
Mašková, Hana, 144
Mathias, Bob, 28 *(sidebar)*
Mathis, Buster, 9-10, 18
Matseke, Lucas, *94*
Matsumura, Yoshiko, 88
Mattila, Topi, 134
McDermott, Terry, 141
McGuire, Edith, *33*
McNamara, John, 53 *(sidebar)*
McQueen, Athol, 10
Medals: Tokyo, *43*, *69*; Grenoble, *121*
Melbourne 1956 Summer Olympics, 27, 29, 30, 31, 53 *(sidebar)*, 70; women's high jump at, 105 *(sidebar)*
Messner, Heinrich, 124, 125
Mexico, 18
Mexico 1968 Summer Olympics, 46, 72, 76, 79, 83; South Africa and, 96
Meyers, Mary, 141
Michine, Alexei, 147
Mills, Billy, *20*, 21-7, *26*, 36, 38, 54, 83, 122; early years, 21
Mir, Isabelle, 131, 133
Miyake, Yoshinobu, 84
Miyamoto, Emiko, 88
Mjoen, Haakon, 127, 128
Mon Repos (IOC headquarters), 93
Monti, Eugenio, *126*, 126 *(sidebar)*
Mördre, Berit, 138
Moscow 1980 Summer Olympics, 97
Moskvina, Tamara, 147
Munich 1972 Summer Olympics, 96
Munkácsi, Antonia, 33
Mustonen, Kaija, *140*, 141

N

Naduit, Georges, *120*
Nagel, Judy, 133
National Gymnasium, 14, *15*, 29, *82*
National medal counts: Grenoble, 166; Tokyo, 155
National Olympic Committees (NOCs), 105, 107-8, *108*
National Stadium, 4 *(sidebar)*, *4*, *15*, 32, 44, 45-47, *48*, 53, 62-3, 69, 70, *90-1*, *95*; opening ceremonies in, 16-17
Native Americans, *20*, 21-27
NBC television network, 109, 121, 144
Netherlands, The, 33, 84-6; speed skating and, 140-2
Neuendorf, Dieter, 134
Nevala, Pauli, 43-5, *45*
New Zealand, 23, 35, 51-8, 63
Nippon Budokan Hall, 14, 84, *85*
Nones, Franco, 135-6, *136*
Norpoth, Harald, 39-40
Northam, Bill, 53 *(sidebar)*
Norway, 43, 45, *122*, 123 *(sidebar)*, 141-2
Norwegian Olympic Committee, 94
Nottet, Petrus, 141-2

O

Odložil, Josef, 57
Oerter, Al, 69-72, *70*, *71*
Olympic Charter, racism and, 95

THE OLYMPIC WORLD
GRENOBLE 1968 WINTER GAMES

▬ *PARTICIPATING COUNTRIES*

North America

CAN . . . . CANADA
USA UNITED STATES OF AMERICA

South America

ARG . . . . ARGENTINA
CHI . . . . CHILE

Europe

AUT . . . . AUSTRIA		
BUL . . . . BULGARIA		
CHE . . . . CZECHOSLOVAKIA	**GBR** . . . . GREAT BRITAIN	**LIE** . . . . LIECHTENSTEIN
DEN . . . . DENMARK	**GDR** . . . . EAST GERMANY	**NED** . . . . THE NETHERLANDS
ESP . . . . SPAIN	**GRE** . . . . GREECE	**NOR** . . . . NORWAY
FIN . . . . FINLAND	**HUN** . . . . HUNGARY	**POL** . . . . POLAND
FRA . . . . FRANCE	**ISL** . . . . ICELAND	**RUM** . . . . RUMANIA
FRG . . . . GERMANY	**ITA** . . . . ITALY	**SUI** . . . . SWITZERLAND